Embrace the

EARTHWAY

and discover . . .

► the link between astrological signs and choosing a life partner
► how to apply celestial guidance to your life
► how the synergistic forces of nature—such as heat, humidity, thunderstorms, or gentle rain— affect you physically and psychologically
► if the wind can "drive you crazy"
► what you need to know about drinking water, including the bottled water available in your supermarket
► the connection between one's aura and vibratory rate
► how genetics—and ethnicity—impacts on vibrations
► the quality most missing from modern life— simplicity—and its effect on happiness
► how to find truth in your dreams—with hundreds of vision symbols explained
► Quantum Meditation and its virtual experience

. . . and more

Mary Summer Rain offers
invaluable lessons, powerful wisdom, and practical guidance
for daily living . . .

BEYOND EARTHWAY

Books by Mary Summer Rain

NONFICTION

Spirit Song

Phoenix Rising

Dreamwalker

Phantoms Afoot

Earthway

Daybreak

Soul Sounds

Whispered Wisdom

Ancient Echoes

Bittersweet

Mary Summer Rain's Guide
  to Dream Symbols

The Visitation

Millennium Memories

Fireside

Eclipse

The Singing Web

Love Never Sleeps

Beyond Earthway

FICTION

The Seventh Mesa

CHILDREN'S

Mountains, Meadows and
  Moonbeams: A Child's
  Spiritual Reader

Star Babies

BOOKS ON TAPE

Spirit Song

Phoenix Rising

Dreamwalker

Phantoms Afoot

The Visitation

BEYOND EARTHWAY

MARY SUMMER RAIN

POCKET BOOKS
New York London Toronto Sydney Singapore

The author of this book is not a physician, and the ideas, procedures, and suggestions in this book are not intended as a substitute for the medical advice of a trained health professional. All matters regarding your health require medical supervision. Consult your physician before adopting the suggestions in this book, as well as about any other condition that may require diagnosis or medical attention. The author and publishers disclaim any liability arising directly or indirectly from the use of this book.

An *Original* Publication of POCKET BOOKS

POCKET BOOKS, a division of Simon & Schuster Inc.
1230 Avenue of the Americas, New York, NY 10020

Library of Congress Cataloging-in-Publication Data

Summer Rain, Mary, 1945–
     Beyond earthway / Mary Summer Rain.
        p. cm.
     includes index.
     ISBN: 0-671-03862-1
  1. Naturopathy.   2. Holistic medicine.   I. Title.

RZ440.S857 2000
615.5'35—dc21   99-055446

First Pocket Books trade paperback printing February 2000

10 9 8 7 6 5 4 3 2 1

Cover design by Tom McKeveny
Book design by Helene Berinsky

Printed in the U.S.A.

RRDH/✄

*For Fire Raven. His reach and depth of love
transcend Space and Time. His Light far
outshines the grand shimmering cosmos.
Fire Raven, ever Timeless and Eternal,
thank you for finding me once more.
Thank you for loving me . . . again.*

CONTENTS

Foreword   ix

SECTION ONE
THE BODY
The Soil of Sacred Ground   1

Part I ▶ The Cosmic Umbilical   3
Sharing the Celestial Genetic Coding of the Sky and Heavens

1 STARSTUFF—Celestial Affinity   5

2 SKYSTUFF—Meteorologic/Geologic Relatedness   47

Part II ▶ The Earth Mother's Umbilical   75
The Womb's Life Force of Earthway Living

3 HEARTSOUNDS—Mean Vibratory Rates   77

4 EARTHWAY GENETICS—Dietary and Healing Aspects   105

SECTION TWO
THE MIND
The Seed of Fruitful Knowledge   149

1 THE TOXIN—Contaminating Attitudes and Emotions   151

2 THE ANTIDOTE—Dream Interpretation   206

SECTION THREE
THE SPIRIT

The Blossom of Eternal Life   271

1 THE CRYSTAL STREAM—Quantum Consciousness
  and Virtual Meditation   273

2 THE KNOWING AND THE GREAT ALONE—
  Wisdom and Spiritual Philosophy   311

Afterword   371
Index   373
About the Author   389

FOREWORD

Since *Earthway* was first published in 1990, I've received count-less letters regarding the material contained within the book. My readers have given a great deal of thought to the various subject matters *Earthway* encompassed and wrote me with thought-provoking questions that this material generated. From inquiries about dream symbology to questions associated with attitudes and emotions, the readership response to *Earthway* has been over-whelmingly embracing and warmly appreciative. This has been evidenced through my correspondents' high interest in the sub-ject matters and their subsequent expressed desire to gain a deeper, more thorough, and heightened understanding of their own nature's tightly woven interconnectedness to Nature and how effectively they synergically affect and complement one another in a multitude of ways. *Earthway* clearly pointed out that the nature of humans is not isolated, is not independent, but is, rather, intricately bonded to the Nature of All, whereby every liv-ing cell of every vitally alive species has an emanating vibrational force field that is capable of affecting the energy fields of all other life species. We are not alone upon this planet. We share it with all other life-forms and, in doing so, we are but a fragment of the liv-ing, breathing life upon the fine and delicate strands that form the

Great Web of Life. Human life is but a singular strand upon that shimmering, undulating web. Human life is but a minuscule living component that binds with all other living component aspects of life to create a magnificently beautiful totality of Life, a totality that shimmers and vibrates with incredible tenacity and vitality. Each component affects the others. Each fragmented aspect of life creates a uniquely individualized vibration upon the whole, each gaining benefits from the healthful state of the other, each subtly sensing the dynamic presence of the other. Therefore, we are directly related to every living thing with a grand cohesiveness, pulsating with the lifeblood of energy circulating throughout the universe.

This is the concept *Earthway* presented. This is the concept readers grasped and, in coming to this enlightening conclusion, intellectually reached further through expanded thought and deep contemplation. These, then, naturally led to inspired questions that were the main focus of hundreds of letters to me. My correspondents have clearly expressed a heartfelt desire for me to address these inquiries, and since I've always placed a strong priority on conveying concepts with clarity and simplicity, I give you *Beyond Earthway* as my way of personally responding to these requests.

SECTION
ONE

THE
B·O·D·Y

The Soil of
Sacred Ground

P A R T

I

THE COSMIC UMBILICAL

Sharing the Celestial Genetic Coding of the Sky and Heavens

Too oft we perceive ourselves as composed of skin and bones, hair and organs, yet rarely do we look beyond our gross anatomy to the finer facets of same, for within us is a shimmering cosmos undulating with the pulse of Life.

1

STARSTUFF
Celestial Affinity

▶ *Is astrology really a viable aspect of astronomy?*

Astrology presents the definitive *relationship* the celestial bodies have with all of life as evidenced through their natural magnetic influences, which emanate powerful specific and unique qualities. You must keep in mind that astronomy is the study of the celestial bodies and the universe as a whole, whereas astrology is the study of the separate *influence* each heavenly body possesses. Though they are two entirely different fields, they are certainly so closely related as to be firmly intertwined. Some astronomers scoff at the idea of celestial bodies' giving off vibrational emanations that have the power to affect human character, yet that same skepticism does not negate the fact that those emanations exist. Reality needs no human verification or belief to sustain itself. Reality exists of its own dynamic volition and requires no human intervention or nod of approving recognition to maintain its viability. Once this is realized, society as a whole will understand that reality is not based on the ideology that the opinion of the majority rules but that rather reality rules *despite* the majority's opinion of it. The opinion of the majority never becomes the qualifying criterion defining a fact. A fact stands on its own. Some recognize it as a clearly perceptible means of substance, whereas others view it as a mist of the imagination. Astrology is a viable issue. Who believes in it is not germane, is it? All humanity is entitled to the right to have an opinion based on personal perspective and one's level of innate intuitiveness. Not only is the *Earthway* material regarding this issue clearly based on a personal, intuitive knowing that the celestial bodies have specific influences upon all life-forms but it is also supported by hundreds of years of research and development through which solid correlations have been evinced. From the time of the three wise men up to today, astrology has been taken seriously by all those who've studied it and witnessed the clear proof of its highly influential manifestations. And, we ask ourselves, how is it that so many people can accurately identify a stranger's birth sign by merely observing his or her mannerisms and animated characteristics? Lucky guess? Sure, I wouldn't doubt that some of them are lucky guesses, but the number of accurate hits far outweighs the number of inaccurate ones and exemplifies the folly of astrology's being relegated to the status of pure guesswork.

You see, astrology deals with influences that sometimes carry great magnetic strength and at other times manifest as a gentle and subtle sway. The entire concept of influence is not a touchable and seeable entity for the people of mainstream science—the astronomers—therefore, they are wont to remain noncommittal regarding it. The ideology of these celestial influences is not considered to be within their realm of science or expertise; they are the first to admit it. You'll find astronomers who debunk astrology and you'll also find those who will be scientifically bold enough to give it the benefit of the doubt and admit to the possibility of its viability. As with all concepts, whether scientific or philosophical, there will be strict adherents, those who are on the proverbial fence, and the confirmed skeptics. In the end, it's all up to the individual, who has the right and freedom to believe as he or she feels within the heart. This decision making is done by examining a concept through generalized reading and then spending time expanding that introductory information by going deeper into it with further research, looking at the evidence, contemplating that which has been discovered. Through these methods, we come to our own conclusions. Never should a decision of belief or acceptance be made on face value, subliminal knowledge, or surface appearances.

▶ *In* Earthway *you stated that the Anasazi planetary belief system, though "roughly similar to present-day astrology, but only superficially," was far more advanced and accurate. Taking this statement to heart, should I just ignore the currently accepted form of astrology?*

Ignore in deference to what, though? I understand your intent, but since the entire system of the Anasazi's astrological knowledge is currently lost to us, with what other celestial interpretation system would you replace it? Remember, the Anasazi were a Starborn race who had highly advanced knowledge of the universe. Their form of astrology would naturally be developed to a far greater degree and much finer tuned than ours because of their understanding of the complete contents of the cosmos. Though earthly humankind is knowledgeable of its universe and is still in its infancy, it is intellectually growing in that developing knowledge through increasing space technology and continuing space discovery. We are reaching farther and farther into that Unknown, and by doing this, we enhance our current base of information with new and exciting breakthroughs. Therefore, we work within our level of comprehension. We operate within the knowns that our science and technology have revealed to us. Our level of advancement is no higher and no greater than what our discoveries create. As those technologies allow us to push the envelope further and further with each small, tentative step, so too does our comprehension of reality widen and expand in a like-wise manner—one step at a time. We are right where we should be. Think about how far we've come since the signing of the Declaration of Independence back in 1776. Take some time to really think about how far we've come in just under 230 years. Actually it's pretty amazing.

One of the main tenets I've always tried to stress to my readers as a priority in life is to "live the moment." That means to take advantage of every opportunity that comes your way to practice unconditional goodness, keep your awareness heightened so you can recognize each blessing that subtly presents itself, and embrace the knowledge that's available for your personal development. This last is what we're dealing with here, to embrace the knowledge that's available. To want more, as this questioner is implying, is to be as a small child in the first grade wanting to skip the one-plus-one stage and speed right to the trigonometry. That child isn't ready for the advanced math. That child isn't understanding that he or she must first learn and comprehend the beginning basics to be able to appreciate and understand the more complex facts. We live in the moment. We cherish that which is within our realm of reality, and then we embrace the brilliance of the epiphanies as they come through inspiration or discovery.

So then, to conclude, we do not ignore a current stage of development on the probable grounds of its being better, expanded, or more advanced at some future date. Seize the day and its knowledge.

▸ *Astrologically speaking, what about the hiring of employees? I run a small company and was thinking about hiring only those whose birth signs were compatible with mine. Would that be immoral?*

Though I understand your desire to have employees who are compatible with the boss, it doesn't seem to me to be a moral kind of thing to do. It's certainly discriminatory. You can't disqualify a talented and skilled individual from employment solely on the basis of the month he or she was born. You can't do that. We already have too much prejudice and discrimination in this world of ours to exacerbate it by extending selectivity to include birthdates too. Putting it in black and white this way even makes it sound downright ridiculous, don't you think? I believe you were looking at this theoretically. In that respect, sure, it might be nice to have all the employees within a company be completely compatible; then again, there'd be a downside to that: there's a strong probability that that same compatibility would eventually elicit a stagnation of ideas and creativity. There'd be such a state of commonality that the overall workforce aura would ultimately become stale and static. Diversity—what you really want is diversity of intelligence, personality, creativity, and character enveloped within compatibility. That's a tall order, but not so tall as to be unachievable. Having a company full of clones stunts growth. Cherish your employees' individuality. Recognize the specialized uniqueness of each person. A stained-glass window is so much more striking and pleasing to the eye when all its vibrantly faceted panes are different colors and shapes. Those unique panes unite to create a beautiful and expressive whole.

► *What was Jesus' astrological birth sign?*

Contrary to the religious party line, his astrological birth sign was Gemini.

► *Will my parents' astrological influences somehow pass on to me through genetic coding?*

Apples an' oranges. Astrological influences are influences that affect the character and personality traits; they are not biological factors entwined within the genetic coding of DNA. Astrological influences are an affecting element *outside* the body, whereas genetic factors are *within* it and are purely physiological. Let's really simplify my point. If your mother was pregnant and received a sunburn, would the infant she birthed also have that sunburn? You see, *outside* influences that affect that pregnant mother don't have a carry-over effect upon the child. So the celestial influences that affected your mother wouldn't carry over to have the same effect upon her child because of the fact that celestial influences are not a biological DNA facet of one's physiology.

► *Is the embryo affected by the astrological influence at the time of conception?*

Nope. Nada. At the moment an infant is born, that child is "showered," so to speak, by the existing magnetic influences of the celestial bodies dominating the heavens at that precise moment in time. That child is *imprinted* with those potent influences that serve to create indelible and dynamic facets to his or her personality. In other words, the child, upon physical exit from the protected womb, is *exposed* to the celestial influences currently existing in his or her new outside-world reality. An analogy would be this: You are inside your house and it's raining outside. Your being in the house is the same as the embryo's being inside the womb. You are not affected by the pouring rain because you are *within* a sheltering environment and the rain is *without*— you are protected from that outside influence of the rain. But then you go outside without a coat or umbrella and you are immediately affected by that rain. You have entered an outside environment where you're exposed to its existing elements. And this is why an embryo is not affected by the celestial positioning at the moment of conception but rather is exposed to it at the moment of birth.

► *I really love someone and want to marry him, but our charts are terribly incompatible. What should I do?*

First of all, I want to stress—firmly—that you should never, ever make a marriage decision on the basis of the opinion or attitude of another. Marriage is an extremely personal and individual issue. It is based on love—or it should be. Your love for this man is your determining factor here. If love is deep enough, if it's true, then what his chart looks like will have no bearing and will not even be a consideration. Since this question came up, are you sure you love this individual enough? I can't imagine a chart causing any kind of anxiety or making a problematic issue that affects one's level of love or consideration of marriage. The greatest depth of love surpasses all superficial aspects of an individual or relationship. It goes far beyond the occupation, religious persuasion, ethnicity, astrological chart, or even gender of one's mate. Asking about this chart is like asking if you should marry someone who has red hair instead of the blond hair you're more attracted to and have always idealized your marriage partner as having. It's just not germane when you weigh that insignificant aspect against that of love.

We've all heard that love is blind. It's true, you know. Love, a deeply enduring true sense of love, sees not. It sees not the faults or the idiosyncratic character peculiarities of another. It sees not the eccentricities or the color of skin. Why is love so blind? Because love is not a sight at all . . . love is a feeling. Love is the very pulse of the heart. Love is a great power in and of itself. And that power transcends all else. Its potentiality is limitless, boundless, and bottomless. It has no shape to conform it within. It is fluid. It is free of constraints and unaffected by societal and personal mores.

This questioner is attempting to qualify her love for her mate, to push and shove it into the form of a specific chart's shape because she thinks that particularly defined shape will enhance the relationship and ensure long-lived compatibility. Theoretically, she perceives this as an ideal situation, but is it? Do we really want a mate who is so like ourselves and so compatibly similar that we appear as twins in character and interests? Are we looking for a mate who is just like us? A mirror image? How boring that would be. I believe we're all looking for love, just love—love that is deep, true, and enduring. That is the priority. And it's the *differences* between mates that keep the relationship interesting, exciting, and openly spontaneous. Chart incompatibility? Phooey! Look not to the chart; rather, look within self . . . to the heart.

▸ *Is planetary influence a significant factor regarding a spirit entity's choice of reentry time into the physical?*

No, it's not. Before reincarnating into the physical, a spirit looks for certain key associative elements that will enhance his or her chances for attaining success regarding a specifically intended purpose. These main elements are ethnicity and geographical location. It's not important if the spirit's mother is married or if she's wealthy or poor. Whether there are other children in the family is insignificant. Likewise, the social status or character of the mother is not a consideration. Oftentimes, the spirit foresees the possibility of the mother's giving up the newborn to adoption and, in this case, the spirit chooses this mother *because* of the new *surrogate* mother by which it sees itself ending up being raised.

The idea of needing to factor in an astrological birth time is absolutely frivolous and of no concern to the spirit entity preparing to reincarnate. That'd be absolutely as narcissistic as wanting to be born a blonde. Those types of characteristics are physical, and physical attributes are factors to which spirits don't give a mote of thought.

You have to remember that spirits wishing to reincarnate are full of a powerful sense of purpose. That purpose is their ideal, their singular goal. It's the whole reason for making the effort in the first place. To focus on planetary alignments whose influence endows the new infant with the most pleasing characteristics would be a sign of egotistical thought toward self, and self is nowhere to be found within these entities—only purpose. So then, the final answer to this question is no. A spirit entity gives no consideration to celestial positioning when determining the best birth circumstances to enter within.

▸ *When a volcano erupts, is its future activity governed by astrological influences?*

Only indirectly. As above, so below. Because of life's interconnectedness by way of the Great Web of Life, all aspects of reality have relationship. This relationship between celestial bodies and the earth's physiological activity is a subtle one. More to the point of your question, the physics of geology and its manifestations are due to the inherent qualities of its innate nature. Plate movement, internal temperature, pressure buildup, ocean currents, air flow, and so forth all contribute to how the physical facets of the earth behave. Meteorology and geology are siblings, whereas astrology and geology are far distant cousins.

▶ *I don't like the sign I was born under. Can I change it? I see other signs that would better suit my goals and purposes.*

What? You can't change your birth sign any more than you can change your birthdate. Well, sure, you could lie about your birthdate and alter records to agree with whatever astrological birth sign you wish to have, but that still won't change the underlying fact of your true birthdate and true sign. No matter how you rearrange the dates on paper, in reality they cannot be altered. You will always be affected by the influences of whatever sign you were born under. At your birth, this celestial arrangement manifested an intangible imprint upon your beingness, your personality and character. It becomes part of you. It delineates your tendencies, attitudes, emotional traits, and so on.

Now, although the above characteristics of a particular birth sign may be displeasing, they don't necessarily negate change either. An individual born as a Virgo will supposedly exhibit preciseness. This person has to have an ordered life, has to be efficient and fastidious. However, just because the sign outlines these traits doesn't also mean that they can't be altered through a conscious desire to do so. You still have your own mind that makes choices and life decisions for you. An astrological sign is just that—a sign. It *implies* influence—a *general* influence upon one's personality. It does not define one's total beingness, because who we are today is a beautiful composite of all our experiential lifetimes. The "who" of us is contained within the totality of our spirit's multifaceted consciousness, not solely confined to this one life's existence. We are a *totality* of consciousness, not a fragment of same.

In this lifetime, you are experiencing and developing new growth, so to speak. That new growth is actually carving out a brand-new facet to the main crystal that is your spirit's totality. Every life lived creates an entirely new facet to yourself—your true self. Every life lived adds another interesting and varied dimension to that true self and its magnificent totality. And it is through experiencing differing personality traits that we become well rounded and complete in the ability to reach goals, fulfill potentialities, and sustain their level of energy so that we can advance to new heights of endeavor.

To this inquirer, I would say accept the who of you. Denial prevents growth. Everyone on this beautiful planet of ours is a unique and extremely special individual. Everyone is different and each adds a colorful dimension to the patchwork quilt that is humanity. Diversity—cherish it. Without it, this would be a very boring place full of sameness—monochromatic hues of one tiring color.

Accept who you are. Love who you are. Make the most of who you are. In this manner, every individual makes a difference simply because he or she is a *unique* individual.

▶ *I'm planning a future pregnancy. Is it wrong to try to plan the birth for a specific astrological influence?*

I'm not going to emphatically tell you that that'd be wrong; however, consider this: If a spirit entity gives no credence to the astrological alignment as a determining factor for reincarnating, why should you? You're going for a "designer" personality for your child, and in reality, is that significant? Don't you want your child to be his- or herself? Don't you want to let your child be affected by whatever alignment is going to be *naturally* inherent?

Advancements in biophysics have created the capability to choose a child's gender, and gene splicing has manifested the potentiality to alter disease susceptibility by manipulating DNA. Do we also want to control a child's personality by dictating what celestial influences will be imprinted upon him or her?

Besides this, *every* astrological sign has its commendable aspects and its less desirable ones. Within each sign is a balance. There are signs that enhance the characteristics of others and there are signs that conflict with the traits of others, yet all signs are uniquely individualized and exceptional. Some signs impart a tendency toward an artistic profession and others inspire philosophical thought. Some generate an analytical intelligence, whereas others instill one drawn more to conceptualized ideology. We need that diversity. Society needs the freethinkers along with the traditionalists. Don't try to control your child's professional or intellectual tendencies. One of the most beautiful aspects of a young child is his or her purity of nature. He or she is like a precious seed the Divine gifts us with. We nurture and care for it. We let it germinate in fertile soil and allow it to grow into the sunlight and experience the strengthening elements of the wind and rainfall. And without any other interference from us, we are, one bright day, suddenly quite surprised to be presented with the beautiful blossom our wonderful gift became—a blossom with personality, intelligence, sense of humor, character attributes, talent and skill, hopes and dreams.

To want to "design" that child is to want to specifically "improve" the seed that was so lovingly gifted to you. That ideology says, "Thanks, God, but I want this gift to look like *this* or act like *that* instead of what You present to me." Huh? It says, "I don't want an artist in the family; I want a scientist."

Our children are incredibly dynamic individuals. Let's perceive them as such. Unique unto themselves. Love yourself. Love your child.

► *When my dog was born, was it affected by astrological influences? If so, do the same celestial laws apply to animals that apply to humans?*

This answer is going to be succinct. All of life is affected by all other aspects of life because of the basic fact that all of life—all your relations—is interconnected. Remember, in a previously answered question, I explained that the celestial aspects are *subtle* influences. The effects on animals of astrological alignments present at an animal's birth time will not be nearly as noticeable as they are in humans because people still don't understand that animals have personality and are receptive to the same external influences as we are.

▸ *In the situation of multiple births, will all the siblings be affected by the same astrological influences and develop to be nearly identical to one another in personality and character traits?*

I find this to be an extremely interesting question because it shows some deeper thought.

Although there has been strong evidence regarding twins, especially identical twins, that shows an amazing correlation between the two siblings in character traits, likes and dislikes, inherent skills, and professional leanings, they are still individual entities. One twin is not the clone of the other. Twins are not exact and precise replicas or mirror images.

There is a hidden aspect to this concept of multiple births— the spiritual aspect. Every individual in the physical is merely a minuscule facet of his or her spirit's totality of consciousness— an animated fragment of his or her beautiful totality of consciousness, which consists of every person that spirit ever was while experiencing a series of sequential lifetimes. So although a child may be a twin, a triplet, or even one of sextuplets, that child is still an individual and carries with him or her a shining totality of consciousness consisting of every personality ever experienced in the past. In this manner, each person is a quintessentially unique individual whether or not he or she shared the womb with others. And this is also why triplets can grow up to follow paths that are greatly divergent from those of their siblings. One could be a child prodigy—a concert cellist, one could be a master auto mechanic, and one could be a dedicated social worker. When one is looking at a singular, generalized concept, it's important to factor in all aspects to come to a knowledgeable conclusion. Who we were in past lives and what our experiential history was are as important to consider as the current astrological alignments under which we were born in this lifetime. Both affect our beingness. Both converge to create a coherency of absolute traits defining the new individual.

Society, particularly new parents, perceives the brand-new life of a newborn as a blank slate to be written on. Society views this new life as a piece of precious clay to be molded and formed, but in reality, that new life already has a long history of consciousness to draw from. That history will present itself from time to time throughout the child's life as nebulous past-life memories or inclinations. That child will have preformed relationships with certain individuals. That child will have a natural but inexplicable magnetic draw to certain people, occupations, or causes. That newborn child is full of experiences that may or may not be recalled or have a likewise significant influence upon his or her current life.

So then, the individual children of multiple births indeed do have unexplainable bonds and emotional ties to one another, yet they also have bonds and ties to their own historical pasts that are powerful behavioral influences.

► *Do astrological influences from past lives carry over to affect my current incarnation?*

Yes, indirectly, because those same influences that were imprinted upon your past life personality helped to form the who of you in that historical experience. See? Every past life incarnation was lived under the affectation of that life's birth sign. And since your spirit's consciousness is an amalgamation of all those lives and personalities you exhibited, your current consciousness carries, deep within it, the influences of those same past selves.

We are indeed a blend of everyone we ever were, of every

experience we've ever had . . . we just don't consciously recall them all; that's why they frequently come to the fore in dreams. We are so much more than who we think we are. We are a composite of everyone we ever were. Our histories are rich and full. Each one of us, if we could manage total recall—I mean *total* spirit recall—could combine our memories and fill in all the gaping holes in history and dispel every seeming mysterious enigma of it. Yet, the Divine, in Her/His great wisdom, has seen the necessity of our selective amnesia, for to recall all would be to hinder the ability to effectively focus on today.

▶ *What planet does God live on?*

What? Are you serious? Well, yes, I think we can all agree that society has this generally held idea that God is "out there" or "up there" somewhere, but a planet? On an actual planet? As John Denver would probably have said about that idea, "That's far out!" And he'd have been right too.

The divine aspects of the Trinity are of a *spirit* nature, whereas a planet is of the three-dimensional *physical*. The Divine is everywhere. Her/His nature *imbues* all rather than being trapped by the constraint of being in only one place at a time. It is the Divine Consciousness that binds all life together upon the fine strands of the Great Web of Life. That Consciousness is everywhere. That Consciousness *is* Life. It is the very breath that sustains us. The Divine is not relegated to here or to there. The Divine is not up, not down. The Divine is within the pulsating DNA of the All.

God does not live on a planet. God . . . just . . . exists.

▶ *Is a war or political conflict (the bombing of Pearl Harbor, for example) influenced by astrological factors? If so, could the outcome of such an event also be predicted by those same specific influences at its inception?*

Several world cultures hold with consulting the stars to determine the "most propitious" time for beginning major life phases or making decisions regarding wedding dates, journeys, and so on, yet wars are not influenced by the stars because they are so gross in what and who they encompass. Weddings involve two individuals; by consulting the planetary positioning in the heavens and calculating an alignment between the astrological signs of the respective bride and groom, one can identify a window of time as providing a tentative "propitious" choice of dates. The same applies to proposed journeys planned by individuals. Rather than the positioning of the stars and planets, military technology and the strategies of the *participants* determine the outcome of wars.

► *Are returned completed spirits affected by the planetary influences at the time of their entry into the physical?*

Sure they are. They aren't immune to any aspect associated with the physical world they enter into. Your question implies the assumption that completed spirits are somehow special, that they're "protected" from that which affects all others. That's just not the way of it. The astrological alignment at the time of his birth affected Jesus just as much as the alignment at the time of your birth influenced you. Being a completed spirit back on earth does not negate one's receptivity to the natural forces existing within the whole of the cosmos. One's spiritual mission cannot be effectively addressed or brought to fruition through any manner of isolation or protective shield. One must be as a sister or brother to the other members of the human family. And that means that the body is susceptible to viruses, emotionality, human and planetary influences, and so on. To be otherwise would mean one is the Divine.

► *Are inanimate objects such as cars and computers affected by astrological influences relating to the time they were manufactured?*

Initially, when I read this question, I felt compelled to think it was sent to me as a joke, but upon further consideration, realized that it was a valid one. I always told my children to never be embarrassed to ask a question, to never think a question—any question—is a stupid one. Otherwise, how would we ever learn? So I concluded that this was a bona fide inquiry and will treat it as such.

Inanimate objects are not affected by the arrangement of celestial bodies in the heavens at the time the object was manufactured—they are not affected by celestial bodies at all. However, there is another aspect to this questioner's issue: the fact that the inanimate object itself, if created from "natural" substances, emits its own field of energy that is specific and unique unto its inherent natural characteristics of composition. So although this object would not be affected by any celestial factor at the time it was made, the object still emanates a unique vibrational field of energy.

▶ *I've been trying to plan my life according to astrological influences and nothing is working. How come?*

Nothing is working because you're attempting to create your own reality as one aligned with the stars and planets. You're trying to make a "designer" life based on heavenly arrangements instead of allowing life to take its natural course. Rather than accepting that which presents itself upon your life path, you are trying to choose what will appear upon the path. This method of trying to control and manipulate your life is a dependent one whereby all elements of that life are contingent on the shape of a heavenly pattern, not leaving you free to make decisions on the basis of logic and reason. Now I'm not saying that consulting the stars is not a reasonable thing to do now and again. What I *am* saying is that it's not reasonable or logical to *constantly* do it, to do it so often that it becomes a habit—an addiction—that precludes independent thinking.

When we're ready to set out on a trip, we usually check the weather conditions. That's reasonable. That's a logical action. When we arrive at an airport, we check the posted schedule of flights to verify if our plane's been delayed or canceled. That's logical. Every so often, we check the fluids in our vehicle engines to ensure smooth running. That's reasonable and necessary. But when people check an astrological chart before they make every move or decision in life, that's not logical or reasonable. That's being dependent and not being self-reliant on one's own resources of intelligence and reason.

Each individual is responsible for his or her own decisions and choices made in life. Those choices cannot be solely subject to their relationship with the stars but must rather be arrived at after being given considerable analysis and contemplation. You see, depending on the stars as a sole criterion for decision making removes all personal responsibility from your self. It says, "I don't have to make this decision because the stars will tell me what I should do." It's the same as using a psychic as a habitual consultant for every move you make in life. You're still using a crutch for personal responsibility, shifting that responsibility to someone else or some other outside factor when it should come from within.

Your life is not unfolding as you'd like it because you're avoiding personal responsibility. You can ease your life path in a general direction according to a plan to work toward a specific goal, but you cannot continually allow your every move to be contingent upon celestial alignments. That makes as much sense as consulting the child's magic Eight Ball for an answer to your every question regarding choices and decisions.

The important choices that present themselves in life are not singular facets. That is, they are not independent elements because most often they affect relationships, occupation considerations, emotionality, relocation, and so on. And gaining acuity and clear perspective regarding these issues brings a decision into sharper focus. When all associated elements have been considered to their fullest, a specific decision will eventually dominate all other possible alternatives.

The issue of this questioner's inquiry can be split into two main important concepts—that of the importance of *taking personal responsibility* and that of *developing acceptance* for whatever situations or conditions are present upon one's life path. Acceptance—for years, I've emphasized this beautiful attribute because it's such a wonderful and stress-relieving characteristic. Acceptance means that we acknowledge when we cannot change something or when we have no right to change something through interference or manipulation. Having this beautiful attribute ingrained within us as a true attitude allows many of life's negatives to easily roll off our backs instead of spearing into our emotions and causing psychological (and physical) havoc. Acceptance keeps many of those negatives from being internalized. It brings about observance of an event, situation, or action rather than a personal participation in it. Acceptance maintains an outsider perspective, which serves as an insulating factor against emotional pain, against being drawn into eliciting a negative knee-jerk reaction, against causing harm to another, and against ending up being an interfering factor in another's life. We accept what life offers and change what we can through personal and wise decisions. That which we cannot change, we accept. It's simple. Life can be a lot simpler if people understand that they don't have to depend on crutches but can instead make their own choices and decisions. Life can be a lot simpler if people comprehend the beauty of having acceptance. Life can be simpler if people just take personal responsibility for that life and realize that nobody can live their life for them and that no one or anything else can make their decisions for them. Each of us is a beautiful and unique individual who makes his or her own specialized mark in the world. Whether that mark will look like all the others because of a lack of individuality or will have no comparison because of individuality is all up to you. It's the difference between independence and dependence. It's the difference between acceptance and bucking the natural current of life. It's the difference between individualized thought and complete nonthought.

If all our decisions and life choices were based on what the heavens displayed at a specific time or were based on what a psychic said, how, then, would we ever have the opportunity to feel responsible? Instead, wouldn't we feel that decisions came from without? From an outside source other than the self? In that situation, we could also have an outside source to place blame on if our choices were less than perfect—a scapegoat. Aha! The *stars* made me do it! A psychic *told* me to do it! It wasn't *me!* But you know what? No matter who or what advised you to do it, it was still *you* who went ahead and did it. So what is the real bottom line here? No matter who or what advises or tells you to do something, to make this or that choice, it's still *you* who are responsible for your actions. Though you seek out advice and consult others, you are the one who ultimately must act on that advice. It's you who must take or leave that advice according to your own conscience. Therefore, the entire idea of a scapegoat to place blame on is in actuality a shallow and groundless excuse for your actions.

▶ *I'm getting ready to build a new house. Is it reasonable to ask the contractors their birth signs as part of the interview process?*

This is a highly unusual question, to be sure, but it's not reasonable if you're intending their answers to be the determining criteria for hire. As I said earlier, you can't hire or fire based on such a discriminatory element as astrological birth sign; rather, your decision should be based on skill and integrity. Even the factor of the contractor's experience shouldn't necessarily be considered, because although this may be his or her first job, the individual may be far more qualified than someone who has years of experience under the belt. Everyone has to start somewhere. Everyone has a beginning.

▶ *Do you foresee a major realignment of the planets in the near future?*

No, not in the "near" future.

▶ *If the Starborn races come from other universes and all of our own astrological influences are based on the constellations within our solar system, do the Starborn have a correlating system of astrology that they recognize?*

Sure they do. It's based on the celestial alignments of their own galaxies. How would it be otherwise? They couldn't base their astrological concept on ours because our planets wouldn't have any influential vibrationary affect upon their own birthings. They have their own planets that emit these similar affects upon individuals and life-forms.

▶ *Are there animal totems associated with the astrological signs?*

It's been generally put forth that there are, but in actuality, an animal totem is a highly individualized concept unique to each person. A generalized totem encompassing all folks born under one sign is too broad in scope; it's far too undefined for a particular personal totem because, after all, a personal totem comes by way of a powerful dream, vision, or strong affinity.

▶ *I heard that every birth sign also carries a specific color with it. Is that true?*

As with the above question, sometimes people generalize. There is supposedly a general color associated with every astrological sign; however, this is also an extremely broad scope concept. One's natural attraction to a specific color is derived from a multitude of factors, such as past-life experiences, personal vibrational fields, biological magnetism, individual energy potentiality, and emotions, psychological profile.

Because they are unique individuals, all affected by innumerable life factors, all individuals born between May 21 and June 20 will not be drawn to the color orange. If every birth sign were truly associated with a specific color, wouldn't twins or triplets all be partial to the same color? Logic and a good measure of reason must be applied when we are dealing with generalized concepts. We can't take them as concrete validations that hold true for all, because each of us is so incredibly different in so many ways.

► *I know a Virgo who is so messy and nonchalant about it that nobody would guess he was born under that sign. How come? I thought Virgos were fastidious and orderly.*

Well, then, this is a prime example of what I just got through explaining in the previous response. Each of us is a unique individual. That uniqueness is based on a wide variety of factors, only one of which is the astrological element. It's not logical or reasonable to stuff every person born under the Virgo sign into a box labeled ORDERLY or FASTIDIOUS, because every one of them is different and is not necessarily orderly or fastidious. Every one of them will possess differing degrees of those qualities. Some will drive you absolutely crazy with the need to have every little thing in its designated place, whereas others won't give a rat's hat about where things are strewn. And then there will be a whole gamut of those who fit well in between the two extremes, each one behaving exactly how a multitude of factors affect their psychological makeup.

The astrological alignment at birth does indeed shower an individual with a generalized birth sign, but the *specifics* of that sign are as varied in degrees of physical and psychological evidence as the sands on a wild ocean beach. Towering tall above all conceptual theories stands the preeminent and immutable fact that first of all, we are individuals—unique and multifaceted. Consequently, these theories' minuscule effects are eclipsed by it.

Enter the evidence of your Virgo friend who does not conform to the stringent mold within which the astrological sign of Virgo would confine him. He is not concerned with household order but rather contrarily prefers a more relaxed environment where the "proper" place for things is right where they are at any given time. So? Does that negate his Virgoness? No, certainly not; it only shows his individuality—his sense of *freedom* to show his individuality. Do you think he cares a whit that his sign characterizes him as meticulous and tidy? Do you think he cares about those qualities defining his personality? No, because he's not letting the astrological factor define who he is—his identity. He is who he is regardless of what some celestial alignment says he must be. You see? Freedom. Freedom to just . . . *be.* And what a wonderfully light and airy attitude that freedom is when you recognize it and really understand it for its priceless value in life! It's a blessing few are truly aware of. It's a blessing few identify and acknowledge as a true blessing existing for the taking.

▶ *If two people are in a relationship, which is the best-case scenario—to have complementary signs or contrasting ones?*

Neither. Either. A relationship isn't defined by the astrological signs of its participants but rather is nourished by their love for one another. Like sign characteristics may appear to present the condition of compatibility, yet it would seem to me that this would have the probability of generating a boring and eventually stagnant relationship. Though most people look for a partner or significant other who has like interests and philosophies, these are not the sole criteria that mark a lasting and meaningful relationship. I've known people who were complete opposites and their commitment to one another was rock solid and unshakable, yet I've also known folks whose partnership endured with deep love while they were nearly mirror images of each other. There is no preferred situation in regard to astrological alignments of partners because, in the final analysis, it's the individuals themselves who make or break the union. There are times when a great chasm of personality, interests, occupation, and so forth exist between couples and this situation opens up an incredibly wide scoped lens through which both end up perceiving their world view. Differences can be a blessing or a curse, depending on how one sees those differences. They can be an element in one's life that causes continual stress and agitation or they can be a powerful force that serves as a strong impetus to expand one's experiential base, knowledge, and potential. You see, it's not so much *what* exists in our life but rather how we *use* what exists. The existence of differences in a relationship is a prime example of how life affords us unlimited opportunities for self-expansion and personal growth.

Don't perceive a partner's differentness as being a snag in the relationship's fabric; rather, view it as being threads of gold that enhance and strengthen the whole.

► *My son's astrological chart shows that his ideal occupation is one involving science or some type of research. I'm at continual odds with him over this because he wants to be an interior designer, of all things. Help!*

I can't help unless you give some serious thought to the suggestions and concepts I present regarding this issue.

First, you need to answer an important question: Why are you trying to manipulate your son's life? He's twenty-two years old. He's an individual. He must live his life according to his own conscience—how he is guided within himself—not by outside influences or forces. Not by what Mother wishes him to be or do. It's time to cut the apron strings, Mom. It's time to open your eyes to the fact that your son is no longer your little Davey, but David—an adult with a mind and life of his very own. He is now responsible for every decision and choice he makes in life. Those are no longer your responsibility as his parent. Yes, I concede that it is still your right to offer opinions and suggestions, to give advice and help, but only when asked. Otherwise, you could very well be perceived as a nagging mother who constantly interferes in her son's life. There comes a time when the line between parental interference and simple advice is very thin. A wise parent recognizes that point and acknowledges respect for it.

I have children, too—three grown daughters. They've made some choices I've cringed at and they've made decisions that have made me proud to be their mom. I give advice when asked. I keep silent when it proves prudent to do so. Wisdom is knowing when to do which. Sometimes parents, through experiential living, know too well the pitfalls of certain life decisions yet, in spite of that knowing, must allow the child to discover those same pitfalls on his or her own. This is so because oftentimes, no matter how vehemently or how often you attempt to expose those pitfalls involved with a particular choice in life, the child will be deaf to your words. For whatever reason, the child will not hear what you're saying and will be in complete denial about any negatives associated with a planned course of action. These are cases when the parent, through continual harping, can become a nagging interference in the child's life or, after repeatedly stressing the pitfalls, can accept the child's determination and just . . . well, keep quiet and hope for the best. It's only natural for a parent to want the best for the child, to want him or her to succeed and avoid hurtful experiences due to unwise choices, but the other side to that coin is loving the child enough to let the child *learn* and *grow* through self-made decisions. That's part of how every individual becomes independent and develops wisdom. Allowing an adult child the freedom of independent thinking is one of the greatest gifts of love with which a parent can bless a child. No matter how old that child gets, he or she will always be your child, but how you treat that child is what determines if you as a parent are selfishly foolish or selflessly wise.

Okay, getting back to the issue of your son's occupation . . . so what if he wants to be an interior designer? Think about that. So what? Are you having a difficult time accepting his choice because you think he'll fail? Do you think it's not "manly" enough? Or because being an interior decorator doesn't garner the social status that a being scientist or researcher would? What? What is it that's causing you so much grief? You need to get to the heart of the matter here. You need to examine your attitudes regarding occupation, status, your son, social mores, your philosophy on lifestyles, and so forth. You need to do this with complete honesty, because using an astrological chart for your prime basis of argument is transparent and shallow. There's more behind your argument—a lot more.

Let's get down to the ground issue of occupation or profession as presupposed within one's personal astrological chart. Okay, the chart suggests an occupation that best suits that birth sign along with all the multiple, correspondingly interactive chart elements, yet does that mean or even imply that all people born at that same moment in time should be a scientist or researcher to succeed in life or reach their ultimate potentiality? Nope. It doesn't mean that at all. Though it may appear that that's what it's saying, it's not. It implies only that folks born then *may* have a greater *inclination* toward those fields of endeavor. Do you see the difference here between *may* and *must? Inclination* and *proficiency?*

Your son might have been a master architect in a past life. He might also have been an accomplished, even world-famous, artist in another. His entire *spirit's* experiential past may have been in artistic fields, and all of these are a viable part of his current consciousness. Keeping that in mind, wouldn't it be quite natural to have a strong, magnetic pull toward another life developing those artistic experiential skills that are so solidly ingrained into the consciousness? In reality, he's merely *continuing* to enhance his natural talents and inherent skills. Can't you see your way clear to allowing him that opportunity? To love him enough to take joy in his having a creative life, doing what he wants and loves to do? Yes, you can. When you really think about it, you can. Rather than fight with him over this, accept his choice. Rather than cause you both undue stress over this, encourage his talent. Rather than widen the distance between you, close it with love and understanding.

▶ *Why is it that people who are really into astrology can never guess my sign?*

Because you clearly enjoy freedom of personal expression. You are a unique individual, and you aren't reluctant to be who you are. And the "who" of you is not based on your birth sign. You obviously have strong past-life influences that overshadow any or most of your current possible astrological affectations. You freely display the effects of a composite spirit consciousness within your current physical life. That's good. That's as it should be, for within, you are many aspects of those varied personalities that you've been in the past, all having equally as many historical experiences.

▶ *I know that the precise positioning of the planets can influence a person's personality at the time of birth, so I was wondering—what about comets and meteor showers?*

Comets or meteor showers that are in evidence at an individual's birth moment do not emanate influential forces of energy as the constellations do; therefore, there is no "imprinting" made on the newborn's character and personality by these events.

▶ *Are comets an omen or some type of harbinger of the future?*

Only in the minds of the doomsday-sayers and fearmongers. In reality, comets and like celestial events are natural phenomena, and their occurrence is completely unrelated to any human or societal affair taking place in the present or in the future.

The idea that comets and such are harbingers of future religious or geologically catastrophic events is strongly reminiscent of the Middle Ages, an age of ignorance in which some believed such things as birthmarks or unusually shaped moles to be the marks of a witch. Not only is the idea of a comet being an omen or special sign ignorant, it's also incredibly arrogant. Long before this planet of ours was inhabited by humanoids, comets and meteor showers were flaming through the heavens for millions of years. Now, enter the egotistical and self-possessed humans who think Nature is there for them instead of the other way around. They think Nature *performs* just for them as a bringer of signs and portents of doom. Jeez Louise, get a clue. Thus, nigh on the cusp of the twenty-first century, have we learned nothing of the reality of nature, physics, and our world environment? How can it be that so many people are intellectually caught in the thought of the Middle Ages? From masses of devotees coming from far and wide to venerate a shadow cast on an office building wall to religious hysterics over an imagined alien mother ship hidden in the tail of a comet. Where has reason and intelligence fled to? Is society so depraved of spirituality that it even craves the ridiculous and grasps it as being truth? As being reality? Has society's perceptual sight deteriorated that badly? Has it gone so far as to obscure all reason and logic?

Earthly humankind is not the end-all of creation. It is not the epitome life-form of the universe, nor does it cause the mighty solar system to revolve around it. Human arrogance has reached the point where it's bumping against its own hard ceiling in an attempt to elevate itself to even loftier heights, yet all the bumping and bruising doesn't appear to be teaching anything because the message isn't getting through.

The stars don't twinkle just for us. We didn't orchestrate the recorded hum of the universe. We don't sit at the controls that operate the solar system's machinations. Meteor showers don't come merely as an awesome show for human enjoyment. And since the daybreak of creation, comets have streaked through the sky . . . long before a human foot ever made a crude imprint upon the moist antediluvian soil of earth.

► *I'm a Libra and, according to my chart, my priority should be directed toward marriage and enduring partnerships. I'm not the least bit inclined to get married, nor am I particularly interested in having a significant other right now. I'm perfectly happy remaining single. What's wrong with me?*

Not a thing. You are who you are, not who a chart says you must be. That's the bottom line here. No one can direct, control, or manipulate your life for you unless you allow him or her to do so. And no chart can cause you to be something you're not or do something you're not naturally inclined to do. People are so ingrained to think they need to exhibit chart characteristics that they think there's something wrong with them if they don't—like you. But you're forgetting that you're a composite of everyone you've ever been. Your spirit consciousness retains a historical memory of those personalities in your current subconsciousness and your current personage retains some carry-over traits of those same past identities. Who you are today is not your whole identity but rather is a minuscule facet of many preformed aspects of a "mother" crystal (my analogy) that contains *all* facets of your self. To expect your beautiful totality to be identified solely by an astrological chart based on your *current* physical life is ludicrous. That'd be like reading only the last chapter of a book and claiming that that chapter is the complete totality of its content, that there was nothing associated with it that came before or that led up to it. See what I mean?

So if your current birth chart claims that you have a priority of marriage and/or close partnerships when in actuality you have other goals that take priority, then that simply gives evidence that you have some strong carry-over personality traits from past-life experiences that still influence the attitudes and choices in this current life. This is normal. It's natural. It's how the reality of one's spirit consciousness totality works. These carry-over traits are never more clearly evidenced than in a child prodigy who retains the memory and skill of a past-life personality who was a master painter or accomplished pianist. This example represents the more visible evidence, yet the psychological traits and those defining our personal interests are more subtle. Still, they explain why we don't seem to fit into the confines of an astrological birth chart.

If marriage is not for you, then so be it. You are an individual and as such are responsible for every decision you make in life. Social mores are finally being seen for the prejudicial and judgmental elements they are. More and more people are opting for the single life. There's absolutely nothing wrong with that. And any-one who tells you that it's a selfish choice is either jealous or self-righteous. They don't live your life; they don't make your choices.

Every single person on this planet must live life according to his or her own conscience. Each of us must follow individual inner promptings for lifestyle, profession, location of residence, spiritual beliefs, philosophies, and so on. We were not created clones of each other. We were created as shimmering spiritual intelligences clothed in physical forms . . . each one different from the other, each one special and amazingly unique.

► *I was born when intensive solar flares were taking place. What does that mean?*

It means that you were born when intensive solar flares were taking place. I'm not being sarcastic, either; it just doesn't mean anything more than that. The same with the meteor showers and comets, remember? Please keep this issue in perspective. Nature is Nature. Nature is not made for—nor does it perform solely for—humanity.

► *My astrological chart shows that I could become a great spir-itual teacher. Does that mean that I could be the reincarnation of some great religious person from ancient times?*

Not necessarily. Not even probably. Let's not jump the gun here and let the ego cloud reason.

I need to reiterate the fact that astrological charts give indica-tions and *possible* influences. Their details are *tentative* traits and characteristics that *may* exist if other past-life characteristics are not predominant factors. Charts represent strong possibilities, not immutable facts. Therefore, you must keep this firmly in mind when reviewing a chart. This is why everyone who has a chart done not only will find exact depictions of their personality but will also discover qualities listed that are completely off the mark.

A chart is not a method of carved-in-stone prognostication. It does not predict or forecast one's destined future in respect to occupation, lifestyle, relationships, or otherwise. It does not reveal past-life identities—or even imply that it can, so you're taking this chart and really stretching it. I mean *really* s- t- r- e- t- c- h- i- n- g it. Though you may not consciously realize it, your ego is getting in the way of rationale. It's unwise to read something that isn't there. It's foolish to make assumptions when there's not been even a hint of an implication made.

Your chart is merely stating that you *may* have a natural *tendency* toward becoming a spiritual teacher in this life. The key here is the word *may*. It in no way implies that you *will*. See the difference? This is much like my correspondents who write that a psychic told them that they're going to be a great prophetess or medicine woman someday yet they know nothing about such things. They write wanting to know how this can be possible. Well, sure, it makes me wonder too, because nobody can tell you what to be. I believe that a bona fide psychic wouldn't reveal a client's future occupation or purpose if it was foreseen. I believe this because I know how problematic such a revelation can be and how much inner confusion and turmoil can result if the individual is in no way ready to set foot upon that specific path yet. These things come quite naturally and in their own time as one progresses and grows throughout life. To be told long before one has any inclination or tendency toward such a purpose is futile and greatly damaging. So for someone to tell you you're to one day be a great prophetess or medicine woman when today, you're completely involved in taking care of a household full of young children is, to me, quite irresponsible. Because of this fact, I seriously doubt this particular psychic's credibility and validity. There are ethics involved here that were seriously breeched.

I think the man who wrote me with the original astrological question was simply openly honest with a curious wonderment. Though that wonderment was subconsciously ego inspired, I don't believe he was coming from an arrogant attitude of possible self-aggrandizement. The lesson here is to not take a grain of sand and perceive it as a mountain. Perceptual clarity is the goal to shoot for. Keeping within the bounds of rationale and solid facts is the key to comprehension and is the fertile ground in which wisdom ultimately sinks its roots. Astrological charts should be viewed solely as *possibilities*—possible tendencies or possible inclinations toward one's character, occupation, personality traits, goal orientation, lifestyle, and so forth. Keep these in perspective, for your life is your own and is not defined by or confined to a diagram of the stars purported to chart same.

Perhaps this correspondent will end up being a great spiritual teacher; perhaps he'll turn out to be a world-renowned environmentalist or a garage mechanic. Wherever destiny leads him, his footfalls must follow his heart, his conscience, his *natural* inclinations in order for him to reach the ultimate potential of his intended purpose for being here.

▸ *Is astrology the work of Satan?*

Oh, please—the heinous mentality of the Inquisition was over hundreds of years ago. Why does every natural aspect of Nature's reality have to end up being bastardized and satanized by religious ignorance?

Most of Nature's reality is merely evidence of physics. The more scientific discoveries physicists uncover, the more human beings realize how tightly the fields of science and spirituality are interwoven into a converging tapestry of reality. This reality is the inherent nature of our world. It's evidence of what is and how it works and behaves. The concept of astrology is simply another discovery of how the magnetic fields of specific planetary alignments emanate a vibrational influence over all of life. That's it. No hoodoo involved. No magic or witchcraft behind it. And certainly, no little red-tailed goblins with horns and three-tined pitchforks trying to woo us to the dark side with it.

The Nature of our world is part of the Divine's creative forces.

The Nature of our world emanated from divine thought. How then . . . how in the *world* can people be so intellectually confused and perceptually blind as to look at Nature and think they see demons? Religious schizophrenia? Fanaticism? An obsession with the Devil? The whole idea of astrology as the work of Satan is baffling and utterly incredible. It's just absurd.

▶ *Is there a difference between computer-generated astrological charts and ones figured out manually by an insightful astrologer?*

Though computers are highly touted and are replacing a lot of manual and technical work, they cannot duplicate or surpass human skill coupled with perceptive insight.

▶ *I know that a meteor shower doesn't affect one's birth time, but does it in any way have the capacity to interfere with the astrological alignment influences?*

No. A meteor shower no more interferes with a celestial alignment's influence than the wind can interfere with sunlight or a shadow can block the wind.

▶ *What does earth's moon represent?*

Wisdom. Enlightenment.

The moon, throughout history, has been represented by the goddess Luna, now commonly, but sadly, replaced by the generalized term *lunar*. Many ancient cultures believed the moon symbolized wisdom and its attainment. A full moon signified full knowledge and the potential to gain it. A new moon denoted lost or hidden knowledge, mystery or esoteric elements. And a lunar eclipse meant knowledge temporarily forgotten or consciously denied.

The most popular and generally held belief about the full moon is that it brings out the "crazies"—moon madness. Police seem to dread full-moon nights, and emergency-department personnel make jokes, in the afternoon preceding a full moon, about gearing up for the full moon because there is a noticeable increase in unusual incidents during a full moon. But why is that? What makes the night of a full moon so different from the nights of all the other moon phases? Well, the general consensus is that it's due to the strong magnetic pull that the celestial body has on the fluids of our planet. The tides bear this out. Not only are our planetary waters affected but our bodily fluids are affected. The blood flow from open wounds, during hospital operations, and during a woman's menstrual time will be greater when the moon is full. And the chemicals within our body are stimulated into increased activity, including those of the brain and hypothalamus. This situation alone accounts for the escalated incidences of such behavioral events as violence and rage, the greater frequency of such stress-related occurrences as domestic abuse, and the increased accidents due to unawareness and fragmented thought.

Many cultures had (and still maintain) a belief in a separate women's spirituality/nature, in which the moon was seen as having a direct influence on women's matters, specifically menstruation, called the moon time. There are various historical belief systems related to the moon; you may find it quite interesting to do a little research on the subject.

I would be remiss if I left the topic of the moon without including the related aspect of horticulture. A cursory scan of any farmer's almanac will confirm the importance of planting times as associated with the varying moon phases. This schedule of planting and harvesting guidelines has been devised after many years of experimentation and analysis. It's not merely folklore, as so many people perceive it to be; it's real and it's effective.

▸ *If astrology is based on the specific qualities of planetary magnetic pull and the influences these have on earthly life, why isn't the concept more generally accepted as fact?*

Because everyone has his or her own opinion on the various aspects of physics, just as for all other elements in life. Not everyone believes in the Bible, yet those who do swear that it's the indisputable and definitive word of God. You see, it's the aspect of personal opinion that comes into play here. Even if a particular concept is indeed a proven fact, folks still have the free will to choose whether to believe it. Just as some think the Bible is the word of God, there are many others who perceive it as a book composed of hearsay and secondhand stories that were altered over time by the hands of many translators. It's a fact of physics that the moon's innate quality exerts a magnetic pull on earthly fluids, yet many folks (though believing in the movement of the tides) do not believe the moon has any corresponding effect on human bodily fluids. People pick and choose that which they want to believe. They frequently fragment concepts by saying, "Well, I believe *this* about it, but I don't believe *that* about it."

Some astronomers believe in the technicalities of astrology and some think it's a bunch of hogwash to which only crackpots hold. Some astronomers believe there is the strong probability for intelligent life existing in other galaxies and some think that's so much crock. So there you have it—personal opinion. It comes down to the individuality of perspective, one's extent and quality of analytical thought, reasoning skill, and rationale. I've witnessed the tendency in a preponderance of folks to immediately reject ideas out of hand before applying any mental energy to the concept in question.

I listen to people voice firm opinions, and when I have occasion to inquire how the opinion was derived, I most often receive a short and somewhat amused retort something like this: "Well . . . everyone knows that." This tells me that the individual has formed an opinion of the concept on a superficial level, that the person has not really given the idea any sort of contemplative, analytical, or research time. On the whole, people need to think more. They need to curb the inclination toward mental laziness and rein in their tendency to go along with public opinion or the conceptual status quo. Copernicus deduced that the sun was the center of our solar system and, consequently, was deemed a heretic for voicing his analytical thought. Why? Well, because "everyone knows" that the *earth* is the center of the solar system and that everything else revolves around it. So what does this ultimately say? It says that what "everyone knows" is not necessarily true. It says that what everyone knows may not be a fact at all and that the oddball who thinks and says otherwise is the only one who possesses the chutzpah to diametrically oppose public opinion and stand up for his or her intellectual abilities.

Society, on the whole, is fearful of individual thought. People seem reticent to voice a new thought for fear of ridicule or being dubbed a kook. Copernicus was called a heretic for his contrary belief, yet time proved him right. He was not afraid of public opinion or concerned that his ego might get bruised. He applied analytical thought to astronomical observations and deduced a fact of reality. He did this despite society's general opinion. So should we. New discoveries and revealing epiphanies concerning the magnificent totality of our world reality cannot be uncovered unless we spend time in wonder and, through that inspired curiosity, extend our mind into realms just waiting for our maiden voyage. To be content with the status quo is to be satisfied with an ongoing state of voluntary stagnation where growth is forever stunted and new thought is a taboo.

Everyone "knows" that the moon influences the ebb and flow of the ocean tides, so why doesn't everyone also know that the moon likewise affects the ebb and flow of the inner tides of human physiology? Both are facts, yet both are not universally held beliefs. And the explanation for this is personal opinion based on selectivity.

► *Will a baby be imprinted with the mother's astrological influences through the amniotic fluid surrounding the infant before birth?*

No, because the baby is not exposed to the celestial influences until it enters the outside atmosphere of the physical.

I understood what you were getting at, but two conceptual

elements were a bit confused. You were thinking that the mother's amniotic fluid contains her own markers for *her* specific planetary influences, and since the fluid surrounds the embryo, her markers could affect the growing infant through symbiosis—at least I think that was your thought on it. But no, an embryo will not absorb the mother's own astrological characteristics through her amniotic waters. They are not transferable in this manner, nor are they passed genetically to be included in the baby's DNA composition. Good question. It shows some deeper thought.

▸ *Some astrological signs supposedly bestow a characteristic for psychism. How can that be when I thought everyone had this ability as a spiritually inherent talent?*

Everyone does, to varying degrees. What we're talking about here isn't the New Age idea of being psychic, as in having the strong skill of psychokinesis or telepathy, but rather the more subtle elements of insight, intuition, and inspiration. These are characteristics everyone does have. Some call them woman's intuition; some refer to them as gut feelings. These are natural to us, as much a part of our makeup as skin and bones. It's a fact that we all get *feelings* about things. And these feelings can manifest themselves in a wide variety of ways. Sometimes they'll come as goose bumps. Sometimes they'll show themselves by the hair on the back of your neck standing up or by a sinking, sick feeling in the pit of your stomach. Other times they appear as a sense of foreboding or strong positive inclination. And frequently they will come as an unexplainable knowing, in that you feel that you just *know* something without being able to give any logical reason as to *why* you know it. No matter what form they manifest in, they all represent a form of inexplicable intuition and insight that we all have and experience.

Now, astrologically speaking, when a chart lists psychism as one of its influencing qualities, it usually refers to a marked increase in the strength of these skills that approaches the level of being exceptional. This, then, is when the natural characteristics of intuition and insight extend beyond the norm and reach into the refined subclasses commonly referred to as psychokinesis, prognostication, psychometry, visions, and so forth.

Yes, everyone is psychic with intuition and the ability for insight, but some people also have additional qualities that have been instilled through the means of their specific astrological influences.

► *Will one's astrological chart reveal major events in one's life—events such as an assassination?*

Not specifically. A well-worked and well-researched chart computed by a skilled astrologer will reveal a time in which such a devastating and monumental event is most probable to occur. As to pinpointing and identifying the exact type of event, well, that's fairly impossible because of the law of probabilities, which works in tandem with the multiple elements of free will choices. A qualified astrologer can examine a chart and recognize a questionable time period for the client. This is pointed out, and it's up to the individual to give it credence with increased awareness during that time or to ignore it with denial or nonchalance. A chart won't—and can't—be so exacting as to define a major event like an assassination or a lottery win, but the associative elements converging on that time period will usually, at the very least, show up as an event carrying positive or negative connotations.

► *Does every culture have some form of astrological belief?*

Though these beliefs are not identically aligned with the specifics of the generally held one, I think every culture has beliefs associated with celestial bodies. Much of today's mythology comes from Greek and Roman ancient beliefs in the gods and goddesses related to the planets and constellations. Many cultures believe in Nature goddesses, those of the waters, air, earth, and fire. The Polynesians have their Madame Pele, for instance. Native peoples' cultures are rich in stories of Nature beings and sky people. Yes, I believe all cultures have some type of traditional beliefs related to the heavens.

▶ *If someone was born on the first day of a new sign, wouldn't that person also have some characteristics of the sign whose time period just ended?*

Well, sure. That's called being born on the cusp. The cusp is the transition time in which the last day of one sign is turning into the first day of a new sign. An individual born during this cusp time may be influenced by both signs, making for a very interesting chart with added dimensions.

▶ *If Jesus were reincarnated, what would his chart look like? Would it reveal his identity?*

You haven't thought this out. Many people are born on the same day. And many of those same individuals make their entry into this world at the same hour—down to the same minute. Would every one of their charts reveal a Jesus type of personality? For sure, they'd all be very similar, perhaps even exact, so how can one chart rise above the others to be so extraordinarily different as to actually herald Jesus' return? See what I mean? And what if Jesus were a twin or born as one of quadruplets? Which child would be truly him? How would you determine that? No, if Jesus were to return to the physical, his chart wouldn't single him out from any other child born at the same time. His recognition wouldn't come from that venue.

▶ *The Wise Men were astrologers. What celestial body did they really see? I keep having a nagging sense that it really wasn't a star at all.*

My goodness, this is an interesting question.

There are ancient writings that were secreted away and hidden. They are commonly referred to as the Gnostic Gospels and were originally placed in large jug-type pottery and either buried or set far back in desert caves in the Qumrān Valley and Naj^c Hammādī region. In December 1945, those scrolls and codices were discovered at the Naj^c Hammādī site. Between the two hidden locations, much new information has been revealed regarding the time of Jesus.

One of the scrolls describes the Bethlehem scene at the time of Jesus' birth. It describes how, for several minutes, time froze. The people and animals surrounding the sheltered cave (the stable, as currently believed) were placed in suspended animation. The writing tells of animals' mouths frozen open as they were suspended in time while eating grass. It tells of shepherds' feet stopped in the air while caught in midstep. And it tells of a great, blinding light in the sky directly above the birthing place—a great, blinding *light.*

Two thousand years ago, there were no airplanes, dirigibles, and helicopters to explain such a light; therefore, what else could it be but a star? You see, conclusions can be derived only from knowns. And the only known object that shed light in the sky was a star. So forever after, that specific birth-time light has been classified as a star.

Now, let me add another element here. I live in a modest cabin located in a semi-remote mountain region. The cabin is up on the side of a hill overlooking a large secluded valley. One night that valley had large, brilliant orbs of white light floating around each other in a cluster. It seemed as though they were almost dancing in the moonlight. One appeared to be the size of a large beach ball; the other two moving around it were a bit smaller in size. If those orbs of light hadn't been down level with the cabin and just fifty feet in front of it, instead of higher in the sky, they would've been mistakenly identified as helicopter lights or stars. I've had other nighttime mountain experiences with brilliant orbs of light that either slowly floated over my head or sped quickly by me. Because of these, taken in tandem with Jesus' birth-time scene

recorded in the secreted ancient texts, I cannot in all clear conscience state that the Christmas light was a real star. I don't believe
it was, because my own experience with orbs of brilliant, moving
white light interjects the existence of other possibilities. And connecting this element to the eyewitness account in the texts of suspended animation gives greater strength to the validity of my
perspective.

And so this ends up being one of those personal opinion situations. Whether the Christmas light was an actual star is up to
each individual to believe or speculate on. One thing I do know . . .
time eventually proves all. Time eventually dispels the obscuring
mist of mystery. One day, after the proper amount of time has
passed, we'll all know—without a shred of doubt—if the answer
is a star or some other source of light.

▸ *Do you personally consult an astrologer?*

No. I've had charts sent to me by my readers who gleaned my
birthdate from one of my books, but other than that, I've never
been specifically inclined to check out the stars regarding life decisions. My philosophy is to take one day at a time and handle whatever presents itself at any given moment in time, a philosophy that
has served me well.

▸ *Will there be an extraordinary celestial event marking the
end times? Will this show up on astrology charts?*

No to both questions.

This end times thing has been blown way out of proportion
and become a runaway concept for too many people. The world is
not going to end. Yes, there will be an axis shift and geological
events will continue to happen upon the earth—just as they
always have—and some of them will be quite dramatic, yet this
does not equate to the end of the world, as in exploded, inciner-
ated, imploded, or dead and gone. With this in mind, why would
there be an extraordinary celestial event marking this theorized

scenario? And how could such an event appear on astrological charts when these diagrams depict planetary positionings?

Though it's prudent to have made preparations for the probable eventuality of electrical outages, an interruption in the shipment of goods, incapacitating blizzards, and so on, let's not carry the likelihood of these occurrences further than the actual bounds of their reality. Let's use practical terminology regarding this currently distorted concept. *Bad* times, not *end* times. People just aren't applying sound reason to this issue. Isn't there supposed to be one thousand years of peace at some point? How can that prophecy manifest if the world ends? Let's get real here. There will always be a mix of good times and bad times. There is a strong indication that the bad times will increase in severity, but eventually, so will the good times be amplified in quality and joy. So logically, we must keep our perspective on this well within the range of reality to facilitate proper planning; we must maintain a mindset focused on actuality instead of exaggerated presumptions of doomsday scenarios.

▸ *Will an astrological chart show if one will come down with a fatal disease at some point in one's life?*

The chart may show a window of time in which a negative event appears to be most probable to occur. A chart won't pinpoint a specific disease or its onset.

▸ *How come the chart of my significant other is diametrically opposed to mine, yet we are totally compatible and have the same attitudes toward everything? We are nearly like identical twins in thought and philosophy.*

This is evidence of past-life characteristics dominating the possible influences of your celestial birth alignments. Your inherent personality—that is, the *composite* beingness of your self's totality of consciousness—is closely aligned with that of your partner's.

The inherent characteristics associated with a person's totality of spirit consciousness supersedes any external influences upon that individual. Astrological influences are external; they are from *without* and act as affectations of energy influence. However, the totality of one's spirit consciousness is *within* self and is therefore the dominant force. This is why the entire concept of astrology, though valid in itself, is not to be perceived as the final word on one's character and destiny.

► *I have a strange question. What do the charts of twins look like if the birth time is spread out so that each child is born on the opposing sides of a transitory cusp?*

For those who don't quite understand this question, the inquirer is asking how the individual charts of each twin will look when one is born on the last day of one astrological sign and the other is born on the first day of the new sign.

Let's discuss an example, using Taurus and Gemini. Okay, one twin is born at two minutes *before* midnight on May 20, making that child a Taurus. The second child waited until three minutes *after* midnight, making his or her birthdate May 21 and that child a Gemini. The child born first would have more personality influences representative of a Taurus but would also have affecting influences from the Gemini sign. Likewise, the child born second would have more personality influences associated with Gemini yet also have affecting influences from the Taurus sign. What's important here is to also remember that each child is the sum total of his or her own spirit consciousness totality, which makes each a unique individual even before the astrological influences were imprinted.

This really was an interesting question. Being a mother myself, I think it'd be hilariously amusing to have twins with separate birthdays and different signs. My grown girls are a Virgo, an Aries, and a cusp Libra who was almost a Virgo.

SKYSTUFF
Meteorologic/Geologic Relatedness

▶ *You stated in* **Earthway** *that whenever the earth's magnetic field is disturbed there is a corresponding increase in human psychological aberrations. Can I override this magnetic influence somehow?*

The physics of this disturbance is likened to the magnetic pull of a full moon (see related question in the previous chapter, pages 36–37). This is a naturally occurring phenomenon of nature. Human response is equally natural. The point is this: if you've taken note that the full moon has some affect on you, then you'd most likely also be affected by a disturbance in the earth's magnetic field. This doesn't necessarily mean you'd experience a negative reaction; it means only that you'd be ultrasensitive to it. The full moon has an affect on me. Even if I'm not aware intellectually that a particular night has a full moon, I can always tell anyway because I toss and turn all night long, which is extremely frustrating. This is the only physiological reaction I have in the way of sensitivity to a full moon. My point is this, just because you notice a personal sensitivity to the magnetic force of a full moon doesn't *necessarily* mean that you'll also act irrationally during a disturbance in the earth's magnetic field. A statement of fact for one person doesn't necessarily hold true for every single individual. As with the increase in violence on full moon nights witnessed by police and emergency-department professionals in hospitals, some folks appear to evidence an increase of aggressive behavior during these times. Some people are more intensely affected than others, having an underlying level of pent-up stress and rage.

▸ *You've stated that living at an altitude of seven thousand feet or more is so much healthier for the human body than is living at lower elevations. Does this hold true for all ethnic groups?*

This correspondent, within the body of her letter, specifically qualified the original question by asking about the black race. The statement made in *Earthway* was meant not to be racially selective but rather to be all inclusive. The human body is the human body. The separatism of ethnicity has no bearing on a concept meant to encompass everyone.

▸ *What makes birds, cats, and other animals react erratically before an earthquake?*

The reaction is their response to a sudden fluctuation in the earth's magnetic field. It could be likened to your comfortably sitting before a cozy, warm fireplace in the dead of winter and then being blasted by arctic air from an opened door when someone comes in with firewood. In both scenarios, there is a sudden change in the atmosphere that elicits an immediate response. Animals are extremely sensitive to their surroundings. They sense quickly altered temperature, atmospheric pressure, and magnetic field changes. Consequently, they have a natural response to all of these.

▸ *You've written about how the earth's magnetic field affects our health. Recently, in catalogs, I've noticed jewelry that has magnets attached. Is there any benefit to this?*

This is a touchy question because unless the jewelry is designed correctly and has the proper metallic ratio, it won't have much effect on one's body. Using magnets for healing is an ancient technique. There are powerful benefits derived from such treatments, yet as with all forms of healing, harm can also be done if the technique is not used correctly. I wouldn't be concerned with the jewelry form, but those who want to use major magnets on the body shouldn't do so before conducting a thorough study of the technique.

▶ *In* Earthway *you stressed how the different weather patterns affect our physical and psychological aspects. With things like El Niño and all the other climatological extremes the planet has been experiencing lately, aren't people gonna be really screwed up?*

Somewhat. Not only the human life, but nature, too. As I sit here typing this response into the computer, I shift my attention past the monitor screen and look out the window. I see an incredibly blue sky with not a cloud to be found. Also not to be found is a speck of snow. I live in the Rocky Mountains at an elevation of nearly ten thousand feet. The date is January 10 and . . . there is no snow *anywhere* on my forested property. It looks more like late October out there. And the temperature is mild enough for me to go out on the deck and sit in the sun for a spell. I've lived in the Colorado mountains for twenty-two years and have never experienced a January that brought absolutely no snow to shovel and plow. Indeed, the weather is becoming stranger, its oddity a frequent conversation topic. Mother Nature is showing her eccentric side. Her increasingly atypical behavior not only perplexes and confuses the human psychological processes but it also bewilders and disorients all other interconnected components of Nature. The barren trees and shrubs think it's time to sprout buds, bears can't figure out why it's not naptime, blades of green grass are spearing up from the dried yellow fields, the internal migrating clocks of some bird species appear to have stopped ticking, and the coyotes are still romping and pouncing down in my valley with the field mice. If this situation continues through the rest of the winter, the underground springs and rivers will not have received their annual amount of replacement waters from snowmelt. The routine measure of snowfall keeps the springtime streams running and the rivers and reservoirs at a normal level. Unless the lack of snowfall is not replaced by a greater amount of spring rainfall, the mountains will be in drought come summer. And a mountain drought makes for a critically dry condition, which primes the forests for wildfires. So you see how tightly all aspects of Nature are interwoven. A singular anomaly can have far-reaching ramifications down the road for every dependently connected facet of nature, including humankind. If the mountains don't receive a certain amount of snowfall, all western states that depend on that water will be in trouble, so it's not only these mountains that will feel the negative effects of this current lack of snow; the result will be felt as far away as Nevada, Arizona, New Mexico, and Utah. In all my previous years here I've had to don snow boots and warm outerwear to go out into the woods on this date, but today I can go woods walking without a jacket over my flannel shirt and nothing more substantial on my feet than sandals. Though it's an undeniably unusual experience and feels wonderful not having to deal with the shoveling and plowing (my driveway is a quarter mile long through pine and aspen woods), I'm also very concerned about the underground water tables. Last year at this time, I had four feet of snowfall around the cabin. This January—none. And . . . if the water we need now comes in the spring as rainfall, will that cause a deluge for these mountains? Will it fill the underground streams and rivers and cause record-breaking mudslides and devastation to homes, roadways, and ranches? I have seven underground springs on my property along with a running creek and a peat bog down in the valley floor. They won't do me much good if it doesn't start snowing soon and the rains don't come in spring. I think I'd like Grandmother Earth to have a talk with her daugh-

ter, Mother Nature—just a little chat about her recent uncharacteristic behavior.

Yes, El Niño and similar meteorological oddities, especially
when occurring sequentially—one following on the heels of the
other—certainly cause havoc with Nature and within the human
psyche. We, as human beings, are closely bonded with Nature,
with our surrounding environment. We, like Nature, have internal time clocks that are biologically attuned to one another's time
pieces. We have a subtle yet tenacious receptivity and reciprocity
with Nature. It responds in a corresponding manner to our moods
and actions, too. We are dependent upon one another for care and
sustenance.

We don't usually give our own inner timing mechanisms
much thought or consideration, but just experience one incidence of jet lag and you'll see how quickly these mechanisms
move to a front-and-center position within your consciousness.
Oh yes, we certainly do have an internal timepiece ticking
within our systems, both physiological and psychological. The
psychological one may be even more nebulous than the physical
one, but journey up north into the Land of the Midnight Sun
and give it a good test. My own inner clock is so precisely calibrated that I mentally notice a huge change in perception just
from being exposed to Daylight Saving Time: In the afternoon,
I'll think it should be four o'clock when in actuality it's only
around two. That's how finely attuned our bodies and psyches are
with the multitude of elements comprising our natural surroundings.

On the whole, we journey through life with our minds narrowly focused on the immediate issues of job, family, relationships, finances, and so forth, giving little attention to Nature on
which we are so tangibly codependent. We watch the evening
news and take subliminal note that many areas of the Rocky
Mountains aren't receiving snow and think, *Humph,* and then
don't give it another thought. But because of the Great Web of

Life that connects everything with every other thing, that lack of snowfall may end up seriously affecting you in the near future. We don't think about the interconnectedness of all of life when, if we truly understand the glaring reality of it, we should. If you live on the coast and the Midwest or Florida is experiencing a severe drought, the availability of corn, beef, oranges, and grapefruit is going to affect you. Life is a synergistic relationship. No one is an island. No geographical region is an island unto itself. What devastates one area climatologically will have a corresponding influence on other geographical regions and people far away. You don't have to personally witness the catastrophic event firsthand to ultimately feel its effects. In some manner, you'll be indirectly touched by it—if not physically, then at least through empathy for those lives that have been devastated. Emotionally, your psyche should be affected. If it's not—if you can sit in your living room and eat your dinner watching pain and suffering taking place in another part of the country or somewhere on the other side of the world—then you need to get back in touch with your world, with the reality of life.

Being a human being means you are not an only child. We are all related—all sisters and brothers—in the family of humankind. Whether or not you want to believe that the weather affects you doesn't negate the fact that it surely does. Whether or not you want to admit that the pain and loss of others touches you doesn't keep the event from being imprinted on your psyche in some way.

Precipitation or the lack of it, humankind's alterations of time, humidity, air currents, temperature, world events, and the happenings in other people's lives all have an affect on us. What makes those effects tolerable is the manner in which we each process and make personal adjustments to those influencing elements. We are intelligent beings. Though we are affected by our world, we also have the capacity to make internal and external adjustments; we can facilitate a personal "correction" to maintain inner and outer balance. However, this cannot be accomplished unless we first recognize and acknowledge that we are each uniquely related to all other facets of life.

► *I moved to Colorado from Florida and now I burn instead of tan; before, in Florida, I never did. Is this due to some chemical change within my system?*

I don't know if your system had some type of chemical change within it, but most often people experience sunburn in Colorado because of the elevation. When you're in Colorado, you're at a much higher altitude than in most other regions of the country. At a high land elevation, the air is so much clearer and rarified. It is above the pollution and other contaminants of cities and the lower areas that contribute to a denser atmosphere, which serves to cloak the sun somewhat and make it less intense. You're just closer to the sun at a higher land elevation. Though the temperatures are cooler in Colorado than elsewhere, the Colorado sun's intensity is so much greater and more powerful that you won't even realize you're burning until you come in out of the sunshine and look in the mirror. Living in Colorado, I could get a suntan all winter long if I chose to. The sun shines with what I call "blue sky days" almost all winter (and summer) long. Colorado winters are nothing like those in the East or Midwest. The skies are rarely gray in Colorado because winter is a sunny time of year. Consequently, the summer sun is even more potent because of the extended amount of daylight exposure time. In respect to tanning, or just being outside, we perceive sunlight as a fairly universal constant and give little thought to its potential strength in relation to land elevation. This simple yet important oversight has caused serious sunburns on the skin surface of innumerable unsuspecting people. Being out in the sunshine is a tremendously relaxing source of enjoyment, yet moderation is still the key to good health and full knowledge is still the basis for making wise choices.

▶ *Can the intensity of the earth's magnetic field be determined by a fluctuation in temperature?*

Increased atomic activity or strength of any element of natural physics causes a rise in temperature. This also holds true with a concentrated or centered amount of magnetic activity. And this is why magnets are used as a special tool for healing—their inherent nature acts to increase blood circulation and balance internal vibrational fields of energy within the physiological system. The temperature within an area of land where the magnetic field is intensified will be slightly warmer.

▶ *Does living in a geographic locale where an active volcano exists create any health problems? I live near one that occasionally rumbles and lets off steam.*

Geologically, as long as the volcano is letting off steam, it may be satisfying its need to ultimately blow because it's routinely releasing building pressure. However, historically, this hasn't proved a safeguard against buildup of additional levels of pressure to cause a major blow in the future. Active and semiactive volcanos indicate the presence of great pressure beneath the earth's surface. Correspondingly, this below-ground pressure has an indirect affect on those living above it, evidenced by an increased level of subtle and subconscious stress sensitivity.

▶ *Is it best to live where the humidity is at a lower level—where it's drier?*

Let me first state that the best place to live is wherever your inclinations lead you. It's not unusual for individuals to have an inexplicably strong draw toward a specific geographical region of the country. This draw may not even be accompanied by a clear and logical reason for its existence; the individual just feels compelled to relocate there. This magnetic pull is usually generated from one's inner self and is directly related to destiny or purpose. This, then, is the primary consideration given to relocation choices . . . what *feels* right for *you*, not if it's more humid than you'd like or if the location is desert rather than wooded mountains. One of our clues to life purpose and destiny is that nebulous inner prompting that frequently comes to the forefront of the consciousness and whispers in a tiny voice, "New Mexico is a nice place to live," or "Wouldn't you really rather be in Montana?" These sudden thoughts come for a reason, for your higher self is attempting to get your attention. Destiny cares not for the tangential aspects of a location if that location is where your purpose will best be served.

If there has been no subconscious leaning toward a particular relocation area, then you're fairly free to live anywhere. Generally, the higher the humidity in a region, the greater potential there is for some type of illness to take hold. Humidity is a prime condition under which spores grow. That fact alone makes those in humid locales more vulnerable to viruses and molds. High humidity also conducts temperature easier than do dry conditions. This exacerbates our sensitivity to heat and cold. Ten degrees can feel like forty on a sunny winter Colorado day, yet in Minnesota or Michigan that same temperature could feel more like a bitter, biting ten *below* because the humidity sends that temperature right through you. The situation is the same with warm temperatures. Ninety degrees will feel more like one hundred ten in Orlando or Kansas City but more like eighty in Utah or Colorado. Living up at nearly ten thousand feet in the Colorado mountains, I count the dryness as a blessing. It warms cold winter days and cools hot summer days—well, up here, it never gets above eighty degrees anyway. The constant plugged nose from sinus problems and colds I had growing up in Michigan all disappeared when I moved out here. Though the dry air sucks all the moisture out of my many houseplants and I have to give them daily morning drinks, I can't think of any other drawbacks to living in a dry clime. Well, yes, come to think of it, there is one other—it depletes the body's moisture. You have to use a shampoo with moisturizer in it and also give your skin a good drink of lotion after showering. Lips also become dry, so applying a moisturizer in the form of lip balm or lipstick is a given. A drier climate increases one's energy level, heightens one's level of exuberance, and evinces a lower incidence of respiratory, heart, and circulatory problems. Healthwise, a drier locale is better overall for both physiological and psychological systems.

▸ *How does low barometric pressure affect the system?*

By exerting pressure upon the body. Low barometric pressure (when it's falling) exerts a subtle force upon the physiological system. This is why more premature births can occur during this time. This atmospheric condition affects blood circulation and respiratory functioning. It also influences the human psychological system by deepening any existing depression and making any other mental disorders worse.

▸ *I live at a relatively high elevation and I'd like to know why I seem to get so tired and irritated when I travel to lower ones.*

I experience a similar phenomenon, only I get more of a suffocating sense. Higher elevations have thinner air than lower ones do. More energy is needed to function in lower altitudes than in higher ones; therefore, that's probably why you feel more tired. Irritated? Perhaps the more subtle differences in atmosphere make you feel so. Humidity affects me that way. At any rate, it's the difference in an elevation's atmosphere that causes these symptoms. The contrast in air quality may not be something you consciously take note of because it's not something that hits you in the face, yet your highly sensitive physiology picks up the nuances and reacts in a variety of ways.

Six years ago, during a book-signing tour across the nation that ended at the East Coast, the August humidity in Kansas City nearly bowled me over. I was just not used to it and it seemed stifling. When I reached the coast of Virginia, it was so bad that I felt as though I was being suffocated. My breathing was sometimes labored. At times I felt as though the water content in the air outweighed the oxygen and as though I needed gills rather than lungs to get enough oxygen. My entire body felt as though the air itself were pressing in all around me, as though the air were extremely weighted and dense. *Dense* is the only way I can describe it because it had a very discernible heavy *volume* to it, in great contrast to the air I was so used to breathing at ten thousand feet. I was so negatively affected by this that I nearly passed out a couple of times. My situation there was due to several factors: the greater humidity in the air, the denser atmospheric conditions of a sea-level elevation, and high summer temperature exacerbated by the humidity.

As with all conditions to which we become physiologically and psychologically accustomed to over an extended length of time, our surroundings become a part of us, albeit an *unnoticed* aspect of our lives . . . until we cut ourselves off from them through travel. In essence, we *become one* with our surroundings.

► *Why does the wind negatively affect so many people? When it blows for days at a time, why do folks say it's driving them crazy?*

People are bothered by the wind for various reasons. Some have highly sensitive ears and, when they're out in it, their ear canal actually hurts because the air is being forced into it. Some folks are annoyed by the constant sound of the wind blowing; it becomes an uninterrupted noise from which they can't find any respite. Imagine that you lived near a running stream. Residing by a babbling brook or rushing creek seems as if it would be so peaceful and serene, yet people don't realize that you can't shut off that sound. It's always there, and at some point, you may desperately want to turn the spigot off to get a moment's worth of quiet. The wind can have the same effect. It's most often the constant noise of it that pushes people to the edge of their mental cliff. Though I've lived by a rushing stream and found that there were days when I wanted to turn off its faucet, I've also been exposed to three straight weeks of a hard, blowing wind that howled down the chimney and whistled through attic rafters. The talk of the town was nothing but "this awful wind," yet I personally thoroughly enjoyed it and couldn't quite gather enough discontent to join in the grumbling.

Psychologically, we are all different. There isn't one of us who could flawlessly match another in respect to identical responses to Nature. Some feel deeply comforted by the roar of the sea and the crashing of waves on the rocks outside their oceanside home, whereas others would find the sounds an incredible mental torture to endure. The specific type of sounds that elicit joy or aggravation are particular to each psyche. The sound of a television droning on all day long drives some people absolutely nuts, but for others, it creates a subliminal sense of comfort and companionship. The sounds of busy city streets with their constant traffic din and wailing sirens will keep a country cousin wide awake all night staring at the ceiling, but her city sister will contribute to the cacophony with her deep-sleep snoring. But do you know what? It works in reverse too. I've had city visitors come up to my mountain cabin. They're what we call flatlanders—people who've never been up a hill higher than those rolling green pastures of Iowa or Wisconsin. The minute they step out of their car, they are literally struck by the silence. The quietness is as a noise to them. With eyes wide, they ask, "How can you *stand* the *silence?*" When I first heard that question, I was thrown for a loop because I'd never in my life imagined anyone who wouldn't appreciate the peace and quiet of this remote wooded valley. It had never occurred to me that that quietness would be a noise to someone else, sound that could drive folks to distraction. What I also discovered was that my visitors' perception was exactly like that of someone shooting off a .357 magnum and experiencing several moments of deafness immediately afterward. Sounds to them were only *temporarily* nonexistent because eventually their hear-

ing became more acute and they could perceive real sounds—
birdsong, the hushed wind whispering through the aspen leaves,
the creek babbling down in the valley, critters skittering through
the underbrush. Though my visitors finally admit that there isn't
total silence up here in the mountains, there just isn't *enough* noise
to make them completely comfortable. I suppose if I can become
so "mountainized" as to be totally frazzled by hectic, noisy traffic
and the people press of mall congestion, then city folks can
become so citified as to be totally disconcerted by my mountain
tranquillity. Works both ways. People become accustomed to their
environment, become one with it. And when they're taken out of
that familiar atmosphere, they feel out of sorts and ill at ease until
they return to it. Some people thrive on the hubbub of city life and
others blossom only with serenity and solitude. Each to her own.

So in conclusion, sounds are an inherent element of our lives.
When new sounds spear into our normal zone of familiarity and
take up residence for a time, they are like an uninvited visitor to
our private space. We balk and grumble; we become restless for it
to take its leave. And our visitor the wind pays us no mind, rudely
continuing to make its voice heard and felt until deciding it's time
to mosey on. What we need to understand with these situations is
that we can lessen the negative effects of an irritant such as a pro-
longed spell of windy weather by making mental adjustments in
our attitude about it. You can't change the element itself, so the
only alternative is to change your attitude toward it. Think of it as
a gift of Nature for spreading seed and pollen where needed. Think
positive thoughts about it rather than dwelling on the negative.
Instead of focusing on how that wind is affecting just *you*, try a bit
of creative thought and come up with ways that the wind is working in a positive manner. Nature loves wind. Just like you should
gently shake your houseplant once in a while to stimulate its internal circulation, the wind has the same effect on the plants and
trees outside. It makes them bend and sway, invigorating circulation and stimulating growth. The wind also culls diseased and

dead standing trees from the woods by felling them. If you really take this to the extreme, the wind will even point out your loose roof shingles that need replacing. An incidence of blowing wind is not a permanent situation; it's only temporary. Altering your perspective on it can go a long way toward alleviating irritation and stress caused by it.

▸ *Why do people get more irritable in hot weather?*

I don't need to be a climatologist or a psychologist to answer this question; neither do you. The answer is simply discomfort. Hot weather, especially in a humid clime, causes people to be physically uncomfortable. Their clothing clings to their skin like cellophane wrap, their sweat drips all over their body, their deodorant isn't working, the pavement's burning through their shoe soles, the air conditioner in the car is working overtime and overheating the engine, and because of the increase in home air-conditioner use there's a brownout or blackout in the city! You get the idea. Hot, muggy weather just has one heck of a huge potential to be an irritant that increases stress and shoots tempers way up through the roof. There's nothing more esoteric about it.

▸ *Why does rain seem to make me sleepy?*

It's a soothing, lulling sound. That's why many relaxation and meditative audiotapes have a track devoted to rainfall. That's why there has been an upsurge in interest by the public in purchasing those small fountains for home and office. The sound of waterfalls and rain is extremely restful.

Also, when it's raining outside, doesn't it make you feel comfy and cozy inside? You're warm and dry. You can snuggle up on your soft couch with a good book or doze a little. Rain is respite. It gives us a time when we have a good excuse to postpone outside projects or errands. Rain relaxes and soothes the psyche. It says, "See? I'm busy giving your garden a good, long drink. I'm refreshing Nature. I'm making things green and healthy. You can relax while I attend to these things. Take a break as I soothe you because . . . everything's right as rain."

► *Why does a gentle rainfall give such a sense of rightness with the world and a thunderstorm instill a subliminal sense of fore-boding?*

Well, for openers, one is gentle and the other one is packing a big gun. It's the difference between a squirt gun and major fire-power. Therefore, the thunderstorm presents a greater potential for severe damage.

Thunderstorms pack the power of positively charged ions, which negatively affect our psychological system. Our moods depress, our awareness dulls, our attention is fragmented, and our mental focus tends to be more easily lost. We become concerned if lightning is going to strike the house or car. The booming thunder vibrates through the ground and frightens the dog and cat as they run for cover beneath the bed. Gathering black clouds begin to form a ceiling of hanging grapes and you start to watch for a whirling tentacle—a tornado—to drop from them. And you want to know why a thunderstorm seems to incite a sense of fore-boding? I think it's quite logical, don't you?

► *I understand why I'd feel melancholy on a rainy day, but sometimes I feel like that on a beautifully sunny one. How could I do that to myself? Could there be an environmental cause to explain such an uncharacteristic reaction?*

Though there may be an environmental cause specific to your geographical region, this is not usually the case. Other than the atmosphere's being loaded with a high level of positive ions, your sunny-day melancholy is most likely a subliminal emotional response to a subconscious issue. There are times when these sub-conscious life issues affect our consciousness without our ever realizing what's going on. Maybe you're worried about a son's trip or a daughter's new relationship and, though you don't think you give undue conscious consideration to the situation, it's still there on your mind.

Another reason for being melancholy on a perfectly beautiful day could be some type of residual emotion left over from an un-remembered dream. Oftentimes when we dream, we'll immediately forget the dream upon awakening, yet the subconscious knows all about it and will "hold" it there for a time. The existence of this dream in your subconscious can frequently cause carry-over emotional responses to bleed into the daily activities performed in the awake state. This is often the explanation for feelings that we cannot explain or pinpoint. You just know that you feel emotionally down or mentally preoccupied, yet you never can put your finger on the reason for it. That's okay. Everyone has days like that. Some days I even have what I call "the Great Nothing," when I have absolutely no impression of tomorrow—it feels totally engulfed in a blackness, a void. I hate that. I hate it because it carries a sense of there *being* no tomorrow for me . . . and I plan on living to be at least ninety-four! So these moods or negative emotions don't always mean that it's necessarily something that you're doing to yourself on purpose; they just manifest all on their own from various causal factors in life. Wracking your brain to figure them out or discern what they could mean is futile and a waste of valuable energy. Rather, put that powerful energy into accepting the fact that these emotional downtimes are a normal fact of life, into focusing your mind on positive elements of your day. Dwelling on the negative only strengthens its hold on you. By doing that, then you truly *do* "do that to [your]self."

I want to reiterate that having down days is just as normal as having those wonderful up days. The mechanics of the human mind have an incredibly complicated and intricate schematic. Trying to understand every little nuance of it is neither a reasonable task to expect success at nor even a logical endeavor, for the fields of psychology and psychiatry are still in their infancy. If neuroscientists are still scratching their heads over a definitive definition of "consciousness," why should you berate yourself for not understanding the cause of every curious mood that comes over you? We accept our emotionality as being part of our unique beingness.

► *Every time I travel back to my mother's place for an extended visit, I feel emotionally drained and physically exhausted. Is this psychological or is there some geographical factor causing this odd occurrence?*

Since you stated in your letter that the relationship between the two of you is good and holds no hidden agendas from the past, I'd tend to think your problem stems from a geographical element. You also wrote that you live in Denver and your mother is on the coast of South Carolina—that could very well be the bugaboo here.

Your situation places you smack dab in the middle of the altitude and humidity aspects of climatological effects on the human physiology. The change in the humidity level alone is a drastic one for you to adjust to. Add the increased atmospheric density to that caused by the sea-level elevation and you get a double-barreled dose of gross effects upon your system. I use the term *gross* to mean "comprehensive" or "overall," as these effects apply to the *total* bodily system.

It's not your mother who's wearing you down emotionally and physically; it's the location of your mother's home. Just as those flatlanders have to experience an adjustment period to acclimate their systems to Denver's high altitude and dry air, so too do those from Denver have to experience an acclimation period when spending an extended time somewhere like South Carolina or anywhere in the Midwest and east.

Certainly my suggestion would be not to stop visiting your mother but to understand the climatological technicalities of your travels and take them into consideration. After arriving at your mother's place, take it easy for a week or so. Rest, take naps, let some time pass before entering into any type of sightseeing or energetic activities. Give your body time to make its adjustments. Your body is quite clever, you know, but you've got to give it a reasonable amount of time to adequately recalibrate itself. Our physiological systems are a marvel. They regenerate cells, they have a unique closed thermoregulatory system, they have an Internet-like communication system, and they have other wonders biophysicists have yet to discover, but we can't expect our systems to readjust as fast as an owl blinks. We need to provide our body with the best possible condition in which to make its readjustments. And that condition is rest. You take it slow and easy and your body will do the rest.

▸ *Our city water comes from a local river, but there's been talk of chemical dumping occurring. Should I have water delivered for drinking? Or have some type of purifier on the tap?*

Pollution is a fact of our world. Even if you hadn't heard any talk of dumping by manufacturers, I think that, in light of the unscrupulous habits of today's world, having a water purifier on your water faucet is a good idea. I'm not sold on the water delivery companies who bring out gallons of their "pure" water to your house. The designer water that has become a fad is usually nothing more than tap water drawn from somewhere else. Testing has shown that most such water is *no less* contaminated than your own home tap water. If some brands claim to be mountain water, then perhaps you've got a greater problem—because mountain water is contaminated by animals. To rid this commercial water of those hazardous health elements, the companies have to purify it. Then what makes the "mountain water" so much better than your own tap water if they both get treated or purified? See what I'm getting at? Once you run your own tap water through a purifying system, it's just as "pure" or even more pure than those gallons delivered to your house or those designer bottles you buy with your restaurant meal. Society needs to use a measure of logic and reason regarding this issue.

My own house water comes from a private ground well. Testing showed the only negative element in it to be overabundant fluoride. This mineral is always present in greater amounts wherever gold is found in the ground. Gold-mining areas will almost always carry an excess of flouride in their groundwater. So I refuse the fluoride treatments at the dentist's and buy natural toothpaste with no fluoride in it to compensate. An overingestion of fluoride will cause the teeth to gray. When it comes to fluoride, more is definitely not better.

Knowledge is the fertile ground that encourages the growth of wisdom within us. To know that our world is indeed populated with unprincipled companies and manufacturers is to know that pollution can exist anywhere. Having that knowledge, in turn, gives us the opportunity to exercise the wisdom and take personal measures to protect ourselves from possible—and often probable—harm. It is far better to err on the side of your family's safety and ignore the ridicule of others than to heed the barbs of others and end up letting your ego make you ill.

I think delivered bottled water is questionable. Same with those fancy-named individual serving–size bottles you buy at the market. If you're truly concerned about the possibility of contaminants in your drinking water, my best suggestion is that you purchase a top-quality home tap purifier that will filter out the finest-size elements possible. There are some brands that will filter out most all minerals and bacteria. The key to using these products effectively is to properly maintain them. If you don't bother to replace the filters, they end up being as good as nonexistent. Replace them more often than the manufacturer suggests in the instructions. If you can't afford one of these top-of-the-line purifiers and you're very concerned about water contaminants, boil your tap water and then keep bottles of it stored in the refrigerator. It's a cost-free way to ensure good-quality water.

If you use a water purifier and think that you're not getting enough natural minerals in your system, there are good overall vitamins with mineral supplements available.

Because of political unrest and the clear possibility of designer germ terrorism against the United States via our water supply, I don't think it's being foolish or cynical to give extra thought to what we ingest. An increase in terrorism committed in U.S. cities has been a prediction I've written about. Whether these acts are perpetrated by citizens or foreigners is not germane and does not change the fact that more incidents are currently being secretly planned and will indeed occur. The evening news broadcasts from stations across the country attest to the strong probability that more such events will manifest in our future. Biological warfare is indeed a danger. Anything we as individuals can do to be prepared is evidence not of cynicism or fearfulness but of wisdom and foresight. Other than releasing airborne bacteria into the air above major cities, breaching the water supply is the next easiest and most covert way to reach and infect an entire regional population with deadly diseases. I'm not a doomsday sayer. My intent for sharing what I see in the future is not to generate fear or to instill fatalism in people but to help folks be forewarned and have the golden opportunity to be prepared.

▸ *My region has begun to experience earth rumblings. It's new to us and I think that perhaps we should move. What's your advice?*

As always, I'd never advise anyone to relocate on the singular basis of geological events. Repeatedly, I've stated that every individual must be wherever he or she is guided to be through personal intuitive promptings. Your question implies that outside factors take priority over inner insight. Though at times these factors can appear to be overwhelmingly compelling, the reality of it is that they still do not take precedence over one's inner inclinations generated by the intellect of the spirit's consciousness.

I want to make it clearly understood that I'm not being a bit sarcastic when I say that we can't allow a perceptual lapse into a Chicken Little mentality to override our intellectual rationale. It serves no logical purpose to run elsewhere at the first sign of trouble or conflict in one's life. Escapism, in the end, serves only to exacerbate and complicate an existing situation. And, I would ask, to where would you run when every region of this beautiful country has the potential for exhibiting at least one negative aspect of the many nuances of Nature?

At the end of the twentieth century we've witnessed an increase in the occurrence of tornados in regions that had never before experienced them. Weather patterns are shifting; air currents are altering. The climatological aspects of the seasons are becoming confused, and we as a society are slowly becoming used to expecting the unexpected. We can no longer count on a specific geographical region's being tornado or earthquake free. Flooding has occurred in unusual places. Droughts can happen anywhere. The earth rumbles and grumbles in new regions. It even snows where snow has previously been an unknown element. Sinkholes are appearing in the middle of interstate highways and their main arteries. So where is safe? Where would you move to and still have the absolute assurance that that location will not also begin to rumble for the first time in history or that that place will not be inundated by an uncharacteristic deluge of spring or summer rainfall?

My point is that the external factors in life are ever changing. They are not a constant. What is a constant is your own personal inner guidance. If you're inspired to live in a particular locale, then that's where you should be. That's where you should be comfortable being in spite of all else because that's where your destiny lies—that's where your purpose can best be manifested according to all associated aspects that serve to effect its greatest potential.

Just as no person is an island, no locale is perfectly safe, possessing the quality of absolute immunity from the elements of

Nature. Therefore, wherever you are (if it's truly where you feel you need to be), those external components add to other facets of your life and serve to make the whole of your existence. What you do with those components—how you use them—determines the quality of your inner growth and your ultimate success in fulfilling your purpose. Earth rumblings shouldn't scare you away from a destined location any more than a rainy day should. Each feature of your life is important, meant to serve a purpose. Many times, that purpose is to aid learning or developmental expansion somehow. Frequently, it's for strengthening inner resolve, determination, or perseverance. Sometimes it's karma related or an integral aspect of achieving a much-needed balance in life.

The proverbial Chicken Little perspective is: "The ground is rumbling; therefore, I run like hell and relocate." The proverbial response exhibited from a perspective based on the spirit's purpose is: "The ground is rumbling; therefore, I fear not and I persevere in spite of it."

A final issue related to this questioner's concern is the importance of individualized thought. Never ever let the opinion, advice, or suggestion of another be the sole factor in decision making. It's okay to make outside inquiries of those you respect or think will offer sound words, but to place all your berries in that one little pail does you a great disservice. Individuality is a precious gift. It's an expression of wisdom to use that gift to its fullest. Nobody is answerable for the actions you take in life or for the many decisions you make; therefore, nobody can be held responsible for them but you—you alone. You alone must decide and act. You alone must take the personal responsibility to analyze and weigh all associated factors—the external aspects and the inner ones—that affect a decision. Both are necessary considerations because they're tightly interwoven. And only *you* are absolutely in full awareness of how they each affect the other. No other person can know these things—these specifics. No other person can be in possession of an absolute picture of your life in respect to its interconnected conditions and situations and relationships. In this manner, each life is as individual and unique as the shimmering stars above, as the wildflowers growing in a high mountain valley. The opinions of others can add a new perspective or expose hidden aspects of a personal issue, but they cannot be the sole determining factor that you allow to control or manipulate your life. Those who look for or use scapegoats to blame for the negative result of a decision are those same people who couldn't or wouldn't take the personal responsibility for making that decision in the first place. When you point a finger at a scapegoat, it's as if you point a finger at yourself and announce, "I didn't take the responsibility for making my own decision, and that person made the wrong decision for me. It's all my fault because I gave control of my life over to another." You see? Rather than take another's advice as your sole criterion, you need to add it to your own considerations to create an enhanced and more developed whole on which to make your final judgment.

Nearly every day, we're faced with decisions to make, some small, others substantial. Daily, we're confronted with myriad choices that have the capability of generating lasting effects upon our lives down the road. Should we give advice or hold our tongue? Should we ask for another's opinion or try to figure things out for ourselves? Either way, the end is the same . . . the final decision is always your responsibility.

► *Why would thunderstorms make me feel emotionally ill? I've tried and tried to discover this reason, but I can't seem to uncover a logical explanation for it. Even more than an emotional sense, it has the feel of coming from somewhere deep within my psyche.*

Though this reaction appears to have a climatological causation, it only looks that way on the surface. From other factors I gleaned from your letter, it sounds to me that your ill feeling is indeed more from the psyche than from some current-day fear of thunderstorms. The anxiety and inner turmoil you experience is probably generated from a strong carry-over event in a past life that either was caused by a thunderstorm or happened during one. Either way, an unpleasant event in your past is closely connected to and directly associated with a thunderstorm. Now when one of these storms happens, the memory of that event (stored in your consciousness) is sparked. Though you don't presently recall the specifics of the event, it's still there and your psyche picks it up through the trigger of the thunderstorm.

Once you understand the technicality of this, future storms should be easier and less stressful for you to experience. For you to get past this current snag you keep encountering, there's no need to have a retrogression session with a hypnotherapist; most times, just being aware of the fact that it's generated from a past-life experience will alleviate the symptomatic reactions.

Nobody likes experiencing fear or anxiety without knowing why. These reactions make it natural to suspect that they're coming from an inner prompting of premonition or intuitive sense of the near future. When that causal factor is eliminated, then the anxiety naturally wanes. Understanding goes a long way toward resolving many things.

▸ *This might sound really off the wall, but can the geological content beneath one's home have some type of effect on the individuals living above it?*

That's not off the wall at all. In fact, it shows some deep thought about the interrelationship between humans and nature. Sure, the underground composition has an effect on life, including human life. All of life emanates energy. Every life emits a specific and unique energy characteristic. Every life is subtly sensitive to the energy output—vibrational frequency—of all other life. This is why minerals and metals are capable of affecting vibrations of other things near them. This is how magnets, copper bracelets, and jewelry-quality metals interact with the energy vibrations humans emit and absorb through responsiveness. Likewise, the geological content beneath your house and in your geographical region will have some nebulous effect on your own vibrations; this content emanates a specific vibration of its own, with which yours will interact.

► *My friends laugh at me because I told them that I can always tell when a summer storm is approaching because I experience the onset of a bad headache. Am I full of baloney or what?*

Or what. An approaching storm, though it might not initially show any discernable physical signs, will be accompanied by low barometric pressure, which affects a wide variety of physical systems and exacerbates the symptoms of existing illnesses. Low barometric pressure will intensify allergies, bronchitis, depression, phlebitis, sinus problems, ulcers, and headaches, just to name a few conditions. (See page 27 of *Earthway* for the complete list.) We as human beings are not independent creatures upon this planet of ours. We are a beautiful living *facet* of that planet, all living facets being a cellular fragment of the living whole. Therefore, we and nature and weather systems and the atmosphere and that which lies underground are all connected. We are all related to one another. Every living facet is, in some manner, affected by the other. It would seem that your laughing friends have a few things to learn.

► *Doesn't the presence of high humidity increase our body's temperature? My friend and I have an ongoing difference of opinion about this.*

Well, you may both be right. When the temperature outside is warm or hot, then yes, high humidity does increase the activity level of the body's thermoregulatory system—resulting in the rapid heat transference you know as perspiration. However, there's another side to this coin. When the temperature outside is cool or cold, high humidity will decrease the activity level of the body's thermoregulatory system. This retains the body's heat. High humidity coupled with *warm or hot* temperatures *increases* the body's temperature. High humidity accompanied by *cool or cold* temperatures *decreases* the body's temperature. See? You're both right. Now you can go on to another topic of debate.

▸ *Does hot weather affect how our bodies assimilate medicine?*

Yes, but cold weather does, too. This issue is somewhat related to the previous one because the atmospheric temperature can affect your absorption of drugs. To put it simply, the ingested dose of prescription drugs should be decreased in hot weather and slightly increased in cold temperatures.

▸ *How come I have severe menstrual cramping only when the weather's bad?*

The low barometric pressure has an effect upon the physiological system. Next time the barometer drops, check the weather. You'll also most likely notice a heavier flow too—perhaps even a greater degree of irritability or stress.

▸ *I get charged up during thunderstorms, whereas others seem to be depressed by them. Why do I seem to be so oddball with this?*

Well, if you perceive your response to a thunderstorm as being oddball behavior, then, sir, you have company. You're not alone— I too get charged up. It's because we are each unique individuals that we react to situations, conditions, and events in a variety of ways. Thunderstorms will make some folks depressed, yet make others buzzed. You and I seem to be among the latter group.

Low barometric pressure most often brings out the depressive side of our psychological aspects. Melancholia, depression, boredom, and the like will surface more often during storms (low pressure times) than when atmospheric high pressures are in evidence with clear skies and sunshine. It's not only visual aesthetics that affect our attitude; it really has to do with the type of pressure in the atmosphere. So why does this low pressure make some folks hyped instead of depressed? There are probably a lot of reasons, all of them personal and individualized. They range from past-life experiences with storms that are subtly imprinted on the consciousness to the fact that some folks just love storms because they have a strong attraction to them and feel some type of affinity with them. For some, it could be as simple as sensing the incredible power of Nature, feeling the electric force of it.

This questioner asked why he seemed to be so oddball with this seemingly uncharacteristic reaction to storms. I can't pinpoint the exact why of it because I don't personally know him; without knowing someone well, I wouldn't attempt to provide a definitive causal factor for something. But sometimes having the need to *know* the precise reasoning for things detracts from the full enjoyment of them. The why isn't nearly as important as the pure and exhilarating sense of freedom to just . . . enjoy. We lose a lot of our beautiful sensitivity and natural reactions to life and Nature through our penchant for analysis. Why this? Why that? Why do I do or say that? Why do I want that or have this kind of reaction? Sometimes it's just better to leave the question out of the equation. Sometimes that's the only path to fulfillment.

THE EARTH MOTHER'S UMBILICAL

The Womb's Life Force of Earthway Living

I look upon the sun-dappled forest floor and spy traces of footfalls that have passed this way before me. Deep in the woods, I hear the screech of a single owl; behind me, rustling in the brush gives evidence that I am not alone—ever. Burnt-orange kinnikinnick leaves touched with red, a glint of mica winking up at me along the trail, the sudden flight of a hidden quail. All—all my relations. And a smile bursts forth from my heart.

HEARTSOUNDS
Mean Vibratory Rates

▶ *According to* **Earthway,** *everyone has a mean vibratory rate that explains why they're attracted to specific life aspects. Should mates have the same rate for optimum compatibility?*

Not necessarily. This question is much like the one in the preceding astrology section that asked if it's best for one's significant other to share the same sign. Again, the same response holds true. It'd be boring to have a mate who was a reflection of oneself. People grow by expanding their horizons, by being exposed to different interests and fields of study. These are naturally supplied by a significant other who is inherently different in nature than you. Differing vibratory rates, when associated with the aspect of life partners, provide an invaluable opportunity and potentiality for personal growth. Hobbies, sports interests, areas of intellectual interest, professional arenas, philosophies, and perspectives are all elements that offer existing venues for self-expansion. They open up leads for conversational debates and analysis, widen experiential horizons, and provide ways to express one's own individuality.

Having the same mean vibratory rate or astrological sign as one's life partner is not a foolproof way to ensure lifelong compatibility; rather, it may be a reason for a relationship to quickly turn stagnant because there are no differential elements to keep it refreshed and therefore more exciting.

In such a close relationship, you don't want to have a clone of yourself. You want to have some differences of individuality to love and cherish, to share and grow from.

▸ *Is one's mean vibratory rate related to his or her occupation or profession?*

It can be. Some personal rates are more suited to a desk job rather than one involving a lot of footwork. Some rates are more attracted to a research lab, whereas others lean toward research in the field. Some are sedentary, whereas others are physical. Some folks are pulled toward the intellectual side of a profession, whereas others want to be involved in the external facilitation of it.

Yet the choice of one's profession is not entirely based on one's mean vibratory rate. The ultimate choice of occupation is derived from a multitude of factors, including past-life influences and the possible carry-over talents and skills from these, environmental aspects, type of personality, individual life perspective, depth of social concern, and effects of one's astrological birth sign. And sometimes situational elements, such as the state of one's finances or one's environment, end up being a determining factor in this choice.

Occupationally speaking, folks do what they do for an endless variety of reasons. Sometimes the work is only temporary; some-times it's a trial-and-error sort of thing; other times it's a tentative testing of the waters to see if one is suited for a particular occu-pation. It's because each one of us is so uniquely different that folks can be satisfied working in all types of occupations. From the factory worker who builds cars to the day-care worker who takes care of the factory worker's children, from the welder to the waitress, from the physicist to the physical therapist, each has a comfortable niche in which to function as a productive facet of society as a whole. Each is a valuable contributor, important and necessary.

► *Is there some sort of detailed chart in existence outlining the various mean vibratory rates as they're associated with compatible specific life elements such as geographical region, architectural style, color, music, pets, and occupation?*

There are none that I know of because this entire concept was entirely unknown to me before I heard it from my mentor. There was no such chart presented to me, and truthfully, I'd have no way of coming up with one without its being devised through assumptions or guesswork. My inclination is to think that such a chart would be, in the end, detrimental. It would be something folks would use as a crutch in place of personal responsibility and individuality. Just as many people refuse to make a life decision or any sort of move without first consulting their personal astrological chart, their astrologer, or psychic advisor, so too would they use a mean vibratory rate chart in the same irresponsible manner.

My mentor's whole idea behind the existence of a mean vibratory rate is that each individual alive is *unique*. Each person is as characteristically matchless with another one as each falling snowflake is quintessentially distinctive in design from its other falling companions. Because of this, each one of us has a remarkably exclusive aura of energy. This aura that emanates from within us is generated solely by our composite vibrations—our mean vibratory rate. Therefore, these rates are so refined, so meticulously developed and finely calibrated that it'd be quite impossible to classify them into separate gross rates. Do you see what I'm saying? One's personal, distinctive rate is a culmination of far too many varying elements to water down into a system of generalized rate classifications. You couldn't do it. No one would be a *precise* match to any of them.

Let me try to simplify what I'm saying. Let's use the concept of color as an example.

Okay, we have the primary colors. Then the color wheel is subdivided into secondary colors derived from a conjoining of the primary colors. Then these are taken further into additional tones, tints, and shades. But there are colors that do not appear on the color wheel. For those colors to have a chart designation you'd have to refine a color wheel so definitively it'd end up being an impossibility. It'd be like taking all the paint chip samples in a paint store and combining them into one huge wheel. Ever been in a paint store and had the pleasure (or chore) of deciding on what shade or tint of the color green to paint your den? Uh-huh. And did you find that every paint store has different shades of color chips? And though you searched every store, was it the case that you still couldn't find the one and only shade you have in your head? This is what I mean by trying to fit all the limitless elements comprising one's singular, distinctive mean vibratory rate onto a specific area of a rate chart. Your specific rate might not even be there; in fact, it's most probable that it wouldn't be.

Every life is lived differently. Every person on this planet has had experiences unlike those of others. Not one individual, even those comprising a set of twins or triplets, has the same historical background in childhood. Each will have his or her own thoughts, likes, dislikes, inclinations, experiences, psychological makeup, world perspective, social attitudes, lifestyle leanings, composite past-life history, and so on. All of these elements make up one's incomparable mean vibratory rate. So . . . how can there be a chart? Just as an astrological chart points to a certain direction, it cannot define the totality of an individual. Neither could a rate chart. It would be a ridiculously futile and highly misleading source to consult.

So no, there is no such chart in existence. I hope to never see one, either, because many would be led into great confusion by it. Many would be led *away* from our responsibility to look within and be sensitive and aware of our own unique intuitive insights.

► *Do animals also have a mean vibratory rate? If so, should I get a dog that has one that matches mine? How does one tell what an animal's rate is, anyway?*

How do you tell what your own is? How do you match a dog's to yours if you don't know what yours is and have no chart to consult?

For the sake of nonargument (we don't want to argue), let's say that there was such a chart in existence. You consult it. You discover that a German shepherd is the dog breed that is compatible with your mean vibratory rate. But, but wait a minute—just a cotton-pickin' minute . . . you're *afraid* of big dogs. You never *liked* German shepherds. You always wanted a little *lap* dog. You always envisioned yourself with a little *Yorkie* following you around the house. So as far as the chart, what's up with that? Indeed! What's up with *that*?

Did the answer shout at you? It should've. The answer to *what's up with that* is that a chart cannot be refined and complete enough to be all inclusive. People's rates are far too distinctive to be correctly classified by a gross chart. How you tell if a dog matches your own rate of vibration is by how you *feel* about it. By which breed you *personally* like. By which pup in that litter you're especially attracted to. See? One's own intuitive inclinations point to matchups and compatibility. *One's own intuitive inclinations.* These, and these alone, comprise the unwritten individualized chart of every human being.

You can't live your life in a "free to be" manner if you run around like a chicken with its head cut off searching out charted life aspects or seeking psychics or other types of consultants to make your decisions for you. The guidelines are not written down. They are not in any reference book; they're not in someone else's head. They're only found in one place—within yourself.

► *Is there a vibratory rate that could possibly account for an individual's chronic violent or abusive behavior?*

This is a good question because it shows some deeper thought. The answer? Indirectly. Indirectly, this is possible. It's possible because each individual is the sum total of all his or her experiences, that sum total comprising past-life experiential events; current-life treatment by society, peers, and relatives; the formation of one's psychological profile; world view perceptions; and so on. If many of these elements, for one person, were negative ones culminating in an overall negative perception of not only one's personal life but also life in general, then that individual would emanate a darker aura, one that reflected his or her mean vibratory rate.

There are clear characteristics in someone such as this that are evidence of the effect of negative elements: generally negative or cynical attitudes, frequent prejudicial or judgmental remarks, arrogance, and a hateful attitude. Inner psychological pressure may find release through physical or psychological violence or abuse. Some individuals with this type of vibratory rate will have a subtly despicable aura that is sensed by others. This person will emotionally bring others down when they're around him or her; there will be a "shadowed" or "depressing" atmosphere around this person. And sometimes the individual will be reclusive because of his or her great intolerance for people in general. People with this type of mean vibratory rate will rarely show happiness or joy, for they feel that there is no reason for such emotions in this world. They are angry at everyone and everything. They are angry that they are forced to live in a certain place or with a certain person, such as a marriage partner. Marriage makes them feel caught or trapped, boxed in with no way out, save frequent violence to fight their way out. Aggressive behavior, whether physical or mental, goes hand in hand with stress, egotism, arrogance, superiority, a judgmental attitude, and the sense that the perpetrator him- or herself is being dealt with unfairly. Each of these attitudes, taken separately, will be destructive for the individual. Taken together, they create a mean vibratory rate carrying an unquestionable high probability for violence and abuse.

► *I want so much to be an artist but have absolutely no talent for it. Does that mean that the profession doesn't match my mean vibratory rate?*

Not by any means. In fact, the opposite is the reality here. Remember, what you *feel* inside—what you're personally *attracted* to and *inclined* toward—will be clear evidence of your vibratory rate making noises for you to hear.

Just because you *think* you have no skill or talent doesn't mean that you don't have a good measure of it in you. Artist is a broad-scope profession, you know. It isn't confined to a singular medium of expression. Being an artist doesn't cubbyhole an individual into painting on canvas with oils, and as you detailed in your letter, that's the only medium you've attempted so far. What about watercolors? Or acrylics? They're different from painting with oils. They have different techniques and offer varying ways of expressing yourself.

What if painting isn't your forte in art? Isn't painting naturally the first medium folks think of when thoughts of being an artist come to mind? There are a great many other mediums. What of stone sculpture? Metal sculpture? Clay? Pottery? Stained glass work? There are all sorts of ways to be an artist and creatively express yourself. You said that you enjoy doing calligraphy. How about developing that inclination into sign painting, or artistic work on business cards, or even expanding it into doing illustrated lettering for publishing companies? How about composing your own book of illustrated verse by creating a beautiful book of famous poems, sonnets, or sayings? Being an artist doesn't mean that you have to labor in front of a standing easel all the long day, forcing something that isn't inherently within you. Let your own self release its natural expression. It has to come from within and flow forth, not be pulled out by some external source. Change your perspective on art. See it for an extension of self—what's inside you—your emotionality, sensitivity, and unique beingness. Then . . . give it rein to show itself through self-expression.

▸ *The color green (forest green) matches my mean vibratory rate because I'm so attracted to it. My significant other is mad about blue (sky blue). How do we decide what color our living room should be painted?*

Why not paint it a mutually liked color and save your respective favorites for other rooms, such as a den or guest bedroom? The fact that two different individuals share one dwelling does not have to mean constant conflict. There's always compromise.

▸ *How do I know where to live to best facilitate my spirit's purpose for reincarnating and also to accommodate my vibratory rate?*

You created two reasons for a geographical choice to reside that are actually one and the same. You've unnecessarily split a hair here. The reason for one's incarnation—that is, the reason for one's spirit purpose—will also be closely aligned to a specific geographical location one is strongly drawn toward. Both elements are direct aspects of a single causal factor. Having a strong, inexplicable pull toward a particular geographical area is most often evidence of a natural prompting by one's spirit. The spirit is attempting to ease you toward its purpose. A geographical magnetic draw is usually the initial marker that destiny is calling. It's implying that the time is approaching for you to begin to involve yourself in what you're here to do or accomplish. The key here is the word *inclination*. That personal inclination is evidence of your individual vibratory rate making itself known to your conscious mind. So the answer to your question is really not with me, but within yourself. Your own inclinations are the guideposts that point out your own path and highlight it as being designated for you alone.

▸ *Do entire countries have a mean vibrational rate?*

Geographically they do because of their specific geologic composition. Yet they also have a secondary element that affects their mean rate, and that's caused by the overall societal vibration of the people living upon that land. If the people are peaceful, the land will be heavily influenced by that benevolence. If the people are violent and warlike, the land will also be affected by those negative vibrations and will usually also evidence this effect through physical release of absorbed stress (earthquakes, volcanos, and so on). As above, so below—never was there a more truthful statement made.

▶ *Is sexual inclination a vibrational rate issue? Heterosexuality, homosexuality, asexuality, and others?*

Sure it is. We are what we are. All of our inclinations, whether they be toward geographical locale, style of clothing, philosophy, choice of profession, or whom we love, are all aspects of our beautiful composite beingness. They are all inherent and natural facets of the who of us. These facets are ingrained. They are like part of each person's DNA. They are the aggregated cells that combine to make us who we are. Just like you can't cut out the inherent inclination to absolutely love the color green in order to change your favorite choice to another color, you can't cut out the cellular influence that draws you to love a particular type of person. Inclinations are natural. You were born with them. They are part of that which *defines* each individual. With that in mind, it's easy to see how sexual inclinations are ingrained and are a definitive aspect of one's unique mean vibratory rate.

▶ *Are the frequently inexplicable responses of attraction and repulsion between two people due to the quality of each one's vibrational frequency?*

Only in the event that these two people do not have any karmic relationship going on. Otherwise, the differences in their vibratory rate, if great enough, will cause a repelling response. Likewise, if these rates are alike enough, there may be a greater attraction. Yet as with all concepts, there is the inevitable exception. Some people who have like rates will absolutely not get along and will not be attracted to one another. Too many influential factors affect this situation to allow an unequivocal yea or nay. Generally, when folks experience an immediate dislike or attraction to another and they can't pinpoint the reason for said response, it's usually from some past-life experiential relationship with the individual.

▶ *What happens when I'm strongly drawn to live in an ocean-side home and my new husband is drawn to New Mexico?*

What doesn't happen is me being put in the middle of this conundrum.

I'm curious as to why this current problem even exists. Didn't you two talk before you tied the knot? This is a major difference of opinion you've got going. It seems to me that something as major as this should've been well discussed long before now. Where a couple would like to eventually live or what geographical location each is individually drawn to should've at least been expressed to one another before now. The waiter brought the meal before you told him what you wanted. Now what?

Well, you could scout out seaside regions that have reasonably close desertlike conditions or neighboring desert areas that are within a reasonable commute. You could live between the two areas (desert and coast) and take regular trips to both. If you could afford it, you could reside for six months of the year in one place and then switch. (Right—who can afford that?) You could . . . let's see . . . you could . . . would any large body of water do? Does it have to be the ocean? You'd have a lot more options if any large body of water would do. I interject this because I once lived on the shore of Lake Superior, which is so expansive that it seemed to me like an ocean (except that it was fresh water instead of the salt sea air and water). What I'm trying to get across is that there are always some workable options hidden within every seeming problem. Every problem is composed of many different elements, and those individual elements oftentimes lead to the very solution one seeks. Compromises can be entertained. Certain types of compromise will better lend themselves to opportunities for resolution. Don't be an unmovable force. Bend. It's in the bending that survival is possible.

▸ *I have a tendency to shun social functions and seem to enjoy solitude over the company of others. Does this preference tie in with my mean vibratory rate?*

All of your personal characteristics tie in with your mean vibratory rate in that they each are evidence of your individuality and the who of you. Preferring solitude over social functions is no longer considered an oddball attitude. More and more people are searching for ways to gain some measure of peace and serenity in this hectic world of ours. Frequently, opting out of social functions is one way for some folks to increase their alone time where they can listen to music, read, meditate, or just veg out for an evening.

The world is full of stress-filled situations and relationships. The workplace can be a prime source of tension and stress. Social situations, though meant to be entertaining and relaxing, are often the opposite because you're still around people; the yakking, the complaining of others, and the expectation for you to participate in conversation can all be a tedious extension of one's workday. Wanting to spend a quiet evening at home instead of being a part of a social scene is not being weird or antisocial; it's recognizing an important inner need for serenity, for getting some much-deserved space, for rejuvenation and peace of mind.

For those who have *always* noticed a tendency for solitude over social functions, this is clearly an inherent facet of their mean vibratory rate. It's part of your character and personality makeup. It's part of who you are, rather than involving any sort of negative attitude such as snobbery, rudeness, or antisocial behavior. Though others may perceive your tendency as rudeness and call it antisocial behavior, it's really not that at all—because you don't hate people or society; you just prefer tranquillity over social noise and commotion.

▸ *Is it possible for someone to not have a personal vibratory rate?*

No, not possible—because one's vibratory rate is one's composite identity. The vibration frequency *emanates* from individuals just as naturally as their breath does, just as the beats of their hearts keep drumming in their chests. Every living facet of life has a vibratory rate that influences other aspects of life. One's mean vibratory rate is necessary as one's very breath.

▸ *Do such choices in life as one's preference in perfume or incense fragrance have a relationship to one's mean vibrational rate?*

Indirectly it does. It's related *in conjunction* with the aspect of past-life influences. The logic of your question sort of put the cart before the horse. It's the past-life influences that existed *first* within your spirit consciousness—*before* your incarnation—and after you were born, those influences became facets of your current totality. This totality exudes a vibrational rate of frequency. So you see, preference in fragrance is indeed due to one's unique vibrational rate, but that rate also includes the influences of everyone you ever were in a past life.

▸ *What would happen if someone completely ignored his or her vibrational rate influences?*

That person would be one very unhappy and frustrated individual.

Remember the earlier question, when I gave an example of using a chart to decide what kind of dog to get, only to find that the chart indicated getting a German shepherd, despite the fact that that breed frightens you? Well, that's a prime example of the confusion I'm talking about with this current question. To ignore one's natural inclinations in deference to alternatives suggested by some outside influence, such as a psychic or astrological chart, is to deny the *nature* of self—the very inherent *beingness* of self.

How does one ignore one's own nature? One's own ingrained beingness? That doesn't compute. And *why* would anyone want to do that in the first place? That's like fighting yourself all the way through life. It'd be like trying to constantly swim upstream against the current instead of going with the natural flow of life. I don't think the situation you're suggesting is possible. I don't believe our natural tendencies can be voluntarily ignored, at least not every one of them.

The ramifications of this idea are so far-reaching that the idea becomes a concept of absurdity. It means that someone who's naturally attracted to hiking through the woods as a leisure activity goes shopping in the mall instead. It means that this individual is emotionally drawn to a like-gender relationship and enters a heterosexual one in spite of natural leanings. It means that this person forces him- or herself to struggle through science courses when he or she wants more than anything to be an artist and has an inherent talent for it. See how frustrating and stressful that sort of person makes life?

Our lives go more smoothly when we follow our own inner promptings. These define our natural course in life. When our surroundings are in alignment with our vibrational frequencies, we experience less stress and greater opportunities for growth. We feel more in tune with life—because we are. To deny our natural vibrational tendencies is to force ourselves to live as a fish out of water or as a bird under water—like trying to force a square peg into a small round hole. It's unnatural. Not to be yourself is to live an unnatural life. To deny one's nature is to deny the nature of the Divine.

► *Can one's mean vibrational rate change? Is it an established specific at birth?*

No, the *mean* vibrational rate never changes. The mean rate means what it says; it's a baseline vibrational characteristic—like a fingerprint—that you bring into the world at birth. However, though it's an established *specific* at birth, experiences, philosophies, and attitudes, among other influencing aspects, serve as *additional* facets as one grows and develops that affect the *originating* mean rate at the time of birth. Just as your attitudes change throughout life by way of experiences and increasing levels of knowledge, so too does your vibratory rate change in relation to the same aspects. It's important to keep these two separate: the *mean* vibrationary rate *always* remains the *same* as it was at birth, but one's *composite* vibrationary rate *changes* with daily affecting factors that cause it to develop and alter. To simplify this, let's make an analogy. Say you're preparing to bake a ham for dinner. The ham itself is the originating foodstuff. The ham equates with your *mean* vibrationary rate. The ham is the ham. It is what it is. So is your *mean* vibrationary rate. Okay, now you spice up that ham. Depending on your flavor preferences, you might add cloves, honey, and brown sugar; or you might like a maple flavor this time and pour maple syrup over that ham; or maybe you want to spread pineapple rings on top; or you just might coat the whole thing with cherry pie filling and have a cherry-spiced ham. These flavoring choices, which were *added* to the base ham, do not change, alter, or negate the ham's inherent and basic existence. It's still there *beneath* the added ingredients. So too is your *mean* vibrationary rate (present at birth) existing there *beneath* the additional vibrational elements you *added* to it throughout life. This mean rate *plus* those added from living life create one's *composite* vibrationary rate. The mean rate never changes, but the composite one does. The composite one changes because throughout life, you are always growing, developing, and changing attitudes and behavior.

Your vibrationary rate changes with the increase of your spirituality. With spiritual *behavior,* the rate increases. With *un*spiritual *behavior,* it decreases. It's always fluctuating. I purposely placed emphasis on the word *behavior* because there are too many people in the world spouting spirituality verbally yet never expressing it—they never walk their talk. All that purporting doesn't hold a drop of pure spirituality unless it's actualized in life through unconditional acts of goodness, without which it's only self-righteous, religious chest pounding. So to merely say that spirituality increases one's vibrationary rate is extremely misleading. It's one's spiritual *behavior* that increases one's composite vibrationary rate—and the lack of spiritual behavior that decreases the rate.

► *I have an obsession with Egyptology. I've never been to Egypt, so would this fascination be a phenomenon due to past-life experiences and their strong carry-over influences, or is it caused by my natural vibratory rate?*

It's caused by the mean vibrationary rate you were born with, because somewhere *within* the fabric of that baseline rate are the preexisting Egyptian influences imprinted on your spirit's consciousness from those past-life experiences. See what I'm saying? In actuality, you could say that influences from past-life experiences and your mean vibrationary rate are one and the same. This is because the *totality* of your spirit's consciousness is composed of *all* your amalgamated personalities of the past. In this case, you've clearly lived one or more lives in Egypt. These are imprinted on your spirit's consciousness and, for some reason, are strong enough influences to bleed through or carry over into your *current* consciousness of *this* life as a strong attraction to the Egyptian culture and geographical region.

► *I'm strongly attracted to natural stone buildings and am wondering if my vibrationary rate has anything to do with that.*

As with the explanation given for the previous question, if you can't solidly equate this attraction to stonework buildings with anything in your *current* life experience, then there's a good probability that this particular inclination is generated from an intense past-life influence. Perhaps you were a stonemason in one of your past lives—not just an ordinary stonemason but one who was called a master at his craft. You could've been an architect who designed stonework monasteries and abbeys. Or you could've been a craftsperson in England who built stone cottages for a living and loved your work. At any rate, when such an influence is strong enough to carry over into a present-day consciousness, as yours has, it usually means that there was a strong emotional factor associated with the influencing aspect. If you were a master stonemason, it's a good bet that you loved your work very much. So then, the experiential time spent as a stonemason is ingrained within the totality of your spirit's composite consciousness. That skill is one fragmented aspect comprising your *current* mean vibratory rate. In conclusion, yes, this has a direct relation to your mean vibratory rate—to one or more past-life experiences.

▸ *I'm a weather nut. Is this interest an indicator that my vibratory rate is telling me that I should be a meteorologist—a weather person on TV?*

You can be a meteorologist without being the TV weatherperson. You can be a weather nut without its esoterically meaning that you need to make meteorology your profession. Have you any idea how many people there are in the world who are weather nuts? Lots. Tons of them. I personally know several of them—my son-in-law expanded his weather interest to become a registered county weather watcher as a hobby aside from his regular job as a casino supervisor.

High interest in a subject matter is not a clear indicator of what one's career should be. You can have a certain skill or talent and make a profession out of it while pursuing your high interests as a supplemental sideline hobby or part-time volunteer work. Usually, one's inherent talents and skills are natural guides to a profession, while the high interests are the ancillary facets to one's life.

▶ *My daughter is so unlike her siblings or parents that some-times I wonder if people don't think she's really adopted. I'm thinking that her differentness is the expression of her unique mean vibratory rate. Am I close?*

You're right on the money. Though siblings have the same genetic origins and are all raised in the same environment, it's the unique composition of one's mean vibratory rate that can make one child stand out from his or her siblings in extraordinary ways. This usually evidences itself not through physical differences, because the current parents were the contributors of all the sib-lings' genes, but through character, personality, and behavior. For instance, if that child spent several incarnations being a devotee of Islam and now he or she enters this new life in a Christian fam-ily, well, you can imagine how different that child's attitudes could be if the carry-over influences from those past lives are strong. The child will have an endless well of curiosity from which to inundate the parents with questions. The child will appear to be far too philosophically knowledgeable for his or her age, and the parents will shake their heads in puzzlement over the child's reluctance to take religious teachings at face value. The child could be perceived as a troublemaker and as incorrigible, stubborn, and having no faith. The ramifications are endless.

And so we must treat each of our children as precious individ-uals and one-of-a-kind human beings. We don't treat them as extensions of ourselves or an arm of the family. They are not a chip off the old block—nor should they ever be perceived as a nonentity because they're under twenty-one. Because of each child's unique composite consciousness based on past-life experi-ential identities, each child represents a special blend of beingness added to society. Not every sibling will want to go to McDonald's. Not every sibling will think a trip to Disneyland is the ultimate vacation. Not every sibling will think a Beanie Baby collection is cool. And certainly, not every little girl is head-over-heels in love with Barbie dolls. One of my daughters didn't care for any doll; all she wanted was to add to her collection of horses. Everything was horses. Another one of my daughters couldn't have cared less about dolls or horses; all she cared about was listening to music. So a parent must understand that every one of his or her children is going to be different. Don't expect to see similarities. Don't be in expectation at all. Be in complete acceptance—for whatever precious beingness your child presents to you. Your job is not to create clones of yourself; it's to nurture your child's individuality and encourage his or her sense of absolute freedom to openly express that individuality . . . in all situations . . . in all ways.

▶ *When the Oriental monks achieve total control of their system's chi energy, are they accomplishing this through maintaining a perfect mean vibrational rate of frequency?*

No, because one's *mean* vibrational rate is not changeable. It's what one is born with. You're mixing concepts here. The mean vibrational rate is totally different from the *chi* energy within us. You can accomplish "perfect" balance of your *chi* energy, but there is no such thing as a "perfect" mean vibrational rate.

What the Oriental monks and like people manage to accomplish is to reach high states of *consciousness*. This brings in a third concept that is separate from the other two. Raising one's consciousness can indeed achieve an increased composite vibrationary rate, and this is probably what you were getting at with your question. Reaching the higher and finer levels of reality is entirely due to one's control of his or her consciousness. This is not contingent on where one's mean vibrationary rate is at or on one's *chi* being in perfect balance and in a condition of clear-flowing energy.

▶ *Is the outward radiation of one's aura (strength and intensity) related to one's mean vibratory rate? If so, can it be voluntarily controlled somehow?*

You stated in your letter that you were interested in being able to control the emanations of your aura because people, though inexplicably, react to its hugeness. You don't like being reacted to in this manner, so you'd like to "bring it in" some so it's not so noticeable and, consequently, embarrassing.

First, I'm curious as to why you're embarrassed by your aura. Clearly, it's a thing of beauty. It's a shimmering extension of yourself, of your beautiful beingness. To want to change the natural appearance of your natural aura's emanations is to want to change the appearance of your face or the natural character of your personality. Your aura is as much a part of your identity as your voice or fingerprint. It's *you*! People react to voices, to personalities, to the way others dress, to the color of another's skin, to absolutely everything that's different from themselves. So, I ask, what makes your aura the one aspect about yourself that you want to change? Maybe somebody doesn't like your hair color or your mannerisms. Would you also want to alter those? Just to please some rude person who didn't have the common courtesy to mask his or her personal opinion? You can't alter every aspect of your beingness in order to please others. You have to cherish the who of you—your beautiful beingness. Every element of yourself is a wonderful facet of your individualized totality. If your eyes are an unusual color, so what? If you have a magnetic personality, don't desire to smother it so you won't be so noticeable and outstanding in a social situation. If you have an unusual hair style and people are ignorant enough to give you side glances, so what? Isn't their ignorance and rudeness *their* problem—a reflection on their own lack of politeness—rather than yours? Sure it is. And if your aura is hugely brilliant, so what? So what if perceptive individuals are taken aback by sensing it? If they're spiritually aware individuals, they'd be *drawn* to that beautiful aura instead of being frightened or repelled by it. Are you getting my drift yet? Love yourself. Cherish your individuality and every single facet of it. Even your enormous, glowing aura.

► *Are "thought forms" and mean vibrationary rates connected in any way?*

No. They're in no way connected.

▶ *When I'm out of body, is my mean vibratory rate different? Does it alter?*

The mean vibratory rate is the amalgamated influences from all past lives that are imprinted upon the spirit's consciousness totality. This is a constant and does not change. It creates the immutable baseline to which future experiential influences are added. This composite vibrational rate of an individual is that of his or her *consciousness*. Consciousness is equated with one's beingness. To go out of body is to raise one's *consciousness* to experience a finer frequency of *reality's* vibration. The logic of your question is the same as for asking this: If I walk into a different room of my house, will my mean vibrationary rate change? See what I'm trying to say? You take your consciousness with you when you journey out of body. It's your *consciousness* that's doing the journeying—that *same* consciousness you have when you're walking around in the mall, that you were born with. The same one with the *same* mean vibrationary rate. Just because you take your consciousness elsewhere—to some other realm of reality—does not also mean that its frequency changes; you're still you no matter what level of reality your consciousness temporarily visits.

This whole concept of consciousness is grossly misunderstood. Today, as we end the twentieth century and begin the twenty-first, neuroscientists are still scratching their heads over how to comprehensively define consciousness. They have this conundrum because their starting position is skewed. They're working from the false premise that consciousness is generated from a mechanized brain and can exist only when electrical impulses fire according to plan in balance with the proper nutrient chemicals. Not so. Not so at all. What do they think one's spirit is? It's consciousness!

▶ *Does each of the different human races possess an "ethnic" mean vibratory rate?*

Yes, each does. Genetics is one of the facets comprising one's mean vibrationary rate and contributes to the reason each person is so individual. Previously, we discussed the issue of having a mean vibratory rate chart made up, but this aspect of ethnicity serves to exemplify why just such a chart would be an impossibility. You'd need separate charts for each separate race, for each of the limitless *combinations* of heritage, and so on.

▶ *Do one's religious beliefs affect his or her mean vibratory rate?*

They couldn't affect the mean vibratory rate because that's the *baseline* rate one is born with, yet they could have some influence on the *composite* vibratory rate that is individually developed throughout one's life.

▶ *Does a belief in God, or the lack thereof, affect one's vibratory rate?*

Only indirectly—because spiritual beliefs usually affect one's behavioral patterns and philosophy. In that respect, they affect one's composite rate.

▶ *If the earthly human race began as a composite species created from a blend of five different interplanetary races, would our mean vibratory rates have an ancient ancestral facet?*

This question shows some deeper thought. Sure, just as one's birth time mean rate includes the effects of one's parental genetic racial coding, so too would all peoples of earth come into this world with a vibrationary imprint of the ancient ancestors who originated human life upon the planet earth.

▶ *I know that the various elements of nature have their own specific energy frequency output. This made me wonder if the vibrational differences were actually more refined than that— that is, all trees possessing the same rate, but perhaps each species of trees having its own, such as all sugar maples having*

*the same vibratory rate and all magnolias having another, and
so forth. Am I making myself clear with this question?*

Oh yes, you're coming in loud and clear, and your idea is right
on the money too.

Just as there are differing mean vibrationary rates associated
with the different human races, so too are there separate vibrational frequencies of energy emanating from the different species
of trees, flowers, minerals, gemstones, and so on. I've devoted an
entire book to detailing the specific energy emanations of all of
Nature's aspects and the unique influences they each have upon
all of life, including humans. You may want to check out this
energy reference book since you were wondering about this subject matter. The book was released in the fall of 1999 and is entitled *The Singing Web.* Its title, of course, is directly associated with
the Great Web of Life and how all of life and its multitude
of energy vibrations affect one another in a very interrelated
manner. The book is a natural *Earthway* and *Beyond Earthway*
supplement.

A tree is not a tree alone. A tree is a *species* of tree, a unique
species with its own set of characteristics and vibrational influences. This is so too for metals, flowers, fish, birds, rocks, and animals. Every type of living vitality upon this earth carries its own
frequency imprint. Consequently, every type of living vitality
upon this earth emanates a specific vibrational frequency that
influences every other life-form. This is the reality of why we're all
related upon the Great Web of Life. We share the cells of a reality
consciousness of the One—of the Divine—from which all of life
is sustained.

► *When my dog got sick, I felt as though her vibratory rate was
altered. Does this happen?*

Oh yes, it does happen. You were probably being highly sensitive and receptive to the state of your pet's aura.

The aura is the emanating energy field of one's vibrational frequency. The aura, if it could be visually perceived by everyone, would be seen to go through a myriad of maneuvers. It spikes when the individual is excited. It flares with anger or fear. It softly pulsates with prayer, meditation, or compassion. When one is healthy, it's strong; conversely, when one is ill, it weakly undulates. And when one is dying, it slowly recedes back into the body.

You were sensitive to your dog's energy vibrations, which were less active during a sickness, and you were receptive to the aura's temporary altered state. You sensed the change. You must be very close to your pet. You must love her very much to be so in tune with her most subtle nature. I was glad to hear she completely recovered.

► *Can one's composite vibrationary rate affect watches, slot machines, and other mechanical equipment, or is that more related to my own energy level?*

Your letter amused me because I too cannot wear wind-up or battery-operated watches and I sometimes can't get my truck engine to turn over because of a specific type of highly charged energy that's spiking from me (a highly agitated mood).

It's not one's vibratory rate that causes this phenomenon but rather one's type of personal energy. Like one's vibrational rate, an individual's energy level and energy quality are unique. Some personal energy characteristics are so intense that they frequently affect mechanical objects; on rare occasions, they manifest as psychokinesis, the movement of an inanimate object by the exertion of a strong force of energy. Sometimes plant leaves or branches will suddenly make a nodding motion if I'm near them and am emanating a particularly strong energy field. I bet this happens to you too, but you haven't yet made the connection to yourself as the causal factor. This plant movement isn't something that's managed in a voluntary manner; it is more of a spontaneous event that comes quite suddenly and unexpected. By this I mean that I couldn't just sit beside a plant and intentionally will it to move. This movement isn't necessarily done with the mind or by forcing one's energy on the leaf; it happens spontaneously and because of a particular burst of one's energy.

Mechanized objects that are affected by one's energy are also affected by one's magnetism. Everyone possesses some level of bodily magnetism. It's biological. It's inherently natural. This magnetism, *combined* with a particular type of personal energy level, creates the dynamic duality of force that has the potentiality to stop watches and engines, move objects, and inexplicably affect other people who are naturally sensitive to such fields of energy.

Through my explanation of this concept, I don't intend to imply that one's composite vibrational rate is completely uninvolved in the activation of this phenomenon. People's vibrations definitely affect living life-forms like botanicals and animals. When there is ongoing discord within a home, the plants will respond in kind by not faring well. The opposite also holds true: When a plant's environment is filled with upbeat, happy, and content vibrations, it will thrive and even evidence spurts of growth. Emotions are real things. The vibrations those same emotions send out are real things. Real things affect other real things.

So let's separate out the two concepts that were involved here: One's composite vibrational rate, coupled with one's personal type of magnetism, affects inanimate objects. One's emotional vibrations affect other living life-forms.

► *I'm an artist. When I create a piece, does my personal composite vibrational rate become an inherent facet of that work?*

Yes. Everything you put energy into retains a measure of that energy. Have you ever been in a secondhand shop or antique store and, after picking up and handling different objects, gotten some type of qualified *feel* from them? It comes as a subtle (or sometimes strong) sense. A friend of mind once gifted me with an old steamer trunk to refinish and use as a cedar chest. Initially, I was so thrilled with it, but that first night when I had it sitting in the middle of the bedroom floor, the shivers that rippled through my psyche and the aura of darkness that emanated from it made it an outcast in relation to fitting in with and being compatible with the rest of my things. It was a dark horse; its vibrations were disturbing. It would have to go. Sheepishly, I explained the situation to my friend. Thankfully, she understood and I returned the chest to the shop for an exchange piece.

The above example verifies that people's vibrations can be *imprinted* upon any object they come in contact with or affect through a close approximation. So for you to actually *create* an object, such as a piece of artwork, with your own hands makes that piece heavily imbued with your personally imprinted vibrations. My own cabin is literally saturated with my vibrations because I bought it unfinished and stained and varnished each piece of knotty pine board that went up on all the walls. Aspects of myself have been absorbed by everything I worked on. And this is also why you may get a certain feel from a place, as when you walk into someone's house for the first time. You may get a cold feel or one of warmth. You may sense stress there, or you might immediately get a welcoming feel. Folks who enter my cabin for the first time stop for a minute and make various comments relating to the "nest" feel it has or how cozy it makes them feel.

Every home has a vibrational atmosphere to it that gives visitors a sense for it. Every piece of handcrafted goods has been influenced by its creator. Everywhere we live, we leave an imprint to mark our passing.

► *It seems to me that every person's personal vibratory rate would be as uniquely distinctive as his or her fingerprints. Would this be correct?*

Absolutely. That's why it'd be impossible to come up with some type of chart for these rates. There are just too many variables. In fact, every individual is his or her own variable.

► *Does being exposed to an electrically charged work environment (computers, printers, faxes, and so on) negatively affect my vibratory rate? There's so much current flowing through the work atmosphere that I can actually hear a hum in the office. Some days I go home feeling depressed without knowing why. Am I off base attributing this dark mood to the electrical current exposure?*

I wouldn't say you're off base with your theory. It's been proven that folks living beneath or close to high-powered electrical lines experience all manner of psychological and physiological negative effects from their proximity to them. In a busy office filled with wall-to-wall electrical equipment, there will certainly be radiating energy influences affecting the people who have to be in the same room for extended periods of time. Tiredness, headaches, irritability, anxiety, stress, and mild depression all are evidence of the effects that ongoing electrical current exposure can have on people. Try to break up the consistency of it if you can. Take your breaks and lunchtime outside the office. Get a breath of fresh air periodically. Any time away from the exposure acts as a type of circuit breaker for your system and shuts off the atmospheric current your body is exposed to. Most often, just taking intermittent respite periods from the constant exposure is an effective solution.

► *People talk about energizing crystals. If they really do this, does it alter the composition or vibrationary rate of the stone?*

No, because the crystal itself, just as do all minerals, metals, and rocks, has its own innate vibrational frequency nature. It can't be changed; it has its own energy. That's what folks don't understand. People also do a lot of talking about "clearing" stones and crystals. Clear the stones and crystals of what? I understand that people think they want to clear such a stone or crystal of any and all vibrations it might have absorbed from another handler, yet that stone or crystal's inherent quality or effectiveness will not be hampered by such superficial influences. Those inconsequential vibrations in no way cause an indelible or lasting interference with the stone or crystal's natural composition or the emanations from same. This idea of energizing or clearing is only for the psychological placation of the individual; it has absolutely no physical effect upon the stone or crystal. Any residual vibrations attached to a stone or crystal will not in any way block or alter its basic effectiveness in relation to its own vibrationary influence.

▶ *Are people's vibratory rates more emotional (psychological) or biological?*

The mean vibrational rate is the baseline one you "inherit" through accumulative characteristics of your past-life experiences, the astrological influence you were born under, and the genetic coding of your parents. The composite vibrational rate, which is an ongoing formation caused by the additional aspects added to the mean rate as one develops and grows throughout life, can come from every element that enters the realm of the individual's world reality. This, then, means that every emotion, every psychological facet, attitude, and philosophy and the behavioral evidence of same, affects the vibrational rate. Taking a wider view, the psychological aspects exert a greater influence upon the vibrational rate than biological or external elements. Why is this? It's because our behavior carries more influential weight than do other factors when it comes to elements capable of altering the vibratory rate.

▶ *Do drugs affect one's vibratory rate? What about the type of foods we eat?*

Drugs affect the vibratory rate because they have a direct influence upon the biological or psychological systems, depending on the type of drug ingested. The one constant element related to one's individual vibratory rate is its state of flux. It's like a light meter you carry around with you, its needle constantly in motion depending on the intensity and quality of light you're in. Drugs affect that "light meter," as do the type of foods you ingest.

► *Does a mentally ill person have a different vibratory rate than a normal person?*

Mental illness affects the vibratory rate because psychological aspects create related responsive behavior. Both psychological and behavioral elements affect the vibratory rate. So yes, a mentally ill person will have a different vibratory rate. So will an alcoholic.

► *Will one's specific religious belief show up in one's vibratory rate?*

I'm not absolutely clear on the intent of your question. If you mean could it reveal if you're a Christian or Moslem, then the answer is no. But remember, it's one's behavior that affects the rate of vibration. So perhaps through one's spiritual *behavior* one's religious/spiritual beliefs could be determined and, in that sense, a ballpark rate might be perceived. Yet there are so many other subsidiary factors that comprise one's rate and are all contingent on specific behavior that it'd be nearly impossible to gauge anything closer than a generalized rate. That's why we're all so uniquely different. Vibrationally speaking, no two people can be identical. Again, this is why even siblings in multiple births, from twins to sextuplets, can each be so different from one another. There are just too many factors comprising our inherent being-ness—our nature.

If there was such a piece of equipment that could gauge one's vibratory rate, it'd have to be so incredibly refined that it'd have to have a separate measurement for every living person on this planet. No two people would have the exact same readout.

EARTHWAY GENETICS
Dietary and Healing Aspects

▶ *I became a vegetarian because I thought that ingesting meat was a contributing factor to human illness and diseases such as cancer, but I don't seem to be experiencing any type of healthier state than I was before I switched my diet style. How come?*

Several interrelated factors are involved here. Attitude or personal perspective is one of them. If your general attitude toward your life has not changed, how can you expect the type of food you ingest to do it for you? Attitude, perspective, behavior, psychological elements, all have a definitive effect on how ingested food affects the physiological system. If you're living in a constant state of stress and anxiety, anger, or frustration, switching from meat to veggies won't keep colds, cold sores, or intestinal flu away from your door. Health and the wellness of the body are managed more by psychological state than by what one eats. You were expecting an outside source to alter and improve that which must be generated from an internal or inner source—your mental state. With an illness, you can do everything right—take the prescribed medicine, add the corresponding natural herbs, take extra vitamins, drink your chicken soup like Mom tells you to do—but if your attitude is depressed, so will your prognosis for a quick recovery be depressed. If your emotional state is down, so will your immune system be held down. As above, so below; as with the mental, so with the physical. Every physical manifestation was first a thought. Sometimes it's one's reason for becoming a vegetarian that results in unmet expectations. Remember, it's all in attitude. The mental is as much a healthful tool as are herbs, acupuncture, massage, antibiotics, and an apple or five almonds a day.

▸ *I go to a homeopathy practitioner on a regular basis. What I can't figure is how a person who's knowledgeable and skilled in healing can be chronically sick.*

That's much like asking why the psychic who was walking down the city street didn't foresee the piano falling out the window six stories above him. Your logic is based on the false premise that professionals are perfect, that humans cannot err, that we have the ability to know and see all.

Statistics reveal that psychiatrists commit suicide and physicians get cancer. Mechanics own vehicles they can't seem to fix. Psychics are never one hundred percent accurate and there is much they cannot foresee. Herbalists get sick. Chiropractors have back problems. And homeopathic therapists can have chronic physical complaints. Having a profession, whether in the field of science, medicine, natural history, or art, does not make one infallible in that professional endeavor or immune to imperfections. There is no perfection in this world, at least not regarding humans or human ability. Specialized knowledge and skills are gifts given to us for the sole purpose of sharing them with or helping others. Having that specialized knowledge or skill does not mean that one has reached the state of perfection in that field. To think that is to make a false assumption, and throughout our lives, we want to avoid making assumptions as much as possible.

▸ *Do you know a secret weight-loss diet that's really effective?*

I wouldn't begin to address this with a ten-yard pole. There are so many crank diet plans out there that I stay clear of the whole issue. What's interesting, though, is the fact that so many ideologies are presented regarding all the special diet plans—one addresses the issue of carbohydrates, another focuses on calories, and yet another singles out one or two specific foods to eat, forsaking all others. Some center on a particular type of exercise coupled with a specially formulated powdered concoction you have to pay an arm and a leg for. Others swear their revolutionary exercise machine will melt the fat off. From liposuction to cellulite eaters, it's enough to turn your stomach and make you vomit your calories away.

I want to know what's wrong with simplicity. What's wrong with using good ol' logic? Pure and simple reason? It costs nothing to use. There's no plan to join, no weighing in. It takes no extra energy. It doesn't leave you stuck on a toilet all day, busy voiding all your extra pounds of waste. It doesn't leave you in a wall-clawing state of craving your favorite food. It doesn't shrivel your insides with starvation. And there are no membership fees. Geez Louise, what could be simpler?

So . . . what is it? What is this great diet secret? Well it's nothing faddish, that's for sure. It's no esoteric new concept, either. Like I already said, it's just logic and reason: It's nothing more mysterious than the simplicity of *moderation*. Moderation isn't anything new by a long shot. Back in the 1920s and 1930s, Edgar Cayce was strongly suggesting moderation of diet as a natural means of weight loss and general maintenance. The idea is as valid today as it was back then—maybe even more so in light of the recent history of AMA (American Medical Association) announcements.

I'm referring to the AMA's history of denouncing this food or that food and then, several months later, retracting those statements on the basis of additional testing. The AMA should be blushing after making so many medical reversals in the last few years. On topics from "bad-news" eggs to the red wine and beer that were to save us from heart disease, America's most prestigious and respected medical periodical, the *New England Journal of Medicine,* has repeatedly reported reversals of the conclusions of research findings. This journal covers all facets of medicine and related research. Opinions and research on the various highly touted fad diets constitute one of these related issues the magazine has covered over the years. And, after debunking most such diets and later reversing specific suggestions for the inclusion of particular foodstuffs in your diet if you want to lose weight, the latest suggestion this professional periodical offered was one of general *moderation* in one's routine eating habits.

So what does *moderation* mean, anyway? It means that a well-rounded general diet that includes foodstuffs from every food group has been proven to be healthiest when not overdone in any one area. Moderation = smaller portions. Moderation = not stuffing oneself at any one sitting. Moderation = a little of this and a bit of that. Don't make an entire week's meals from beef products, or fowl, or pork. Remember, some of this and some of that. *Variety* is as essentially important as the concept of moderation. Variety *and* smaller portions. Never eat so much at one sitting that you feel like you need to unbutton your pants to get breathing space.

There are a few little hints to reducing your body's fat ratio. Replace carbonated drinks with water or juice (fruit or vegetable). I once did a little experiment out of personal curiosity. I love Pepsi—not the diet variety, either. I decided to drink a glass of water instead of Pepsi every time I had the urge to reach into the refrigerator for the Pepsi bottle. I did this for two weeks. To my amazement, I lost eight pounds—just from omitting the calories in the soda pop. It's a small amount, I know, but think about how all those small things can add up to your routine intake of calories. By cutting down through choosing alternative drinks or foodstuffs, you can lose weight without even adding any more exercise than your normal, daily routine. Instead of grabbing two pieces of those tempting little bite-size bits of Nestlé Treasures (chocolate-covered peanut butter) from your counter candy jar, just take one. Instead of the usual portion of pie or cake, cut a piece that's a bit smaller than you normally would, or have that dessert every *other* day instead of every day. Alternate your routine. It's so much easier than stressing yourself out and getting frustrated with complete self-denial. If you use moderation, you can eat well and still lose the weight.

Moderation in conjunction with exercise will result in a noticeable difference when you look down between your feet at the number on your scale. The best exercise is still walking. Now remember, we're not addressing the issue of toning up or strengthening specific areas of the body here, we're just talking about excercise for overall weight loss and maintenance. Not only does walking burn calories but it also strengthens respiration, which in turn helps to cleanse the lungs and blood supply. Walking aids in circulation, is wonderful for the heart, and greatly benefits digestive function through muscle stimulation. Many digestive problems, especially constipation, result from a sedentary lifestyle with little or no walking. Keeping waste moving through the system in a regular manner is paramount to good health and weight loss.

Then there is the psychological factor of attitude. Do you know that a happy and optimistic perspective will burn more calories than a melancholy, depressed, or pessimistic one? The latter is the psychological equivalent to being physically sedentary. It *absorbs* rather than *sheds*. It *soaks up* rather than *emanates*. It's a *heaviness* rather than a *lightness*. Everything about pessimism and the wide variety of moods by which the mind's darker side can be shadowed will impair health and the healing process in a limitless variety of ways. A state of depression is counterproductive to the concept of moderation because it will say, "The heck with *this*," and you'll grab a whole handful of those chocolaty peanut butter Treasures instead of just the one you know is best to reach for. A depressed mood will most frequently shout in your ear, "I *deserve* this candy!" But do you? Does the healthy state of your body really *deserve* an *unhealthy* portion of calories? Isn't improved health and fewer calories what you really deserve? Dark moods and attitudes will play games with your goals, with your reason and logic. Dark moods will skew the rationality of your intellect.

So though I don't have a magic potion for weight loss, I do know that when one ingests a *wide variety* of food in *moderation,* while in an *optimistic* frame of mind, and routinely takes *walks,* one's weight will decrease and general health will improve. No mumbo-jumbo. No hoodoo-voodoo. Just logic, plain and simple.

► *I need to meet you so you can teach me all about herbs and which ones are best for my own system. When's a good time?*

There's no time like the present . . . to research herb books.

What is it with the "I need a teacher" syndrome? If people can't learn from books, why do universities bother with them? Why libraries? Bookstores? Internet book outlets? And mail-order catalogs brimming with available titles? This question and other similar ones never fail to confound me. Over the years, I've received hundreds of them from folks who think I'm the end-all source for information on herbs. I'm not. I never said or even implied such an absurd idea. I don't specialize in any one subject matter. There are many people who do. They're called herbalists, dietitians, nutritionists, and so on.

If you want to learn about rocks, you read all you can about geology, talk to rock shop owners, take a course in geology, join a rock hunters' club, and have discussions with a geologist. When you have a particular interest, you go to an expert in that field.

This correspondent is wanting knowledge of herbs as related to his own specific health problems or needs. In his letter, he mentioned that he'd not been to a physician in many years. One thing about getting into herbs is *knowing* what your own body is *lacking* so you can make an intellectual choice as to what it *needs*. This particular individual is wanting herbs that his specific body may not need or require.

This general issue was brought to my attention through a personal experience I had with a friend of mine. I have an elderly woman living with me who is my friend's mother. It was clear from her physical condition that her body was missing some essential nutrients. So how do you decide which ones are lacking? A blood test. Now I know that a blood test is associated with traditional medicine, yet good medicine is a *blend* of *all* forms of medicine. And what that blood test showed for that woman was a clear, dangerous lack of nearly all of the B vitamins. So that simple test revealed where we needed to start. You can't make guesses. You need to know the status of the existing condition before you can go from there—some type of baseline that points you in the right direction for the proper use of specific elements.

Good medicine is broad scope. It's not only diet. It's not only vegetables or grapefruit. The attainment, maintenance, and practice of good health is accomplished by taking advantage of all forms of medicine and types of healing. From the practices of the ancient Chinese to laser surgery to the Earth Mother's natural offerings, we use whatever knowledge and proven methods are available. They are all gifts wrapped in a variety of colorful wrapping papers.

I don't teach because I'm not a teacher. I don't give medical advice to individuals. I'm not a consultant. I'm not any type of practitioner. I relay the knowns and share what I've learned throughout life. To this correspondent, my best suggestion would be to research the writings of a respected and skilled herbalist. I would also suggest that before doing this, he make sure he knows his own body and its baseline condition. Without knowing that, you can't begin to know where to start from. In order to get anywhere, you first have to know where you are.

▸ *Is cancer caused by or exacerbated by diet?*

There is a specific gene associated with the *susceptibility* or high *potentiality* of developing this disease. Cancer is not specifically caused by a particular type of foodstuff but rather is a condition that is highly sensitive and responsive to stress and intense negative emotionality. This means that although an individual may have a gene marker for the disease in his or her DNA makeup, which may indicate a dormant tendency for the disease, the disease may not manifest unless it is awakened and activated through stress, depression, anger, or any of the intense negative psychological conditions serving as the disease's prime impetus.

► *Does chiropractic treatment serve any real healing purpose?*

Whenever bones are out of alignment the body's flow of energy (*chi*) through the entire system is impeded or blocked. When this happens, the body may experience innumerable ill effects. Proper alignment of the bone structure is as important as good circulation, ingesting the minimum amount of vitamins and minerals every day, eating in moderation, getting adequate exercise, and making sure you get sufficient rest and peace of mind.

► *If my doctor determines that my being overweight is not due to any physiological dysfunctions or genetic factors, does that mean that I'm causing it myself? Is it a psychological problem?*

In your letter, you did admit that you love to eat. It sounds as though your physician might not have spelled it out as you would've wished. You need to be straightforward with your doctor and not be timid in asking her to clarify the information she's conveying to you. Too many times, people leave their doctor's office with too many unanswered questions and confused about what was said.

If your doctor said that there was no physiological dysfunctioning or genetic factors causing you to be overweight, it's probable that she was trying to tell you that you're either eating too much of the wrong things or that you're not getting enough exercise—perhaps both. You know what your eating habits are. You know if you're getting enough exercise. You, above all others, can pinpoint where the problem is, especially when tests have shown that there's no genetic or other type of physical cause.

You say you love to eat. Well, you can still love to eat—just change what you eat. If you can't manage to make a complete change, then at least alternate your favorites with something a little less fattening. Drink more water. Alternate water and your other drinks. Don't go to the grocery market when you're hungry; eat something nutritious before you go. Snack on wheat crackers instead of chips and the like.

Keep your television remote on top of the TV so you get up to change channels.

If you're really interested in losing some weight, you won't think it's too much trouble to sit down and give the subject some deep thought. There are a multitude of ways you can decrease your calorie intake and give yourself a little added exercise to boot. Sometimes, though we don't particularly think of ourselves as being lazy, we can get in slump phases when we just aren't interested in expending any more energy than we think is necessary. This is when your determination to lose that weight has to kick in. You have to decide what you want more, being laid back or expending that bit of extra energy that, deep in your heart, you know will do you good and help you slim down.

And then there is that old "I deserve" excuse. "I *deserve* to have this extra piece of chocolate. I *deserve* to sit here all evening with the remote. I deserve to *drive* myself up the street to visit my neighbor instead of *walking* up." Where this "deserve" thing comes from, I'm not sure. I suppose there's a wide variety of reasons why folks use this psychological mechanism to soothe themselves. Yet what makes us so all-deserving in the first place? Aren't we all hard at work toward our individual goals? We all do the normal chores involved in keeping a house or apartment. We do laundry, go grocery shopping, vacuum, make a living, and so on. So what is it that makes one person stand out more than another so much so that he or she feels deserving of a reward? I once overhead someone once say, "I worked so hard on my diet and did so good that I deserve to treat myself to this marzipan." Huh? Where's the logic in that? Why wouldn't that individual think that what she *deserved* was to *feel good about herself* instead of voluntarily doing something to sabotage the gains she'd made? Perhaps what she really deserved was to go out and buy herself a new pair of jeans or a dress (in a smaller size). Now, that'd be a real reward for her efforts. You don't reward yourself with that from which you've been trying to stay away. That makes no sense. That's childish logic. That's like someone who quits smoking and is so successful that he rewards himself by having a cigarette. See what I mean? I'm not implying that the fight with one's weight—the old battle of the bulge—is an easy one. All I'm saying is that your weight is part of your ongoing lifestyle of which you must be aware. Its maintenance becomes a way of living because you won't keep excess weight off if you work at doing so for only a specified span of time—say, until you get to a certain weight goal. After that goal is reached, your attention to your body can't end. Maintenance takes diligence too.

If this correspondent is eating for self-gratification or for self-soothing, then there is some aspect in her life that is psychologically disturbing and, in her conscious mind, she feels a need to placate it or make some type of personally satisfying compensation for its existence. Getting to the root of the life problem is paramount. Eating can be a conflict-resolution placebo—it really won't have any effect on the underlying problem.

► *How come some people have AIDS [acquired immunodeficiency syndrome] and never first had HIV [human immunodeficiency virus]? And how come some folks have had HIV for years and it never developed into a full-blown AIDS condition?*

Because just maybe, HIV is not the singular forerunner of AIDS that the medical community would have us believe. I think the general public has to be more discerning when accepting everything that comes out of the offices of the AMA or appears on the pages of its journal (the *Journal of the American Medical Association*) and also those of the *New England Journal of Medicine*. Over the years, the AMA and these two journals have reversed their positions regarding medical theories, so we need to think for ourselves instead of taking another's statement or conclusion as being the last word. I would like to refer you to a very interesting book written by Kary Mullis, a biochemist who was awarded the Nobel Prize and the Japan Prize in 1993 for chemistry. He is a maverick scientist who is not intimidated by peer pressure to spout the party line. Outspoken and oftentimes amusing, his book is a breath of fresh air to read. It's entitled *Dancing Naked in the Mind Field* (ISBN 0-679-44255-3). Don't be afraid to read it just because it was written by a biochemist. His writing style is very readable and his conceptual clarity is very down-to-earth. The book reads like a science or medical novel. As a carrot in front of your nose, here's a startling little fact: The scientific community *pays* this geneticist/biochemist to *not* speak at its seminars. Hmmm—don't you wonder why? In part, it has to do with his realization that the "incontrovertible" connection between HIV and AIDS has never been solidly established. When he gives speeches, he tends to be vocal about this situation, much to the chagrin of his scientist peers.

▸ *It's been proved that mental visualization is an effective supportive tool for healing, so why don't hospitals have specialized therapists on board to facilitate this method?*

I suppose you'd have to ask a hospital administrator or the hospital governing board. Yes, I certainly agree that mental visualization is a powerfully dynamic tool for stimulating healing activity of the cells and for maintaining wellness. If hospitals are lagging behind in using these techniques, then I think the holistic field of medicine is primed for a newcomer.

I'd never thought of this concept as a separate therapy before now, but this correspondent has sparked the idea for a wonderfully helpful therapy. The visualization therapist would not only have to possess a well-rounded background and understanding of the way visualization works but also be a skilled medical technician, perhaps a nurse. This last would be a prerequisite because to facilitate proper visualization of any medical condition existing within the body, the therapist would have to know all the terminology and specific physiology of the disease or condition. It would be paramount that the client be able to view medical volumes displaying color visuals of the condition as a basis for visualization. For visualization therapy to work at its optimum level, the client's visualizations would have to be as medically—as physiologically—accurate as possible. My suggestion that this therapist be a nurse is only one option. Any individual with a strong background knowledge of medicine and physiology could research a particular condition enough to gather the appropriate medical texts and make aids, such as diagrams, for the client to study before the actual therapy event begins.

I don't see that visualization therapy would legally require any type of certification for the practice of this process. What would be essential would be for the client him- or herself to investigate the therapist regarding medical knowledge or background. The last thing a client wants or needs for this type of healing therapy is to be misguided to visualize the wrong physiology and mechanics associated with his or her condition, so it should be the client's priority to make sure the visualization therapist is knowledgeable about medicine, types of operations, the manifestation of the different diseases, physiology, and so forth. Traditional medicine has learned that biofeedback is a useful aid to healing; now doctors need to take another baby step beyond their rigid thinking to include visualization therapy.

▸ *You need to write a supplement to* Earthway *devoted to beauty secrets.*

I do? Did you think I forgot to include that section in *Earthway*? External beauty is superficial. It has nothing to do with one's true beingness. External beauty is one of the most misleading characteristics an individual possesses. That's the reason a section related to external beauty was purposely omitted from *Earthway*. You see, who we each are—our inner beingness—is not related to external appearances. It's the state of our *inner* self that is reflected through *behavioral* beauty, and that's what *Earthway* was all about. It's all about the different natural aspects of Nature that exist as interrelated facets of ourselves, and about how this powerful interconnectedness benefits humankind in a multitude of ways. By realizing this interconnectedness and using these gifts of Nature, we become beneficiaries of Grandmother Earth's living legacy. Beauty is ours. Beauty is not only skin deep—beauty emanates from *within*.

▸ *We're basically spiritual people. Why wouldn't it be natural for us to depend on faith healing as our sole medical technique?*

Though we may be spiritual people, and the truth of that statement could be debatable in itself, we are in physical bodies. Those physical bodies are affected in positive and negative ways by elements of our natural physical surroundings, by the atmosphere, by climatological elements, by diet and chemical additives, by viruses and toxins. We've also been provided with natural physical aids to counter these, such as natural herbs and botanicals to heal our ills; traditional medicines, which are derivatives of many of those same botanicals; and ongoing advancements in medicine that continually introduce less-invasive and less-endangering methods of surgery. Technology is a child of knowledge. The wisdom to use knowledge in ways to help society become healthier is an element of humanity's natural growth. The Divine gave us the potential for intelligence; to not use that precious gift to help heal and save lives is an act of terrible ungratefulness.

A skill is a gift. Talents are gifts. Whether you believe that these gifts are from the Divine or that they are naturally acquired is not germane. What's relevant is that skills exist for a reason—to be used. The Divine gave us a will to live—to *want* to extend our lives so that we can use those extended years to serve others and practice unconditional goodness.

There is a skewed belief to which some hold that says something like this: "If God wants me to live, I'll be healed." Well, know what? God doesn't interfere in our lives. Instead, that's what the Divine gave us the gift of free will for. To leave healing to "faith in God" or "in God's hands" is to push personal responsibility onto another's shoulders. It's being irresponsible because you don't want to make a major medical decision. You can't say, "Well, if God wants me, He'll allow me to die of this illness." News flash: If God wants you, you don't need an illness to cause your death. You could go in any number of ways. Yet is that even the point? No, because God doesn't cut people's lives short. The Divine wants you to live a productive life of service, one reflecting spiritual behavior. God wants you to be fulfilled, not cut your own life short with misguided thoughts that He's calling you back.

To depend solely on faith healing is not in keeping with why you're here. It's not taking advantage of the opportunities you're given to improve and extend your life.

▶ **What do you think of the theory that a glass of red wine a day helps to prevent heart attacks?**

I'm inclined to agree with it. The French are known for their penchant for having red wine with meals. Studies have shown the French people to have a lower incidence of heart attacks and circulatory problems. Statistically, this ethnic group stood out from others under study. It would appear that the wine was the determining factor in this comparison. Italians also fared well in the study.

▶ **In Earthway you reminded us that bubble bath products aren't good for little girls. What would you suggest as a bubbly alternative?**

Yes, it was publicized that physicians were reporting an increased incidence of vaginal irritation and infection in little girls who used bubble bath products. Parents need to be responsible and use logic when purchasing some products for their children. It's natural to want to treat your young daughter to a fun-filled bathtime, but looking beyond the packaging and weighing possible consequences is part of responsible parenthood.

What's the alternative? Plain liquid soap. A small amount poured under the faucet's running bathwater will make the bubbles you're going for. I suggest using one that has the least additives such as fragrance. Frequently, added fragrance in a hygienic product or lotion causes contact dermatitis (itching or rash) for sensitive individuals. Many wonderful herbal products have been contaminated with additives during the manufacturing process. Watch for these in the ingredient list on the packaging.

► *Are soft drinks okay?*

You're asking me? I'm a Pepsiholic from way back. Let's return to the concept of moderation. It aptly applies here. A *little* of something doesn't do harm, but too much causes problems. Generally, it's best to avoid ingesting too many carbonated drinks. Again, alternate these with water and juices. Grapefruit juice and apple juice are wonderfully healthful. A small juice glass of grape juice taken before a meal helps the digestive system assimilate nutrients. Apple and cranberry juice seem to stave off the formation of kidney stones in individuals susceptible to them. Carbonated drinks are okay once in a while, but not as one's sole choice for fluid intake.

► *What about diet soft drinks?*

Healthwise, as a general rule of thumb, pure sugar is better than the substitutes. Pure sugar is natural, and natural ingredients are more healthful. Where folks go off track with this is in ingesting more than they should. Once again, moderation is the key.

▶ *Should I feel guilty having French fries or pizza?*

I'm not going to tell you whether you should feel guilty, because that depends on your own system, on whether you're on a diet, on what other things you eat, and if you make French fries and pizza your mainstays. If your eating regimen is well rounded and includes a routine intake of salads, lean meat, fish, and such, I don't see that you'd have to feel guilty over having French fries or pizza occasionally. Again, all foods have some merit and nutritional benefit. Variety—a wide variety of foods taken in smaller portions—is best.

▶ *I think that God made perfect human bodies and that all disease is psychosomatic.*

As always, everyone has a right to his or her own opinion on everything, yet this opinion has a bit of a rationale problem. Even objects of perfection are subject to being affected by external influences.

Consider this: When a "perfect" wildflower blossom has its petals marred by a sudden high-mountain hailstorm, did that flower cause the damage to itself? Or was it negatively affected by an *external* natural force? Okay, maybe I didn't use a perfect example, so here's another: When a *human* infant comes down with a bad cold, colic, or the flu, did that infant cause the illness with his or her mind? Even when it hasn't yet developed mental reasoning abilities? Of course not.

The only error in your logic was in adding the word *all*. When you said "*all* disease," that's what made your theory false. I firmly agree that much human illness *is* caused by psychosomatic elements, but we can't say that it *all* is. The mind and its power can exert a dynamic force upon the human physiological system. The mind is the body's mainframe control center that manages all its physiological systems, down to the smallest cellular structure. We see clear evidence of this when an ill person becomes well after being given medication in the form of a placebo. The patient *believes* he or she has taken a strong dose of medicine and therefore the mind's response to that belief acted upon the condition to improve or heal it. This happens when a condition has been generated by the mind itself—a psychosomatic cause. The mind *causes* it and then, with the placebo, the mind *cures* it.

There are innumerable psychological provocations that can induce a psychosomatic situation. Sometimes an individual feels the need for attention and perceives the way to achieve it as being through sympathy from others. The quickest method of gaining this sympathy is through focusing the attention of others on one's new illness or painful physical condition. People who chronically use this medical form of manipulation are what we call hypochondriacs. They dwell on their aches and pains, and no conversation you have with them will ever be without the inclusion of some physical complaint. It's choosing negative attention over positive interaction. And when these people complain often enough, the psychologically induced condition oftentimes becomes real at the mind's continual insistence. The mind can heal the body, and the mind can make it ill. However, the mind does not create *all* the body's illnesses.

► *Your natural healing* Earthway *book was so comprehensive that it covered healing aspects I never would've thought of, yet they were all so obviously interconnected. Do you have any plans on doing a book on explaining the many alternative healing methods, such as therapeutic touch, chiropractic, and acupuncture/acupressure?*

Though I have plans for other types of books, one such as this is not among them. My books, each one of them, has a specific purpose. I write because bringing certain messages and information is the first phase of my purpose for being here. Every book focuses on a particular concept that needs conveying or a subject matter that needs greater clarification. This is my twentieth book and the light at the end of my writing tunnel is getting brighter with the publication of each one. I have a few more to write before I close the cover on the last book. Then I'll be concentrating on the second phase of my work—that of a spiritual/social nature—when I establish the Magdalene Abbey for women as both a spiritual place of solitude and respite and a safe house away from domestic abuse.

To create a book about the various alternative healing methods would be redundant because there are myriad volumes already available on these subjects, both those devoted to the individual alternative healing methods and those detailing the methodology of many of them in a single volume. I'm not interested in creating repetitive information just to add another title to my list of books. Every one of my books was written for a specific reason, and to repeat the work of others is not within the framework of my purpose, nor would it sit well with my conscience.

I thank you for your gift of kind appreciation expressed about *Earthway*, and I hope you'll understand why I won't be doing a book about alternative healing methodologies.

► *What is the best treatment for stretch marks and scars?*

Cocoa butter and peanut oil. Whenever you purchase a cocoa butter product for this purpose, make sure that it has no additives, that it's one hundred percent pure. The Yellow Stick, made by Cocoacare Products, Inc., in Dover, New Jersey, is a wonderful product. It's pure cocoa butter and comes in a convenient push-up tube. If you've ever used pure cocoa butter before, you know that it's a fairly solid product and you have to hold it in your hand for a while before you apply it elsewhere to your body. Your hand temperature liquefies the cocoa butter and, before you know it, you've got a handful of melted emollient in your hand. By buying the product packaged in a tube, you can apply it without getting it anywhere but where you want it to be.

▸ *I've heard that honey is a good healing application for skin infections. Why?*

It's a good skin-healing agent because it has antibiotic properties.

▸ *What's the best type of vegetable oil to use?*

There are several: canola, olive, and peanut oil.

▸ *What eye makeup removal product is the best one on the market to use?*

Petroleum jelly, because it's pure and contains no additives or ingredients that would irritate the eyes. Plus, there's an added bonus—petroleum jelly will nourish the eyelashes.

▸ *Do chemicals and growth hormones in our food cause increased human violence?*

There can be an indirect relationship found here because the hormonal stimulation and development of puberty is brought on at an earlier age when mental and emotional aspects are still immature.

▸ *In* Earthway *you mentioned the importance of maintaining a healthy balance of acid and alkaline within one's system. You listed several food examples, but how can we maintain our systems in a decently balanced state if we don't know the acid-to-alkaline composition of all foods?*

This balance of acid and alkaline foods is not a new concept. There are reference materials available if you're interested in further research. Some of them have a comprehensive listing of foods and will be helpful to you.

No matter what subject matter you're interested in, no matter what philosophy, school of thought, hobby, or special interest, there is a well of information available. Do research. Read. Study. Take the time to be well informed. Never depend on a singular source as a basis for belief. That single source should serve as an ember that sparks an interest. That spark ignites a desire to learn more through extended research and discovery. Having someone tell you the answers is okay, but it's so much more valuable when you discover them in a manner that enriches and develops your personal understanding.

▶ *We can't all eat only of the fruits and vegetables grown in our own geographical locale, so we eat what's available. What of the fruits shipped in from other countries?*

Vibrationally speaking, it's best to eat foodstuffs grown and harvested locally, but there's not a single geographical area that provides the perfect growing conditions of every fruit and vegetable. So sure, you've got to ingest some foodstuffs from other locales. You may be able to grow the perfect juicy tomato in your own garden and your county may produce the best watermelons in the nation, but it can't also produce the oranges and grapefruit that Florida does. Ingesting locally grown foods will give you the *optimum* vibrational balance.

Eating foodstuffs shipped in from farms and orchards in other countries removes the vibrational connection to you one step further. Besides the vibrational aspect, this situation adds another element—that of less safe growing and harvesting practices. Many of the fields of foreign farms are irrigated by polluted water, which is absorbed by the plants. This is how bacteria and such contaminate the end product that is shipped to our markets. World market trading and commerce is a good practice for every nation involved; however, every nation does not have the same health standards in food production and processing as the United States does.

▶ *I've started finding rodent droppings in my silverware drawer. How do I keep my utensils clean?*

If you have rodent droppings, then your silverware also has urine on it. Until you solve your critter problem, you need to keep your eating utensils in a clean and uncontaminated place, a place where they're covered and out of harm's way. I suggest one of those *nonplastic* or *Corningware* storage containers with a tightly fitting cover. Trap the rodents by the method suggested below, but you must keep your dishes and silver, including cookware, in an uncontaminated place.

Since you live in New Mexico, you're probably familiar with the hantavirus pulmonary syndrome (hantavirus) that has been evident mostly in the rural regions of the western United States. This virus is deadly. It has a fatality rate of fifty-one percent. Outbreaks have occurred in twenty-three states, in Canada, and six Latin American countries. The hantavirus is carried by rodents and infects humans through rodent saliva, droppings, and urine. It is transmitted by inhalation of airborne particles or direct contact with the rodents, their droppings, or nesting areas or by receiving a rodent bite. Cleaning out a barn or outbuildings increases one's potential for exposure through breathing in airborne contaminants if they're present. Cleaning a basement and sweeping up droppings can also lead to an infection. And you certainly don't want to use eating utensils that have been exposed to contaminated droppings or urine.

Not all species of rodents carry the hantavirus. The primary carrier is the deer mouse. The cotton rat in the southeast region of the United States is also a known carrier. This virus is not spread from person to person. You can't get it from being around an exposed individual.

The primary symptom of this disease is difficulty in breathing caused by a fluid buildup in the lungs that quickly produces an inability to breathe. The first symptoms are a flulike fever (temperatures of one hundred one to one hundred four degrees Fahrenheit); headache; muscle aches; abdominal, joint, or lower back pain; nausea; and vomiting. Immediate medical attention is necessary. There is no cure or vaccine for the hantavirus infection.

On a personal note, my friend's nephew died from this disease. He was only eighteen. He'd cleaned out the family's barn and died only three days after being hospitalized. Being a young person who had a full and fun life of things to do and places to go, he ignored the fever for a day. Additional symptoms sent him to the hospital. This young man didn't live far from me—on the other side of a ridge, twenty miles down a county road.

I have at least one thousand rosy finches coming at one time to feed on my sunflower seed offerings at my cabin. I also have three feral cats who live in the wild woods around my place. Nearly every morning, though I put out food for the cats, I find one or two dead birds (or the remnants of them) in their food bowl. Why do I keep feeding the feral cats and why don't I get rid of them? Because they also keep the rodent population in check around my cabin and property. Though I'm sad to see the dead birds, those cats are helping to keep the hantavirus at bay in a natural manner, through their predatory nature. If you live in rural areas, especially out in the deep forest as I do, you discover and achieve a fine balance of existence that is interrelated with Nature. In this manner do humans and animals live in and share a respectful relationship with one another.

I strongly suggest closely checking all cupboards where any type of cookware or eating utensil is stored. Here are the cleaning precautions advised by the Colorado Department of Health, Division of Disease Control:

1. Open windows for at least 30 minutes before cleaning. Leave the area until the airing-out period is completed.

2. Set rodent traps inside the house using peanut butter as bait. Use spring-loaded, glue, or live traps. Do not use rodent poisons.

3. Use rubber household gloves.

4. Mix one-half cup of bleach with five cups of water and pour it into an empty spray bottle.

5. Spray the area, then let the area soak thoroughly for ten to fifteen minutes.

6. Pick up the material with rubber gloves and place it all into a plastic bag, then place that into a second sealed plastic bag.

7. Vacuum the material with a wet vacuum. Do *not* vacuum *dry* material; vacuum only wet (soaked) material.

8. Wash the rubber gloves with the bleach mixture and then with soap and water; disinfect in the same way any utensils used.

9. Dispose of the bagged material in a secure trash container.

10. After the above items have been removed, mop floors with the solution described above. Spray dirt floors with the disinfectant solution. Carpets can be cleaned with household bleach, Lysol, or by a commercial-grade steam cleaner or shampooer.

11. Disinfect countertops, cabinets, drawers, and other durable surfaces by washing them with the solution described above.

12. Clean potentially contaminated bedding and clothing with hot water and detergent. Machine-dry laundry on a *high* setting or leave it to air-dry in the sun. (Remember to use rubber or plastic gloves when handling potentially contaminated clothing and to wash gloves after use as described above.)

▶ *Liver is one of the best sources of iron available to us through foodstuff. I don't understand why you suggest avoiding it.*

I suggest avoiding it because the body's liver—any body's—is the system's filter. Would you eat a dirty filter? If you placed a water purifier on your *kitchen* faucet, would you then go to the *bathroom* tap for your glass of water? Why do you wash dishes? You do this so that the next time you need a plate, fork, or glass, you'll have a *clean* one to use. This same theory applies to the ingestion of liver.

▶ *Isn't the ingestion of chocolate okay . . . just once in a while?*

It was my mentor's opinion that chocolate shouldn't be ingested at all . . . period. My personal opinion—and like you, I too have a right to have one—is that once in a while doesn't do harm. Moderation, remember?

Chocolate and peanuts (peanut butter included) have a high concentration of the amino acid L-arginine. When the human body receives a higher dose of this chemical, such as through the routine ingestion of chocolate or peanut butter, the L-arginine will serve as an activator for the herpes virus that is dormant in everyone's system. When herpes is stimulated, people experience an outbreak of cold sores or canker sores.

Chocolate and peanut butter should be eaten as a treat, not daily. Just as a glass of red wine with dinner has been shown to improve blood circulation and stave off heart disease but more than that one glass a day could lead to other types of physical problems, moderation is the key.

▶ *Which is better for the human system, cow's or goat's milk?*

They're both good. Which is best depends on the individual—not only the person's system but also taste preference.

▶ *Aren't foods one makes by hand better than those prepared by a deli or sold on the grocery store shelves?*

This correspondent is referring to readymade sauces, spaghetti, ravioli, boxed bread mixes, and so forth. Vibrationally speaking, those foodstuffs you put together with your own hands at home are better than prepared, processed foods and mixes that may contain some form of harmful ingredients such as certain preservatives. This is because your own vibrational frequency and essence has an effect on the ingredients as a particular meal is prepared and cooked. Purchases from a deli aren't as bad as food taken down from the shelves of the market freezer, such as the frozen meals you bring home and put into the oven. Yet don't misinterpret this. In answer to the *spirit* of this correspondent's question, these sources of food aren't in any way detrimental to you; they just won't be as aligned with your own vibrational frequency as those foods you put together yourself at home.

► *I have some gum problems. What would be good to help this?*

Many times gum problems are a sign of a vitamin A deficiency. You can increase the intake of this vitamin by taking a supplement or by increasing your intake of dairy products, fruits and vegetables, sunflower seeds, or seafood. There is a foodstuff listing for these vitamin A food choices in *Earthway* on page 55.

► *My grandmother likes to smoke a pipe; however, regular tobacco has become so expensive that she can't afford it. What natural herb can I give her as a substitute for regular tobacco?*

The wild-growing tobacco substitutes that will probably be more available to you would be the following: goldenrod (leaf dried), kinnikinnick (leaf dried), lobelia (leaf dried), mullein (leaf dried), sumac (leaf and root dried), sunflower (leaf dried), yarrow (leaf dried).

► *I love raspberries in milk, yet in* Earthway *you stated that it's not good to mix the fruit with milk. I'm doing it anyway and it never seems to cause me any ill effects.*

I love raspberries in milk too.

You misinterpreted the *Earthway* caution. What it said was this: Never mix *citrus* fruits or juices with milk. That means such fruits as oranges, grapefruit, tangerines, and tangelos.

This is an example of what I mean when I've said that "people see but don't see, hear but don't hear, read but don't read." Folks will hear or read something and not quite get it exact when they repeat it or go to use it. They *interpret* rather than take it as is.

Berries in milk are not detrimental to the human physiological system; citrus fruits in milk are.

► *I have a problem with foods not agreeing with me—all foods. Now that I've gone through the full gamut of digestive problem testing, my physician says I've no physiological dysfunctioning or condition to cause this. What's the deal?*

For you specifically, the deal is what you further expressed in your letter to me. You said you were always stressed out. That's the key to your digestive troubles right there. One of the points listed in the "Earthway Dietary Guidelines" section is *Never eat when you're upset, nervous, or angry.*

There was a good reason for listing this all-important dietary tenet. State of mind—your psychological aspects—has a direct connection to the physical body, especially the digestive system. The entire digestive system is so sensitive to emotions that it would appear that it has some form of emotional-trigger response, that it has a specialized network of nerve endings that read and respond to your emotional state. When you are stressed, angry, or upset, those nerve endings within the digestive tract (including stomach) react like the earth does during an earthquake. The whole system vibrates and quivers. Though you may not be aware of this happening, it occurs just the same. Negative emotions set your whole digestive system off and cause a state of internal agitation. It rumbles. Excess acids spew forth. Gases are produced. Then . . . you send food down. What a mess. What a mistake that is—because your internal system is in such utter chaos that it can't process that food in a normal fashion. It's because of this inability to properly process the food when the digestive system is in such a state of turmoil that you experience problems. And if you're *always* stressed, well, no wonder everything you eat causes problems.

Try to practice some calming techniques before eating. After arriving home after work, sit for a while on the couch or in your

favorite chair before rushing right into the kitchen to fix your dinner—rest a bit. Listen to soothing music. Maybe take a calming,
warm bath. Don't use alcohol to calm your nerves. Rather, drink
a cup of chamomile tea (without caffeine). Get in the routine of
postponing the dinner hour until after you've recovered from the
stress of work and the hectic drive home. Eat lighter. Sometimes,
just eating healthy snacks during the day instead of three heavier
meals will greatly help the situation. Munch on saltine crackers
during the day to absorb the excessive stomach acids your emotions are causing. You know your own lifestyle. You alone are the
best one to come up with the most effective ways and methods to
ease your various reasons for emotional stress. Sometimes a small
measure of mental visualization works wonders. Visualize all of
your nerve endings being smoothed out, sort of like applying a
hair conditioner to your hair's split ends. Envision your stomach
and intestinal tract as being calm—softly rising and falling ocean
waves rather than a raging sea in a storm. There are ways. You
can find them.

▶ *I'm a very busy person and am always on the go from morning to night. I'm also way past the age where acne can be a normal tendency, but I still have to deal with it. I hate this. Do you
have any suggestions?*

Since you also wrote that your dermatologist determined that
there was no specific cause, you may want to see whether these
acne outbreaks correspond with your ovulation time. A woman's
menstrual cycle can play havoc with the hormonal and chemical
balance of her system. Also, you mentioned that you had reached
the midway point in menopause. This too alters the hormonal and
chemical balance because your body's in the process of making
readjustments to what the system will interpret as being normal
functioning.

Your admission that you're on the go so much led me to think
that perhaps you're not getting enough rest. Sleep—enough of

it—does wonders for the complexion and emotions. Are your emotions in balance? Are you stressed? Do you accept life more than you try to fight against it?

Also consider your diet. Are you ingesting an overabundance of corn-based products, such as taco shells, chips, salsa, and the like? You need to completely avoid corn, or at least cut way down on your intake of it.

▸ *If wooden cutting boards are so unhealthy to use, why do manufacturers keep making them?*

Probably because people keep buying them—supply and demand.

Cutting boards are for cutting. They save one's counter from getting damaged from knives and the cutting blades of other kitchen utensils. When a piece of raw meat is placed on a cutting board and a knife is drawn through the meat, an indentation from that blade can be made in the cutting board. Left inside this indentation are remnants of the meat product. Inside those remnants are harmful contaminants, such as the bacteria *Escherichia coli*, commonly known as *E. coli*, and *Salmonella*. Cleaning and scrubbing such a cutting board after use will not entirely rid the board of these contaminants, so they'll be present to taint other foods that are set on the board afterward.

You do not want to use a cutting board that can be indented in any way. These indentations are perfect hiding places for dangerous bacteria. You want a glass cutting board that cannot be indented by blades and that can be easily cleaned under running water and bleach. Bleach is the only substance that effectively kills these bacteria. After you clean the cutting board with water and bleach (I set my glass cutting board in the sink and pour straight bleach over both sides of it from the bottle), wash the board with hot water and a strong antibacterial dish soap. And don't stop at the cutting board. Everything you touched with your hands while preparing the raw meat could also be contaminated with bacteria—the skillet or stewpot handle, a towel, a sponge, a water tap handle, the countertop, a cupboard handle, or all the spice containers. Each one needs to be washed off with the bleach solution. Because of germs, I'm a big user of paper towels. I use these instead of a dish sponge for cleanup. I never use a dish sponge on a countertop or range top for cleaning purposes. I always clean these with a watered-down ammonia solution and paper towels. I don't own a dishwasher because I don't want one. The dish sponge is used for nothing but dishes, which are washed in hot soapy water with an antibacterial dish soap and thoroughly rinsed in hot running water. In the dish dryer rack, the dishes just sparkle. I'm not a cleaning fanatic, but I do know the dangers of unsafe kitchen practices and take measures to keep those who eat food from my cabin kitchen as safe from contamination dangers as possible. I don't use any type of wooden cooking or food preparation utensil. However, I do have a wooden bowl to place fresh fruit in.

As long as people care more about the look of wooden cutting boards than the hygienic properties of plain glass or marble ones, manufacturers have no reason to stop producing wooden cutting boards. They make what sells. I would think, though, that the manufacturers would want to make a safer product just out of integrity. Perhaps they could still produce the wooden product but with a glass top or some type of hard, clear substance laminated over the wood. I'm not an expert on such things, but it seems to me that this could be done so that people's desire for a wooden cutting board could be satisfied and everyone would still have a safe product to use.

I too like the look of natural wood and prefer it over glass and plastics, but in some circumstances, wood is not the safest choice.

▸ *I heard on the evening newscast that the AMA announced a new discovery—that research showed that eating a cup of raspberries a day can stop tumor growth. What do you think?*

I think it's been proved that practitioners of so-called traditional medicine are finally discovering the healthful and healing benefits of Grandmother Earth's gifts to us. It appears that it's nearly impossible to be cognizant of absolutely every single healthful benefit that a single foodstuff is capable of providing. Research oftentimes brings unexpected surprises that were not relevant to the original purpose of the tests—healing discoveries made through happenstance. Say the raspberries were being researched as an acne treatment and, quite unexpectedly, observers noticed that tumor growth seemed to be stopped in its tracks after those participating in the tests ingested raspberries. Hmm—a happenstance discovery! So, to test out this new theory, the observers give the raspberries to test subjects with tumors. If the subjects were not given any other substance—chemical or variant foodstuff— the researchers could fairly well deduce that it was the addition of the raspberries to the diet that halted the tumor growth. Many new discoveries are stumbled upon in this manner.

What do I specifically think about it? Perhaps it's true. Maybe it's a real discovery. My mentor never mentioned this, but that doesn't mean that the AMA's recent announcement isn't valid. There were many subject matters my mentor didn't touch upon during our times together. Time is the best validator of truth, so since the AMA has reversed itself so many times over the years, we'll wait and see. At any rate, raspberries are a good natural source for the B vitamins. They're good for you whether they stop tumor growth or not.

▸ *Is brushing one's hair daily good for it, or does daily brushing have the potential of making hair thinner?*

The answer to this question directly depends on the individual's own hair and scalp condition. Brushing the hair stimulates the blood flow beneath the scalp and helps to bring it to the surface, where it aids in nourishing the hair root follicles. Brushing also distributes scalp oils down along the hair shafts, conditioning the scalp and stimulating hair growth.

However, if your scalp and hair are in an unhealthy condition such as being dry and brittle because of hair dyes, bleach, or lack of humidity, brushing may do further damage by breaking it off. And brushing may exacerbate any type of dermatitis of the scalp.

There are nutritional factors that negatively affect hair growth and condition. A lack of certain vitamins, low-protein diets, strict low-fat diets, fasting, and not eating nutritionally all contribute to poor hair and scalp health. Biotin is the key to healthy scalp and hair because it aids in the body's assimilation of protein, vitamin B_{12}, and pantothenic acid. Many times folks exhibiting poor hair and scalp conditions need to ingest a greater amount of biotin in conjunction with folic acid. The folic acid helps keep biotin and the B vitamins from being neutralized and broken down too fast by such canceling factors as alcohol and smoking. The folic acid promotes normal cell growth and cell reproduction.

People with thinning hair, hair that is overtreated with chemicals, or hair that is dry and brittle will usually notice an improvement after ingesting extra biotin along with folic acid. Some natural-food shops stock products that have been specifically formulated for this purpose. Some natural food sources for biotin and folic acid are listed in *Earthway,* on pages 71 through 76.

▶ *What makes metals good or bad for the human system? Aluminum is hazardous to one's health but iron is good for it. What's the deal?*

Well, just because one metal or mineral is healthful doesn't mean that they all are. The determining factor is the inherent makeup of their individual composition. Lead isn't good for you, is it? Lead causes all sorts of physiological ills. The lead in paint, if ingested, can kill you; at the very least, it can lead to liver failure and brain dysfunction. If there's too much lead in the ground water providing your drinking water, it can have a cumulative effect on your system and wreak all sorts of physical and mental damage. So can asbestos. Even an excess of fluoride does harm to the system— rather than being a dental boon, it becomes a dental nightmare.

It just happens that iron strengthens the blood cells through the action of regulating the body's protein metabolism and aiding in the formation of hemoglobin in the blood and myoglobin in the muscle tissue. Iron aids and supports the body's ability to resist infections and flu viruses. Iron is an immunity enhancer that greatly boosts the body's capability to fight off invading elements.

A metal isn't just a metal, a mineral isn't just a mineral, and a vitamin isn't just a vitamin. In every category, the quality and composition of each category member is unique. Each has different positive and negative facets based on its specific composition and how this composition acts on other substances and entities, such as the human body. Just as aluminum is great for some uses, it's not so healthful or wonderful for others. Asbestos has a purpose for existing, but one of those purposes is not for contact with human skin or for inhalation. Iron is essential for human health, but isn't so good for use outdoors because it'll rust. Everything Nature provides us with has a purpose, and some provide more than one benefit. Everything in Nature has the balance of polarity—that is, each thing possesses negative and positive aspects. Think about it. The earth itself—the soil—through its nutrients, grows our foodstuffs and forests and landscapes our property; yet it can also be destructive when it shakes from an earthquake or becomes saturated with moisture from torrential rains and moves in landslides. Every single facet of Nature has polarity and the potentiality to be an aid or a destructive force, including metals and minerals. Of all the wonderful gifts of Nature, none are purely negative or purely positive; they are all in balance.

▸ *In* Earthway, *you listed shellfish as being a good source for various vitamins, yet Edgar Cayce didn't hold with eating any type of shellfish. Why the difference?*

Why not? Anyone can have a personal opinion. I think that Cayce was probably so emphatic about shellfish because they are bottom feeders. Bottom feeders pick up more contaminants than other types of water dwellers. Perhaps he foresaw the increase in water pollution, yet that factor doesn't negate the vitamin content of the foodstuff itself. If you ingest shellfish harvested from unpolluted waters, the health benefit is a positive effect. If you happen to ingest shellfish from polluted waters, as I unknowingly once did, you could get hepatitis or worse from it.

Cayce had strong opinions regarding the ingestion or avoidance of specific foods, just as my mentor did. Each had different priorities regarding what to stress. Now enters an individual who reads this information. This individual has a free will and a mind with which to make decisions. This individual does additional research because he or she is wise enough to seek knowledge before making a decision. This individual will, I hope, make a personal decision after carefully considering the subject and weighing all the information. And this individual will then make an educated decision as to what's best for him- or herself. I do the same thing you do. Cayce may have denounced shellfish, but I happen to think shellfish is good for the body once in a while. So occasionally, I buy it fresh and cook it myself at home. Other so-called dietary experts claim pork is a forbidden food, yet I'll do up a pork roast maybe once a year or include Italian sausage on a home-baked pizza.

Remember that the bottom line on good nutrition and an all-around lifestyle is *moderation*. It's not rational or logical to expect to receive all the body's necessary vitamins and minerals from a narrow selection of foodstuffs. Variety not only is the spice of life—it is a *healthy* life.

Also remember the importance of individual thought. Reference books are great. They're wonderful for gaining knowledge, but don't take one person's opinion on a subject matter as being the final word on everything. When even the experts disagree, when the medical establishment reverses itself, when up-to-the-minute research negates previous findings, it tells you something. It tells you to make personal choices on the basis of what feels right for you. This holds true in all areas of life, not just those aspects related to dietary choices.

▸ *I would like to pick my own mushrooms. Do you think book learning can teach me enough to accomplish this in a safe manner?*

No. My opinion on this is that you should study a clearly illustrated reference book on this subject that depicts and thoroughly explains the types of mushrooms specific to your geographical area, a book that includes the edible and poisonous mushrooms. *Then,* and only then, locate an experienced mushroom expert who is involved in teaching the subject through field guides. There's no better way to learn than by doing. To find the mushroom in its natural habitat, pick it, touch it, examine it, and note all the species' particularities of color, shape, texture, and so on is the best way to learn safe differentiation when going it alone. First the reference book studying, then the hands-on learning with an expert field guide. Then, after you're confident of your newly acquired skill, go out on your own search for wild mushrooms.

▸ *Are the herbal teas made by brand-name manufacturers as good as those obtainable in health-food stores?*

Some of them are. Just like everything else, be aware and discriminating when making purchases. The milk bought in a grocery chain store is usually just as good as the milk bought in a dairy's retail shop. Some market cheese can be just as good as that bought at a roadside dairy farm stand. Herb teas bought from a health-food store and in a grocery store can be nutritiously identical. What you want to do is check the freshness date and the ingredients. Watch for additives if you're specifically searching for pure ingredients. Many teas will have one flavor or type listed on the box but will in reality contain a blend of several. Generally, loose tea is better than tea bags. This is particularly related to green tea. It all comes down to deciding what you're looking for.

Sometimes the choice to purchase your tea from a health-food store is generated by nothing more than a psychological element. Sometimes the teas there are better and fresher; other times, it makes no difference one way or the other. It just depends on the specific type of tea you're looking for.

▸ *Whenever I'm with other people in a social situation where a meal is served, I'm always the last one eating. Even if I'm just sitting in a restaurant by myself, I notice that people seem to eat fast. Is it just my imagination?*

No, it's not just your imagination. I'm always the last one eating too. People eat way too fast. They scarf down their food at an amazing rate and then wonder why they have heartburn or indigestion. This habit seems to go hand in hand with the fast pace today of society. Fast travel, fast communication, fast talk, and fast traffic. The pace of the world's lifestyle has gone from slow and easy to fast and stressful.

This fact was brought home when I was listening to the local TV evening news and the station's reporter physician had chosen the topic of esophagus lacerations. Hospital emergency departments are seeing an increase in throat tear incidents. Why? Because people are eating too fast and not masticating their food enough before they swallow it. The report amazed me. Though I too had noticed how fast people finish a meal, I had no idea the problem had become so bad that folks aren't even chewing their food properly.

At any rate, eating fast and not chewing your food well enough contribute to a multitude of digestive problems. Take your time when sitting down for a meal. You're receiving the blessing of bodily nourishment. Mealtime should be relaxing and pleasurable. It should be enjoyable and an act of appreciation.

You know, people get so caught up in their own little circle of life that seeing starving children and entire villages of starving people on the television no longer has any effect on them. People have distanced themselves from the rest of the world. They've forgotten that we're all related to each other—each of us is an individual member of the human family. Every bite of food taken is a blessing. It's a sign that we should be grateful that we too are not starving. Yet how many times have you sat in front of your television watching these sad newscasts while shoveling in the food off your plate? How many times have you done this and realized you never felt one twinge of guilt? American society has become so distant and removed from the rest of the world, from having any *feelings* for those across the oceans that such news reports seem like movies.

The abundance of foodstuffs in the United States is a blessed bounty that Americans take for granted. You can see this is so by the manner in which people eat. People need to be more aware. They need to *receive* their blessings with *respect*, not *take* them with *indifference*.

► *Does the atmosphere of a restaurant affect how food is assimilated?*

Believe it or not, it can. This question shows some thought, some awareness.

Restaurant decor, such as style of furniture, period setting, use of color, and background music, plays a major role in setting an environmental atmosphere for the purpose of dining. That atmosphere greatly contributes to the type of mood presented as an aesthetic enhancement of the dining experience.

A fast-food eatery will not be decorated for the purpose of detaining its guests. Its decor usually consists of vibrant colors (reds in particular) and the mood is set to give a "hurry up and order, eat, and leave" message to the customer. Just the fact that you have to stand at a counter to order your food creates a rushed atmosphere that pushes you to move along so the guy behind you can place his order. And so on and so forth. Then you have the middle-ground restaurants that have a wider variety to their menus yet still don't present a "rest, relax, and enjoy your meal" atmosphere. The music in these places might be loud or the kitchen and food preparation area can be seen by the dining public. You might hear dishes clattering in the background, and the the staff members' complaining or joking is within easy earshot. And then you have the quiet restaurants—muted background music, low lights, soft-speaking waiters and waitresses, high-backed booths, and private tables. The soothing, relaxing atmosphere of the latter is designed for leisurely dining. It invites people to stay awhile and make their meal a pleasurable experience. It invites you to leave your stress outside.

Sure, a restaurant's atmosphere affects the dining experience. I'd love to design a restaurant that would be an example for others to follow. I've been in a couple that had excellent atmosphere—wonderfully tranquil and extremely enjoyable.

▸ *Does freeze-drying rob food of its nutrients?*
Generally, no.

▸ *Do you have any suggestions above and beyond the redundant lists of survival supplies for storage that other authors provide?*
I'm not sure because I haven't seen these lists.

One item I tell my readers to include as an essential element of their survival or emergency supply is vitamins. Folks don't usually think of vitamins when they're making a supply list, but they're a necessity. You may not have all your daily nutritional needs covered by the foodstuffs you've stored. In the event of a real long-term emergency, you're stuck with whatever you have on hand, and scurvy is a real threat. So having a reasonable stock of a good multivitamin with minerals among your long-term supplies is a wise move on your part.

Water-purifying tablets can be used up too quickly. Bleach goes much further because all you need is a few drops of bleach in a gallon of water to purify it for drinking purposes.

I know that many lists include batteries. However, as you know, batteries can lose their stored energy and can leak as they become old. These batteries are mostly meant for use in radios and flashlights. My companion and I have eliminated the need for batteries in regard to these two items. We have two *windup* radios and four *windup* flashlights that need no batteries at all. These products were manufactured for Third World countries and are produced by the BayGen Company under the trademark Freeplay. Once fully charged by winding, the flashlight will run for approximately six hours. You can receive a brochure by calling (800) 946-3234, sending an e-mail message to **freeplay @ freeplay.net**, or visiting BayGen's Website at **freeplay//www.freeplay.net**. These items are a little on the expensive side, but they're incredibly well made and worth the money. In 1999, both items were under one hundred dollars each (between sixty and eighty dollars); each one comes with a five-year warranty.

My good friends Sindy and Pam installed solar and wind power on their remote forty-acre cabin property. They have chickens and ducks (for eggs only), a generator, and a mule and two goats. Now, having a goat is fine, but how does one have a goat for fresh milk when one lives in the city or an apartment? Uh-huh—that's where the boxes of powdered milk come in. Maybe you think you don't drink enough milk to need to include that item in your storage supplies, but milk is an ingredient in a wide variety of meals.

Don't forget hygiene items. Think about all these little odds and ends that you use for your personal hygiene. When it comes to this subject, most folks immediately think of toilet paper. They have toilet paper stocked, but what about women's items, such as tampons and yeast infection treatments? A good antibacterial wash such as Betadine is a must. Some type of pain reliever should be stocked, as should bandages of every size. Herbal black ointment or several tubes of commercial ichthammol or cans of Smile's PRID Salve are essential because you may have a need for a drawing salve and a disinfectant.

A good rule of thumb is to take a thorough inventory of your household supplies. Check through your medicine chest and food cupboards to get a good idea of what you use on a daily basis and try to create a minireplica of those for your emergency cache.

Also, as frivolous as it may first appear, a few beauty or "treat" items may be well worth stocking. If an extended emergency does occur and you're left without goods available from stores for a long while, a piece of chocolate or candy or an application of your favorite perfume can do wonders to lift your spirits. These items are not as insignificant as they may sound. Every little extra to boost morale will be worth its weight in gold.

Make sure you have some salt in your storage supply, and have a variety of spices in your cache to allow for a variety of flavoring in the routine foodstuffs you may be forced to have for a diet for a while. Pasta, a wide variety of it, is an excellent foodstuff to stock because you can prepare it with just boiling water on your wood-stove or camp stove. For more variety purchase the prepared boxes that include the pasta and flavorings. Some of these even come with dried vegetables.

Rather than choosing specific cans of vegetables or fruits, opt for those products that contain a mixed variety. This will save on storage space and also, when needed, provide you with an assortment of nutrition sources. For example, instead of buying cans of peas, cans of carrots, and cans of asparagus, purchase cans with a variety of vegetables in them. Buy cans that contain vegetables *and* meat for protein. The greater *variety* you can amass, the less chance you'll have of experiencing undernourishment when and if an emergency arises.

Last, but certainly not last in importance, is cash. Stash that cash—whatever amount you can afford—on a daily basis. What if you awoke tomorrow morning and your bank had closed its doors? What if ATMs (automated teller machines) were out of commission? What if all computers didn't work? What if the stock market crashed and all your money was tied up in stocks, bonds, and other investments and you couldn't access it? What if all the money you had in the world was what was in your pocket or wallet? What then? If you have foresight enough to have stored food and toiletry supplies in case of an extended emergency, why wouldn't you also have a stash of immediately available cash at your disposal? Seriously, think about it. I repeat, what if you awoke tomorrow morning and all the cash you had in the world was what you could scrounge up from your dresser top, pocket, change jar, or wallet? Think about it . . . think about it. So what if your friends think you're being an alarmist? You don't even have to tell anyone that you're stashing some cash. In fact, you may not want to do that anyway. You have the responsibility to take care of yourself. You may have loved ones or a significant other whom you want to take care of in case of an extended emergency. If you're a responsible individual, you'll have your bases well covered. Being prepared for any eventuality is not being an alarmist; it's having the wisdom to act on the probabilities presented by foresight. Perceiving the reality of societal and geological potentialities is not being a fruitcake, it's being rational. Too many people today jump to the conclusion that preparedness equals alarmist, when in actuality, those same people are choosing to avoid personal responsibility through the psychological cover of denial.

▸ *I think that when food is offered to the public, in such venues as restaurants, county fairs, flea markets, and cafeterias, that leaves the public open to the possibility of terrorist activity via bacteria/designer virus contamination. My friends think I'm being paranoid. Am I?*

Well, no. It's a fact that *any* place food is offered to the public could be a possible vector for terrorists. Same with any building's being a possible target for bomb placement. I think that your friends are not specifically referring to your basic concept but rather your *fear* of its happening. Perhaps they think you're too focused on this idea to the point of it seeming to be a neurotic issue with you and you're presenting a paranoia about public eateries. I can't say for sure if this is their thinking on it, but it seems logical. If this fear is on your mind so much, maybe you have some type of unidentified premonition or subtle sense of an upcoming occurrence. If you can't pinpoint why you're so centered on this idea, it may be generated by some type of subconscious foreknowledge.

It's certainly not unreasonable nor irrational to think that a terrorist or psychologically dysfunctional individual could contaminate a public food source with bacteria or a virus. We've witnessed this type of activity with the 1982 Tylenol scare and other product-tampering incidents in the past. It's not impossible. It's happened before and it will certainly happen again—somewhere.

► *Why do you think wild foods aren't more available in super-markets?*

I agree that their availability is certainly limited. I mean, there is a coffee company that puts out a chicory coffee, but you're wondering where the dandelion root coffee is too. Grocery markets will sometimes offer piñon nuts along with their walnut and almond bulk displays, but you also want to see beech. The best supermarket section for finding any decent variety of wild offerings is usually the tea section.

My opinion on why this is so is that food growers stick with what they know, what's they've found to be tried and true. The farmers aren't likely to be confident enough to change their plantings and harvesting from corn to shepherd's purse because there's no proven popularity or profitability.

Other than that, you'd have to inquire of the food manufacturers and processors themselves for a definitive answer. If you want some of the more natural wild foodstuffs, you still need to shop at a good natural health-food store to get any kind of variety.

▸ *I don't understand why pharmaceutical companies make and market medicines that have negative side effects. Why do doctors prescribe them?*

That'd be a good question for a doctor. I've seen prescription medications come with pamphlets that listed so many possible side effects that I couldn't fathom why anyone would possibly want to ingest them. It would be nice if all medications were perfectly safe and had no adverse side effects, wouldn't it? Yet even some of the common pain relievers can eat away at the stomach lining. Perhaps the problem lies with the formulation of these pills; perhaps the problem lies with their final chemical composition? I don't think that taking willow bark (natural aspirin) instead of taking any of the name-brand aspirins in pill form would cause any stomach problems.

However, the drug digitalis is derived from the foxglove flower. If the medication were taken in its natural form and too great a quantity was ingested, you'd certainly get an adverse reaction from it. So I think your question is directed more to the pharmaceutical companies that do the research and manufacturing from the natural base chemicals. You want to ask them why they spend time and vast amounts of money creating a hair loss treatment product (such as Propecia) for men that turns out to be verboten for pregnant women—they're advised not to even *touch* it. Or why do pharmaceutical companies spend so much energy and money on pills to make *men* more virile? The two most widely touted and publicized recent pharmaceutical breakthroughs of the century were for *men*—increase their hair growth and increase their sexual prowess. Is that medical equality? Where are the breakthroughs for women? The breast cancer cure? All they can come up with for women's breast cancer is to announce that the voluntary elective surgery for double mastectomy will raise a woman's chance of not getting it by a whopping ninety-five percent! And we should be jumping for joy over *that* medical discovery?

Dearest correspondent, I don't know what's going on with the pharmaceutical companies. Their priorities are governed by profit margins. Their "discoveries" and new product lines have more polarities (healing benefits versus adverse side effects) than the public deserves. They have the technology—it isn't that. They have the intelligence—it isn't that. They have the funding—it isn't that. So . . . what is it? Your question is one that is on the minds of many, especially those who suffer from adverse side effects—and especially women.

► *Is it healthy to use a humidifier in dry weather or in a dry climate?*

Sure it is, but too often, people use these machines without changing the filter (sponge material) frequently enough, and that has the potential to cause health problems. Just like you need to clean out your drip pan beneath your refrigerator and change your furnace filter on a monthly basis during the wintertime, you also need to change or clean the interior of the humidifier. Remember that germs and mold culture faster in moist conditions.

► *Did AIDS really come from homosexuals?*

To buy into that one would be as ignorant as believing homosexuals also brought us the common cold. Let's get real here. Sexual orientation does not create a new disease. The basic premise of this question isn't even logical, is it? What if the question were worded like this: Did AIDS really come from *heterosexuals?* You see how ridiculous *that* sounds? Both propositions sound ridiculous. Homosexuals have been singled out as scapegoats for this disease. It's a fact that new diseases, virus mutations, and bacteria strains are cropping up all the time. They are not selective about whom they infect. Human vulnerability knows no cultural, ethnic, social, or gender barriers. Nor is one's choice of life partner a criterion for a virus in targeting a victim. That theory shows no logic. It's ignorant.

▶ *Is colored cereal harmful for kids to eat? How about colored dog and cat food?*

There's really no reason, other than aesthetics, to add coloring to foodstuffs. Several years ago it was discovered that a certain type of red food coloring was harmful to humans and the manufacturers stopped using it. If one type of dye was found to be harmful, why continue coloring food at all? But this was not a lesson learned. My opinion is that it's better to stay away from the multicolored cereals. Dogs and cats—why do they need colored food? They need nutritious food, not a bowl full of Fruity Feed or Kaptain Kat.

▶ *I'm a beautician and work with chemicals all day. Will this have any long-term adverse effects on me?*

Long-term exposure to many different types of chemicals certainly has the potential to leave some type of physical residual effect(s). Though most beauticians nowadays take the precaution of wearing protective gloves, they're still breathing in the fumes of the various chemicals and are taking the chance of developing some type of respiratory condition in the future. I don't think it'd be unreasonable to wear some type of nose and mouth covering (mask) while working with these intense chemicals.

SECTION
TWO

THE
M·I·N·D

The Seed of
Fruitful Knowledge

THE TOXIN
Contaminating Attitudes and Emotions

▶ *What causes jealousy? I don't understand why my sister acts jealous the way she does, especially when I'm not the type of person to flaunt whatever I have.*

You don't have to flaunt your stuff for others to be jealous and envious. You're not causing the negative emotional responses; she is. Her ego is causing it.

The ego is inflated with self-worth that demands material possessions, social status, recognition, financial security, professional superiority, and only the best of the best of everything for self. It says, "I deserve." Yet in reality, nobody deserves anything for which he or she hasn't worked.

Jealousy is a terrible emotional cancer that metastasizes throughout all aspects of one's life. It negatively affects relationships, personality, perspectives, and business dealings and causes constant internal turmoil and stress. It engenders a form of restlessness as one continually strives to be better than another or acquire the "best" material goods. This state of being is one in which the individual never experiences inner peace or tranquillity because of the constant need to outdo others. It's like being in a race, only the feet aren't pounding over a track field—they're thumping, thumping on a never-ending treadmill.

People evincing signs of envy aren't necessarily self-absorbed individuals, but they're of the opinion that it's *they* who deserve the things you have. Also, these emotions stem from a skewed perspective of value, quality, and importance. These people have their life priorities mixed up. You see, they have this idea that what's most important in life is social status, personal recognition, popularity, expensive possessions, a new car (not a Metro, but a BMW), achievement awards, and being in the top tax bracket. Every one of those elements is so shallow, so inconsequential when contrasted to the beautiful higher qualities that are germane to the big picture of life.

Some folks write to me admitting—sheepishly—that they're envious of me. That is a total puzzlement because I'm just being me. I'm no one special. I'm simply doing what my inner promptings inspire me to do and write about. I don't perceive it as being anything special, so I have difficulty understanding why others do. I don't place myself before the public eye for recognition because, quite truthfully, after all these years I'm still the same shy and retiring individual I've always been. I prefer solitude to being in a crowd. I do what I do because that's why I'm here. I don't need to publicize my personal beingness because the emphasis is on the *words* I have to convey . . . not the *identity* of the writer of those words. That person stays behind in her remote mountain cabin while her words go *out* into the world. I think when my correspondents write and, in various ways, express some sort of envious or wishful thoughts of being like me, they interpret my work personally—they envision what it would be like for them to have had some of my experiences and how they would imagine their life as an author of twenty published books. If they're completely honest with themselves, I'm sure they'd admit that what they envision is probably very different from what my life is actually like. They envision popularity, cross-country book signings, speaking tours, lecture engagements, personal recognition on a national scale, and a six-figure income and all it can buy. They've added quite a bit of glamour and fantasy to their vision of my work. All those qualities and activities are not a part of my life. They never were. So people really don't want to be like me and don't have a reason to envy me. I still struggle along to pay my monthly bills just like everyone else does. Don't forget, the more you make, the more Uncle Sam takes as his cut, and sometimes I can barely make that quarterly estimated tax payment when it's due. My life is not anything like that of the famous novelists whose new titles get on the best-seller list every time. I'm a solitary individual, not a public one. I abhor traveling and much prefer the tranquillity of my mountain valley cabin. I am not the typical writer—well, maybe I am after all, because most writers out there are struggling ones. Let me rephrase: I'm not the best-seller type of writer.

What I'm attempting to get across about jealousy is the basic fact that everyone is an individual. No two authors will have an identical career or lifestyle. No two people will envision a particular career in the exact same way. No two people handle publicity the same way. No two people write the same. Everyone is different. Each individual works hard to earn what he or she has. And what an individual ends up having is based on his or her unique perspective regarding priorities and sense of self. What I mean is this: Two individuals might win a lottery, yet how they use that windfall is based on their personal perspective about life and about themselves. One of those two might go out and purchase a Mercedes or a big new house in an upscale neighborhood, whereas the other one might replace a dying vacuum, get his or her vehicle fixed, and give the remainder of the money away to help family members out of financial trouble. See what I mean? So envy is an individualized emotional response directly generated from one's sense of self and life priorities. That's why I say that some of my correspondents just *think* they envy me; whether they want to admit it or not, my voluntary cabin solitude and reclusive lifestyle would drive most folks absolutely bonkers!

Don't ever wish you were someone else. Don't ever wish you had another person's stuff—it's just stuff, for heaven's sake. Stop looking around and wanting what this person has or what that neighbor purchased. Don't you like yourself? Don't you appreciate what you do have? What you have accomplished so far in life? Do you have to have it all . . . *now?* Someone who is always envious is never satisfied with his or her own life and is always looking around—elsewhere—for satisfaction. Whether the criterion is the attainment of specified possessions of the highest quality or whether it's personal status, this type of person will never find inner peace, never realize the serenity of acceptance because he or she is always wanting something more and better. There's not a thing wrong with wanting to improve one's condition or situation, but all in its own time—one step at a time as we walk through life. One foot before the other.

The behavioral evidence of jealousy exposes one's inner discontent. Jealous people exhibit a hatred of self rather than a love of self, a hatred that purportedly comes from not being able to afford what the neighbor or sister has, of not being able to generate the same or higher level of income a sibling or friend does, of not being recognized with admiration equal to that given another. But it really comes down to perspective that is skewed and must be honestly looked at—analyzed. *Why* is status and stuff so all-important? Why isn't practicing unconditional goodness just as important or more so? Why is the opinion of others more important than knowing oneself to be a good person, whether one is a lawyer, doctor, or store clerk? And that "stuff" isn't all it's cracked up to be. Have you ever wanted something really badly and, once you finally got it, it just sort of lost its magical glow? Its importance? That's because it was just stuff! And making that stuff one's priority says reams about who one is and where one is at. Is that where one really wants to be? Truly?

Envy also shows that someone isn't seeing him- or herself, not recognizing and acknowledging personal traits, talents, and qualities. We're each unique, each with individualized qualities. Why would we desire the personalized qualities and traits of another when we each have our own beautiful ones to develop? Why be envious of another's bone structure, artistic skill, creativity, or other attribute when we have our own specialized markers that are unique to each of us? Everyone has a particular beingness that is outwardly expressed through such elements as career choice, inherent talent or skill, choice of home decor, social expression, and use of finances. The actualization of these elements expresses who we are. All personal choices in life, from the geographical location we chose to the style of clothing we're drawn to, are all evidence of individuality. Envy and jealousy are indications that we don't recognize our own individuality and the vast array of choices that individuality gives us in life. Envy denies the existence of self and its innate qualities. It denies free expression and smothers acceptance. It germinates the dark seed of hatred and animosity. It has the capability of growing into a clinging vine that ends up choking individuality and darkening our world view with shadowed and convoluted perspectives.

Jealousy is evidence of spending more time on other people's business than one's own, of attending to the without rather than the within of self. Jealousy shows that one hasn't yet recognized one's own blessings in life. Jealousy is a complete waste of time and valuable energy.

► *Our city government introduced a bill to vote on that gives an employee the right to list his or her homosexual partner as a dependent for medical benefits and as a beneficiary for life insurance. I'm on the fence about this. What do you think?*

One thing I know is that I'm not sitting on the fence about it.

First of all, an employee can list whoever they please as a life insurance beneficiary because there's no law that demands that a beneficiary be a blood relation or a legal marriage partner.

As far as medical benefits for one's life partner go, whether that life partnership is formed by way of a legal marriage, a common-law situation, or a professed commitment shouldn't even be an issue. The fact that an employee has a life partner to claim and include on a form as having benefit rights is enough because a partner is a partner. And, I hope you noticed, my answer didn't even have to address the additional subelement of sexual orientation.

Our society has fragmented itself into a zillion shards of razor-sharp glass, the heinous cutting edges of which can be felt at every turn. They fall upon every segment of society to slice and maim with prejudice, arrogance, racism, superiority, and hatred. This is not opinion. It's fact.

If an employee has a life partner, isn't that the sole issue with the subject of benefits? Why must that employee's partner have to meet further criteria associated with his or her rights? Do the employee forms ask if that life partner is the same race as the employee? The same religion? Of course not. So why is that partner's gender made an issue of? If an employee's partner is entitled to medical, dental, and death benefits, then so be it.

Society has become a self-righteous lot, so much so that it believes it has the right to say who someone can love and who someone cannot love. Don't you think that's hideously intrusive into another's personal life? Don't you think a place of business has no business censoring or even questioning who someone loves? Don't you think a government has no right to exclude anyone's life partner from having equal rights? Then perhaps it's time the government laid down the law to put a stop to this self-righteous and prejudicial behavior of its citizens. Does the Declaration of Independence say that everyone is endowed with certain inalienable rights—*except* homosexuals? Read my lips: *Nobody* can tell another who they can or cannot *love*. Love is *everyone's* inalienable right.

The real issue with this question is prejudice. Prejudice germinates hatred. Hatred incites violence. The bill in question will eradicate prejudice and discrimination associated with employee benefits. Any action that serves as such an impetus is an intellectual move toward societal advancement.

Society has yet to reach the stage of intellectual advancement whereby every individual perceives every other individual as a human being—nothing more, nothing less. People currently see other individuals through a kaleidoscopic lens ground to the specifications of their own perspectives: That person is Chinese, too fat, probably not very bright, looks poor . . . and on and on. People have this urge to categorize everyone they see. They criticize, make disparaging comments to a friend, maybe even point and laugh. Everyone they see is shoved into a cubbyhole, maybe many cubbyholes. Never do they see another as just . . . a . . . human . . . being. They do not perceive with intellectual purity. First, we are all members of one base species—that of human being. All the other differentiating characteristics only add to each human being's uniqueness as an individual—only make each person more fascinating. We are human beings, every one of us, and so every human being *must* have the exact same rights as every other human being on this planet. The right to love is one of those rights. The right to choose *who* one loves is another. No one should be singled out, excluded from rights, or persecuted for whom they love. Until society reaches that level of intelligence, it remains mired in the darkness of hatred born of self-imposed ignorance.

This question also has to do with rights. I'm confounded over how it's anyone's "right" to judge who another person can or cannot love. Love is an emotion. It's a very individualized aspect of one's personal life. It's in no way dependent on or subject to societal input. If society doesn't have the right to tell you which career to have, which house to buy, which make of car to own, it certainly has no right to tell you who you can or cannot love. So how can it be constitutional to make discriminatory laws regarding love? And if society does make such laws, it needs to go back and make laws reversing them. If ethnicity, religion, and gender are put on the books as qualities for which it is illegal to discriminate against a person, then an act must be added that protects the individual's right to love whomever she or he wishes. Remember, the issue here is rights, and nobody in this world has a right to control, manipulate, or persecute others when it comes to the issue of whom they feel love for. A society that thinks it does have that right is steering its ship out into dangerous waters where the churning seas will capsize it beneath the ravaging waves of intolerance, prejudice, hatred, and violence.

▶ *What's so compelling about gossip?*

I don't know. I've always found it repulsive and catty.

Psychologically, people are drawn to gossip because gossip is rarely associated with good and positive issues. Gossip is usually the dirt on someone. It's usually the behind-closed-doors kind of thing where people have some prurient interest in peeking through the keyhole of another's closed door. Gossip is second-hand voyeurism—being a once-removed Peeping Tom and getting cheap thrills.

The negativity of gossip magnetically draws folks' attention and interest because they seem to enjoy hearing of incidents (whether true or not) about others that mar character or good standing. Gossipers and those who listen to their tales put themselves on a pedestal as they shake their heads over the terrible behavior of another. Gossip lowers the subject's standing in society while the gossipers think it raises their own status, as is evident when gossipers exclaim, "Oh no! Why, you wouldn't catch *me* doing that!" or "I can't believe so-and-so would do something sooo *unspiritual!*" In this way, gossipers stroke their own ego. They think, *I'm too good to do a thing like that!* and *I'm too spiritual to do something like that!* It's a behavioral response that switches the attention from the gossip subject to the listener, again stroking the listener's ego.

► *A friend of mine is a real loner. What makes antisocial behavior? Is it a fear of people?*

No, it's not necessarily generated by a fear of people. That'd be like saying that the singular reason some people don't like the color blue is because it reminds them of water and they can't swim.

Since every person is a unique individual, there are equally as many individual reasons why folks exhibit different behavioral tendencies. *Antisocial* is a strong term because for most people it brings to mind frightening behaviors, such as those by mass murderers, the Unabomber, hermits who talk to themselves, and the like. Let's not use the term *antisocial* for the behavior you're talking about because it really doesn't fit in light of the additional information regarding this individual that you supplied in your letter. For the sake of treating your friend fairly, let's use the term *solitary*—your friend prefers a solitary lifestyle.

Many times a preference for a solitary lifestyle is due to a person's shyness or lack of self-confidence. The person is uncomfortable in social situations and with people in general, especially large groups, and crowds raise his or her anxiety level. Noise may be a particular annoyance to the person, or the fast pace of society may unnerve him or her. These are not antisocial traits. They're an indication of someone who requires serenity, someone who needs a prescribed measure of quietude to maintain a balanced inner *chi* (energy) state of beingness.

We have to be careful and give thoughtful consideration when pulling a term out of the blue to use as a label for another person. Sensitivity to others is a sign of wisdom. When an individual possesses a heightened sensitivity to the erratic character of society, that individual will naturally seek solitude for the purpose of maintaining inner peace and balance. That person is not antisocial but is exhibiting wise behavior by seeking out an environment that aligns with his or her composite vibrational rate.

There's another way to clarify the concept of labeling. In your letter, you mentioned that you were a bookworm, that you loved reading and that all your spare time was occupied by studying new books on science and popular physics. Okay, so you love to read and all your friends know this. Would you rather they label you a nerd—or an intellectual? Uh-huh, this is what I mean. Be sensitive to the labels you loosely stick on people. Be considerate. Be accurate.

► *I'm a mom three times over. One of my young daughters is obsessed with Barbie. Am I an awful mother to hate those dolls?*

Well, no, of course not. You'd be surprised to know you can be counted among a growing circle of like-minded mothers.

Please, don't guilt-trip yourself over your attitude, because it's more philosophically sound than you may realize. In my book *Fireside,* I had a lengthy conversation with my friend Sally about how skewed society's perception of women and beauty was. One of my points was that women's beauty is often seen as being related solely to whether women have teeny waists and exaggerated boobs. Yes, I said *boobs* in the book because I'm known for calling a spade a spade—why mince words when you're trying to get to the point? Anyway, my point was that society has always had this grossly skewed and grotesque perception of what the "perfect" woman is and what constitutes feminine beauty. We witness evidence of this perception in the chiseled waistlines and blown-out breasts of today's popular dolls. This particular physical presentation is sending a terrible message to little girls. It's brainwashing them from an early age to think that they need to grow up and have long blond hair, a tiny waist, large breasts, and a model's face to be considered beautiful. Society's emphasis on beauty is not only twisted, it's insidiously damaging to little girls' self-perception and self-worth.

These dolls' clothing adds further insult because they are styles fashioned for the upper crust of society—debutante gowns, cocktail and evening dresses, golf club outfits, and riding habits. These suggest that a goal of being a social climber should be a priority for a little girl. The occupational outfits aren't much better because they're for such professionals as veterinarian, sports star, dancer, teacher, and so on. They give the message that a little girl should either strive to be a professional with a top income or take up a traditionally female profession. Where are the blue-collar outfits? Where is the outfit with the hard hat for the female construction boss? Where's the airplane pilot's uniform? Where is the oil rig worker's outfit? The miner's? The mechanic's? Tsk, tsk.

Okay, as if that wasn't bad enough, let's look at the places that house these dolls. Penthouses? Mansions? Houseboats? Get real. Where's the modular home? The cabin? The apartment building?

And how come these dolls don't come with an old beaten-up pickup like mine that has more than one shade of brown paint on it? Huh? What about that? How come these dolly vehicles are all sports cars or top-of-the-line expensive sport utility vehicles? I wouldn't trade my old four-wheel-drive pickup for any of those flashy machines.

No, Mom, don't guilt-trip yourself for having less than loving thoughts toward your daughter's doll's conglomeration of status accessories. What may make you feel a bit better about them is if you could manage to provide a psychological counterbalance for the false perceptions of womanhood she's receiving. I know it's hard when all she's being inundated with is *Baywatch* women bouncing along the beach and Xena swinging through the jungle; well, to be fair, at least Xena shows that women can take care of themselves. Anyway, try to have conversations with your daughter about the hundreds of other options life presents for girls. Teach her the real meaning of beauty. Explain to her that it's not what is *seen* but what is *felt*. Tell her that real beauty—true beauty—is not any type of physical attribute at all but rather what is felt inside . . . warm and loving emotions. And that true beauty is a selfless character and the exercising of unconditional goodness. True beauty is giving to others without expecting anything in return, not even a thank-you. Mom, you can probably come up with dozens of examples to which your child will specifically relate. Give it some thought before you approach your daughter. Have some good examples ready. Talk to her—and listen. With children, sometimes you get more clues regarding the right thing to say just by listening to your child—really listening. Personally, I think Barbie needs more girlfriends. Her social life is too narrowly confined to Ken and she needs to get a more rounded life.

Go for it, Mom. Start bringing your daughter back to the real world. Buy her a dump truck for Barbie to drive.

What's interesting about this issue is that the same problem exists for little boys. Society's idea of manliness is muscle and power. G.I. Joes started it. Now it's all those hideous warrior action figures with Uzis. Today's society doesn't even think about offering little boys a *gentle* perception of manliness. Society doesn't even think to teach little boys that gentleness carries great power. Instead, it teaches them that power comes only by way of brute force and violence. And oh, how much more powerful and controlling you can be if you have a gun in your hand! The bigger the better! And sadly, little boys grow up believing that brute strength is power, that strength rules, that muscle mass means a beautiful man. Little boys' toys give the same psychologically skewed message as the little girls' toys. For girls, that message is: *Your personal power comes from being beautiful and sexy—use to get what you want in life. Your goal in life is to be a member of the social circle.* For boys, that message is: *Your personal power comes from brute strength—use it to gain and maintain the respect you deserve. Your goal in life is to be manipulative, controlling, and domineering.* What a crock that all is. A gentle man exudes so much more magnetism than does an arrogant muscle man. An independent and intelligent woman is so much more beautiful than a bouncing beach bunny.

Get a clue, world. Get a clue.

► *Do you feel society is losing its respect for life?*

I think the evening newscasts on television stations across the country indicate a general loss of respect for life in our society. When you hear of children shooting and killing other children for their jackets and shoes, of drive-by shootings, that says it all. We do not value human life.

No violence is random violence. That phrase is a misnomer because all crime and violence is committed with intent by the perpetrators. Rage, hatred, and prejudice are running rampant. Religious fanatics filled with the delusion of being God's chosen avengers are consumed with twisted self-righteousness and are acting on their psychotic directives to personally vanquish evil from the earth. The problem with these people is that their perception of who and what is evil is based on prejudicial perceptions—they're personal opinions and not factual. This is how some of the hate crimes manifest. This is why women's centers are targeted and bombed, why gay bashing occurs, and why people are killed just because of their different beliefs or lifestyles. Prejudice, greed, jealousy, religious self-righteousness, and racism are all the real evils that contribute to the increase in hate crimes. When you don't respect another's right to have a different belief, lifestyle, or philosophy, you cannot have a deep respect for life in general.

When people do anything to harm another, whether it be emotionally or physically, they do not have a solid respect for human life. Think about that. To injure another is to do harm to another. To speak ill of another is to do that person harm. To make assumptions or have preconceived notions about another and then spread those as gossip is to do harm to that person. It shows a lack of respect for individuality. It shows prejudgment. And to denigrate others is, in reality, to lower the quality of your own character. But to actually physically attack or kill another because he or she is different is the greatest crime of all. That's not being a soldier of God; it's being the Devil's minion.

Oh yes, there's a great loss of respect for human life bounding across the planet. And the true perpetrators have names—Ego and Self-righteousness.

► *I'm convinced that the world's going to hell in a handbasket because of society's growing obsession with sex. Am I just being neurotic about this?*

Well, sex is a natural part of human beingness. We're here in physical bodies and sexual activity is an integral part of our behavioral, physiological, and psychological character.

I once had a correspondent who thought most of our nation's ills would be resolved if our government just made all addictive substances illegal. I responded to this individual by reminding him that psychiatrists' offices are filled with folks who are addicted to sex. Clearly, this particular correspondent didn't think his solution through.

Though the sex drive is an inherent aspect of human nature, I would agree with this correspondent's opinion that society is obsessed with it. I agree because I've observed no segment of society that sexual innuendos have not invaded. Look at television commercials. They use sexy connotations all the time because they believe sex sells. The late-night talk shows, billboard and magazine print ads, and the film industry all take advantage of sexuality. Look at the nightly television newscasts that advertise upcoming broadcast by leading with a sex-related event to pique viewers' interest. The news magazine programs, such as *Dateline* and *60 Minutes*, have increased their ratio of sex-related stories. And the percentage of offenses that involve domestic abuse and sex crimes has gone through the roof in the past few decades.

I think society is indeed obsessed with sex, but I don't think it's anything new, as this correspondent would imply. In the 1950s, it was verboten to show as much as a navel on television shows. But through the decades, censorship has relaxed. Back then in the 1950s, who would've ever imagined that you could sit in your living room and watch *NYPD Blue* and see Jimmy Smits buck naked making love or getting in a claw-foot bathtub with his lover? This is my point: It's not that society has become more *obsessed* with sex, it's that society has become more *open* about it by shedding its former taboos.

And there were always sex crimes being committed, but they weren't as well publicized as they are today. Just as many little girls were being sexually abused back in the 1940s and 1950s as today, but nobody *told* on the upstanding Ward Cleaver–type man back then. Today there are legal options to pursue and society will no longer sweep such insidious behavior under the rug. It's no longer an attitude of *Let's protect* the socially upstanding father (or uncle); now, it's *Hang 'em!* The secrecy is gone. These vile men are no longer getting away with what they used to; consequently, sexual abuse is much more publicized than it was before.

▸ *Sometimes I think my son was born with an attitude. Is such a thing possible?*

Sure it is. Though it may sound quite impossible, it's more probable than you think.

Remember when, earlier in this book, I addressed the concept of mean vibratory rates? Your question is directly related to that concept. You see, your newborn infant came into this world with a consciousness full of past-life experiences. Your newborn was already in possession of certain attributes of his consciousness that comprise his own specialized mean vibratory rate. He came into the world with his own set of inclinations, natural tendencies, inherent talents, and attitudes. Your son may grow to exhibit an inexplicable talent for drawing and understanding schematic diagrams or have a strong skill for oil painting. He may inherently have an aversion to some type of animal (on the basis of past-life experiences). He may not be attracted to the opposite sex. He may dislike the social scene and prefer solitude. All of these are examples of the attitudes, talents, psychological aspects, philosophical beliefs, and behavioral facets a child can possess as *natural* characteristics of his or her unique mean vibratory rate of beingness.

So yes, your son probably was born with an attitude. We all are to some degree. We are all born with inherent qualities that form the foundation for our current life to build on.

I would suggest that, after understanding the above, you don't worsen the situation by trying to argue with or change your son's inherent nature. Instead, accept. Accept and work with him—not against him. Parents seem to have an ideal vision for each of their children. That's all right, yet a parent must also realize that each child is a unique individual with ideals of her or his own. The correct ideal for a parent to have is the goal of nurturing, supporting, and encouraging the inherent ideal of the child. A child is not a copy or an extension of the parent, not a second life through which a parent lives. A child is a one-of-a-kind special blend of both parents' DNA. A child is a complete individual in and of him- or herself. With this fact in mind, it's easy to see how your child not only can have separate perspectives from yours—and even ones that oppose yours—but can also have entered the world with them.

Perhaps you've seen the common bumper stickers with *Celebrate Diversity* printed on them. Whenever I see one of them I feel a little twinge inside. Although I understand the intent, I think it should be worded more precisely. I think it should read *Celebrate Individuality*. Life is full of diversity in Nature, human beings included in that, yet what makes human beings so diverse is their beautiful individuality—each person vibrating to his or her own life frequency.

So, Mom, work with your son. He is a beautiful human being. He is his own person. Join in sharing the joyful celebration of his individuality. Love your son.

► *Why are the kids these days dressing so sloppily? They all look like bums.*

Not necessarily so. First of all, not *all* of them dress this way. Don't be all-inclusive if it's not a fact. Second, that they dress "sloppily" is not fact either; it's an opinion—your opinion. To them, they're in style. Let's take a quick trip back in time.

There was a time when I wore miniskirts and white go-go boots. I liked the style and enjoyed it while it lasted. To my way of thinking, it was style. My father's strong opinion was that I looked like a slut. But I was in my twenties and I dressed however I pleased because I was an individual with the right to do so.

Today, styles still cause generational differences. You too probably recall a time when you dressed in a manner that was contrary to your parents' preferred style. Every household seems to experience the phase of arguments over the hairstyles and modes of dress to which the children are attracted. It's no different now than it was in the 1950s. Whether a style is viewed as sloppy or as being in fashion is based purely on the opinion of the observer.

Just lately I've heard rumor that I've been called eccentric because of the way I dress. I have no problem at all with that, because if eccentricity means individuality, then that rumor is right on target. So what if I sometimes wear OshKosh bib shorts with striped tights and a T-shirt? So what if I wear long, lace-trimmed calico skirts (handmade) with gauzy, embroidered peasant blouses and knee-high moccasins? So what if I wear Levi's and a camisole top? I wear whatever my mood of the morning happens to call for. If it's a calico skirt, a plaid flannel shirt, and bare feet (which seems to be my routine at-home cabin wear), then so be it, because that combination sure is comfortable. Do I care? If that's considered being eccentric, then maybe I am. If expressing one's individuality is being eccentric, then I think everyone should be eccentric rather than dress to gain the acceptance of others. I don't dress for society's nod of approval—why should the kids? They dress for the approval of their peers, not of the adults. One day, when they grow up, they may attain the wisdom of dressing for self-expression.

► *Why is it so damned hard to be happy in this world?*

Well, I don't know. I guess that would depend on what specific elements in life make an individual feel happiness. For each individual, feelings of happiness are generated by different life aspects. What makes me ecstatically happy wouldn't necessarily make someone else happy and might even leave them stone cold. Happiness is relative, just as humor is. What most people laugh at, I don't even crack a smile over. Same with happiness. What makes some folks happy leaves me nonplussed. Material goods, success, social status, approval of others, and financial security are attainments most people view as elements of happiness and necessities of life. Not me. Give me the basic necessities, such as indoor plumbing, health, my little furry people (Yorkies), companionship, a roof over my head, and the joys of Nature, and I'm set for life.

I can't define the reason why happiness appears to be so elusive for you because its source is so diverse for each one of us. I think it might help if you examine your life and analyze your thought processes. Make a list of life elements that you *think* make you happy. After giving this list a good, hard look, you might discover that many of the items you listed are superficial and not true sources of happiness. You might find that after reviewing this list, your entire perspective on happiness has altered, redefined itself. Sometimes the very things we take for granted in life are the very things we need to feel happiness over. Think about these. Make a list of the things you take for granted—even your indoor plumbing. Now, you may think the example of indoor plumbing is just too ridiculous, yet what if something were to cause your house plumbing to be unusable for a time? Thankfulness for plumbing doesn't sound so ridiculous after all. For me, thankfulness for something so mundane was very real because my companion and I moved into an unfinished cabin—plywood floors, nothing on the walls but some drywall, no bathroom sink, a half-finished deck, no window coverings, and no connection to the main electrical power grid. An old hospital backup generator was wired to the electrical box, and this generator ran on propane, gobbling up four quarts of oil a day and then spitting back out three of them. The first priority on our agenda when we moved in was to build a fenced-in area, thirty feet by thirty feet, for the furry people in the family (four Yorkies). One of them weighs only three pounds, and the owls and hawks in the surrounding woods had immediately shown a hungry interest in the Yorkies—plus, there are coyotes in the area. The entire dog area was then covered with chicken wire to keep the high-flying predators from swooping down in the pen. Okay, with that done, the second priority was that awful generator. We called the local generator company who services the brand. After the service people came out to check it over, they just stood there and laughed. That told us a lot about its condition. The company bought it back from us for parts. We got a whopping fifty dollars for it. Then we had to replace it, so we bought a small generator with a motor. We placed it beneath the front porch, and my friend wired it through the basement and out to the circuit box on the back of the house. It was noisy to run, and though it took four hundred dollars' worth of gasoline each month to run for thirteen hours a day, it supplied us our electrical needs. I say *needs* because we couldn't run a microwave, a coffeepot, electric heaters, computers, the copy machine (that blew when I tried to run it), blow-dryers, curling irons, a washing machine, or a clothes dryer. (We had to schlep dirty clothes thirty miles to the laundromat.) We learned, though. I could use the iron for clothing only after shutting down the main switch for the water pump and water heater. We could vacuum with full power if I unplugged the refrigerator for a few minutes. The refrigerator was off all night long because we ran the generator only during the day. Luckily, we never lost a bit of food because of this. Likewise, we had no lights once we turned off the generator switch, so we kept flashlights around the house and on bedside tables. With the generator off during the night, there was no water for drinks or toilets owing to the fact that we have a well and electricity is needed to pump the water up into the house. Twice when the generator needed servicing and we had to leave it in town for several days, that was when the real roughing it took place. But you learn. You learn to store extra water and make do. It's not so bad. We lived one and a half years that way.

But when my friend brought her elderly mother out here from Overland Park, Kansas, to live with us (she has Alzheimer's), we could in no way expect her to feel her way around in the dark at night (she'd forget about the flashlight or even whose house she was in) and take the chance of falling down the stairs. We bit the bullet and decided the situation would be best served if we hooked the cabin up to the power grid. Because we're in a semiremote mountain area, we had to pay twenty-seven thousand dollars up front to bring the power line down to us. It was installed underground. I love our quarter-mile-long driveway through the forest, but that long, twisting drive just added more to our cost. So now we have lights at night and we feel we've made the cabin much safer and more convenient for an elderly lady who has developed a habit of wandering around during the night—even outside in the woods—in her nightie. One good thing is that we still have the generator and keep plenty of fuel stored for it. If the electricity should go out for any reason for an extended time, we can easily switch back to the generator and still have our basic needs met as before.

The example of my experience was not to talk about me, but to illustrate two points: being prepared, and simplicity. Simplicity is the quality most missing from those life aspects people identify as sources of happiness. We were very happy living on that generator. We wouldn't have brought electricity in if it hadn't been a necessity for the comfort and safety of an elderly woman. Except for the noise the generator made all day, we were perfectly content with a lifestyle some folks would've perceived as being a pain in the backside.

Happiness. Society has forgotten the simple things. Life has gotten so high-tech so fast that people have lost perspective on what brings happiness. I can hear some of you countering my example with thoughts something like this: *well, you didn't have to buy that remote cabin; that was your choice.* Yes, and you'd be absolutely right. It was my choice because it was located in a secluded valley that I'd admired for twenty years. This cabin looks down on that valley and there is only one other house visible to the eye no matter in which direction one looks. And that single house is a summer place that gets visited not more than four weekends a year. The entire valley is pure Nature. Its beauty and serenity is priceless. That is my happiness. An incredible variety of wildlife fill the woodlands. My heart is so full it nearly explodes out of my chest when I watch through my window at a mother bear feeding from the deer grain bin not ten feet from the window, and her cub hilariously swinging from the rim of the birdbath. That sight is my happiness. Seven bucks appeared out of the misty fog one night and, one by one, entered the aura of our house floodlights to congregate, staying for an hour eating the sweet grain and playfully sparring with each other. When they began coming to visit on a regular nightly basis, they began to feel so comfortable and safe that some of them actually lay down by the grain. That was happiness for me. And when a raucous cawing awoke me on the daybreak of my last birthday morn and I flew to the bedroom dormer window to see what the deal was, I was heart-struck to be presented with a once-in-a-life vision of more than a hundred crows mysteriously perched on the bare branches of all the aspens surrounding the cabin! *That* was pure, spine-tingling happiness. Or when the fiery sunsets alight the valley in a blaze of orange ethereal light that fills my cabin in a magic moment of twilight surrealism. Or when hundreds of rosy finches descend on the cabin roof, sounding like a rain of hail, and then settle in hordes upon my porch to dine on the sunflower offerings and, if I should go out to join them, momentarily fly off in a single graceful wave, only to immediately return to surround me and eat at my feet. That's my happiness.

Oh yes, living without that electricity was indeed my choice. Yet you've still missed the point—because that *is* the point. Happiness is what people choose to make it for themselves. It can be for stuff (material possessions) or it can be gained through a recognition of life's simplicity—the simple blessings society has become blind to.

You think it's silly for me to give an example of indoor plumbing as a source of happiness or something to count as a blessing, but just wait until you don't have it. Indoor plumbing is a prime example of those necessities in life that society has blown off as a given that will always be there for them. My God, just having a roof over your head and a warm bed to sleep in is a blessing. Why are people so arrogant and egotistical as to think they deserve these things more than someone else does? So arrogant that they take these things so much for granted that these things are no longer perceived as blessings? The fact that you can walk into your kitchen whenever you please and have a multitude of foods with which to indulge yourself is a blessing. One day you'll understand that. Happiness? It's all around you. You're surrounded by sources of happiness, yet few even acknowledge them or even see them. One day that will change . . . dramatically.

I would invite you to sit down and seriously think of the things that could be different in your life—worst-case scenarios. You could develop a fatal or crippling disease, go bankrupt, lose your house. Your pets could become very sick, all your friends could move away, or a tornado could wipe out all you own. And on and on. When people watch the nightly news, they may shake their heads to witness the hardships of others in the world, but rarely do they interpret what they see as a reminder to count their blessings.

Read the autobiography by Christopher Reeve and, after turning the last page, tell me again that you can't find happiness in your own life, that you haven't anything to be happy about or don't have blessings to count.

Happiness means something different for everyone. Each individual responds to various life elements in a myriad of ways. You are the only one who understands your personalized criteria for happiness. Perhaps your significant other would be absolutely thrilled with a new, state-of-the-art computer, yet you and I couldn't care less about such a thing. Happiness for you would come from different sources. You know what those sources are, even if they're smothered into near oblivion by a lifetime of skewed perspectives.

► *My nieces and nephews never say thank you for the gifts they receive. Is this attitude a sign of society's apathy or of just one set of parents' failure to teach social graces?*

From what I've personally observed, I'm beginning to think it's become a sign of societal apathy because I also see it happening with the adults. In the last few years, I've noticed a marked decrease in people's expression of the social graces (what I call plain common courtesy). I might not have been raised in a family that had its family crest imprinted on gold-embossed stationery, but I was sure taught to say *please* and *thank you* and to not interrupt an ongoing adult conversation unless there was an emergency of some kind. I was respected enough to be offered an opportunity to express my opinion during an adult conversation, but I usually just listened and learned a lot.

The topic of gift acknowledgment has come to the fore in my own life more than I'd like to admit. My companion sends her niece and nephews substantial gifts at Christmastime and on their birthdays yet she never hears back from the children regarding whether they even got the gifts, much less gets a thank-you. I too have experienced this while trying to be a grandma to the two boys to whom one of my daughters is a stepmom. I've recently gotten the hint that I'm not even perceived as a "real" grandma because I'm too far removed. I'm the stepmom's mom—some stranger lady up in the mountains. Okay, I can deal with that—because I accept people's behavior instead of internalizing it and fretting over it until it becomes a horrendous family issue. What good would getting upset do? None. It would get everyone involved all upset and cause hard feelings for a long time.

There's another element to this issue too. What is the purpose of giving a gift? Is it because you feel you absolutely *have* to? Or is it because you just plain *want* to? I give gifts just out of the blue because I want to. I try to remember friends' and relatives' birthdays, with gifts. Holidays too. Sometimes I hear back that someone has complained about the choice of gift I gave. That's bad manners—that's crude. And, being a public person, I receive gifts now and again from my readers. I naturally think it's rude to not acknowledge these gifts, so I always try to send a thank-you card. But then I've heard it rumored that "you have to send Summer Rain a gift to hear anything back from her." So there you are. I hold to the tenets of my perception of common courtesy, but some folks twist it into some kind of self-serving thing to get gifts. Sometimes life presents situations that put you in that old catch-22: You're damned if you do and damned if you don't. But you still have to follow your conscience to maintain some measure of inner peace regarding your actions. Regardless of that ridiculous rumor I heard about me, I still keep sending out thank-you notes for the gifts people send me. Sometimes, owing to the security measures Hampton Roads Publishing Company takes with my packages, the return address of the correspondent is obliterated after the company readdresses the package to me, so I have no address to which to send a thank-you note. Otherwise, I always respond. If some people want to misinterpret common courtesy as being self-serving, then that's their perspective, not mine.

Yes, there is a growing lack of common courtesy in the world. People do seem to be more rude and arrogant. They would rather spout a knee-jerk unkindness than use the wisdom to process it through their intelligence first. They let acts of goodness performed toward them go unrecognized. They don't feel inclined to acknowledge gifts others think to send them. And although you and I have a feel for why road rage exists, others just sit and scratch their heads. The issue of not sending thank-you notes or at least acknowledging gifts with a phone call is but one indicator of how far society has distanced itself from common courtesy. So, what do we do about this? I think that's your implied question.

We can stop sending gifts altogether in an attempt to get the recipient's attention. We can complain to the recipient about her or his lack of courtesy. Or we have the option to keep on trucking just as always, with the exception of adding a good measure of acceptance to our attitude.

I don't think complaining is a solution. Complaining has the tendency to reverse the blame, and make the complainer look like she's nit-picking. Complaining about another's behavior rarely effects a desired outcome. So let's scratch that option.

You could stop sending the gifts. But is that what you really want to do? You probably send them because you want to. You want to be included in your nieces' and nephews' birthday celebrations by showing them you care enough to remember their special days. Okay, that's fine. So, if that's what's truly in your heart, the very act of giving is your own reward because it makes you feel good. It says, "I care about you and want to give you something for your special day." Period. That's what it says. The fact that you *care* and, out of that caring, externally express it through a physical act of goodness makes it also an act of *unconditional* goodness—because in this case you know you'll not receive any type of acknowledgment. And I bet you a photo of a bear on my porch that you never thought of it quite that way before, did you? When we accept people's bad behavior and are kind to them in spite of it, we're practicing unconditional goodness. You give those gifts because you want to. You don't give them to receive gratitude in return—or do you? I tend to think that you don't, because that'd be a selfish reason for giving, and you certainly come across not as a selfish individual but as an aunt concerned over the manners of her nieces and nephews.

Your situation involved another aspect. You informed me that most of your nieces and nephews were rather young but that some of them were old enough to be in college. Okay, this needs addressing.

Very young children need to be taught by their parents that it's the kind and courteous thing to do to acknowledge a gift. My children, when they were very young, always gave their grandmas a phone call or sat and labored over a printed thank-you note after receiving gifts. As a mother, I made sure my girls thanked others for kindness directed toward them. They might have had to wear clothing from the local clothing bank, but cleanliness and politeness was always a routine part of their experience. That takes care of the younger children.

Teenagers and college students have reached the stage in life where their own philosophies and attitudes dominate those with which they grew up. Independence sparks and ignites the young adult's sense and expression of individuality. This is what makes a parent cry, "I didn't raise you like that!" Well, parents, that's true, but now's the time for your child to be independent, so you'll suddenly discover all kinds of attitudes you never knew were there all along . . . within the child's natural mean vibratory rate of unique beingness. This is the time when one's child can seem as though he or she has changed overnight into some unfamiliar stranger. This is the time when inherent tendencies and inclinations take the opportunity of independence to blossom. It's a wonderful time, really. And a parent needs to appreciate this period, no matter what characteristics your child may show. This is where parental acceptance is a boon to the relationship. Acceptance of a child's (or anyone's) individuality, no matter how it's expressed, shows wisdom by way of preventing discord. Acceptance strengthens rather than shreds relationships.

Okay, back to the main issue. Once a child reaches the stage of independence, that child may or may not continue to adhere to the common courtesies he or she was taught as a youngster. Sometimes these young adults don't adhere to certain tenets of their youthful rearing because they have different philosophies, because they're trying to prove their independence, because they have too many other elements of their new state of independence to think about and handle so some of the social graces get forgotten, or because they just plain don't realize that the responsibility of responding to gifts has now fallen on their shoulders instead of on their parents'. When they were younger and living at home, the responsibility of remembering and acknowledging relatives' birthdays and anniversaries was always their parents'. After those youngsters grow into adulthood and are on their own, they then must assume that social responsibility. How they choose to do so is up to them. And, as parents, aunts or uncles, or grandparents, we have to accept that behavioral choice with grace. It doesn't mean that we have to express our displeasure or disagreement with that decision by altering our own pattern of gift giving; it simply means that we accept what those young adults have chosen to do. You see, life choices are the right of each individual. We all have free wills to exercise. What's important to understand is that the behavior choice of another does not necessarily demand that we change how we've been behaving for years. Because others' attitudes differ from ours does not automatically mean that we must alter our long-held philosophies.

Gift giving is a sign of kind and thoughtful remembrance, not an act associated with reciprocity. Gift giving is not dependent on a response from the receiver. Gift giving is an act of goodness; it should be an act of *unconditional* goodness. It's done out of kindness or love . . . nothing else. No response required. However . . . courtesy and respect for the giver is grossly lacking if the gift recipient does not acknowledge the gift. And that's when we practice wisdom by having acceptance for another's bad behavior.

▸ *I grew up with the constant admonishment that "good" girls don't expose their legs by wearing shorts or dressing any way other than a true "lady" would. That attitude really messed me up and damaged my self-esteem as a woman. Comment?*

You bet I'll comment.

First let me express empathy for the psychosexual abuse you were exposed to as a child. That sort of attitude gives a young girl the impression that her body is somehow bad or evil. That's a classic example of psychosexual abuse that can stay with someone throughout her entire adult life, causing subconscious behavior and dysfunction. I'd like to wring some necks when I hear about this type of parental behavior.

I could tell you some real psychological horror stories about abuse to which I was subjected as a young girl by my chauvinistic, bigoted, racist father—abuse that, for an extended time in my adult life, had long-term damaging ramifications. The things he did ranged from laughing at the molded breasts of my cherished Madame Alexander doll to telling me that menstrual blood was really the "evil" coming out of women because they were bad and were created only to serve men. Although a young girl who has been continually exposed to such gender-bashing grows up to realize that such indoctrination is wrong, the years and years of hearing it leaves its residual effects on the consciousness. Amazingly, I got married. After twenty-five years, I began hearing uncharacteristic comments from my husband, such as "Women should just enjoy rape; it doesn't hurt them" and "The sheiks have it made—polygamy was a good idea" and "You can't wear that; your cleavage is showing and it makes you look like a slut." Yet he was interested in having "interests" on the side. Then, the situation escalated. When my friends would telephone me, he'd say I wasn't home. He ranted when I wanted to go out for a few hours in the evening to a woman friend's house to just hang out and watch videos. He began telling his friends that I was abandoning him by not spending all my time at home. He was most happy when I sat beside him on the couch while he watched football games. My attempts to visit friends and exercise my individual rights were met with rages, sometimes violent ones involving his gun. Life became so unpredictable that I feared I would be killed and began sleeping with a gun of my own under my pillow. My next surprise was hearing from friends that he was telling them that I had no interest in sex. That floored me because after repeatedly trying to get him to tell me why he was so unhappy, I'd assumed that it must be a lack of spice in our sexual relationship. And I'd attempted to fix that by going out and buying a massive pine waterbed, its huge canopy lined with mirrors. Nothing changed, and I then made the mistake of suggesting he get professional help. That exacerbated the situation. I finally moved into my tiny writing cabin for sanity and safety, and consequently, he convinced our mutual friends that I'd abandoned him. Not one of them came to me to ask what was going on. But I had one friend who was a main player in some of these events who knew the truth. She was my continual support and mental mainstay. If it hadn't been for her, I don't know how it all would've ended. While I was living in the little cabin, my husband would call me to say, "Nobody will marry me. Will you?" He'd already asked three women the same thing. I told him, "We were married for twenty-nine years and you threw me away." Well yes, that was true, he admitted, but now he wanted me back. Then one evening he called to say that we had to talk, that I needed to get over to his place (the house I had moved out of) to talk. I told him I'd be glad to meet him at a restaurant (a *public* place) to do this talking. He insisted that "what I have to say won't work in a public place." That sent shivers of foreboding up my spine and my scalp tingled. I held my ground regarding the public place, and he hung up on me. The following evening, he got in his truck, inside the garage with the door closed, and ran the engine. I am not the only person who believes his call to me was made with the intention of getting me over to his place for the purpose of taking me with him. Now

I live one day at a time. Now I'm okay. Now I love being who I am . . . a woman who loves her femininity and every expression of it. I have risen above the psychosexual abuse I took as a child and an adult. I have survived. I have survived to love my beingness.

I've recounted these experiences for two reasons. One is that my readers have written hundreds of letters asking about what happened to my marriage. There were incredibly horrible rumors about my husband's death. These wildly inaccurate speculations were emotionally painful for my family and this is a way of responding to those rumors with the facts, so the public can cease its speculations and my family can put the past to rest. The second reason is to encourage women everywhere to realize that, though they are married, they are still individuals with rights. Every married woman has the right to have friends of both genders. Every married woman has the right to the telephone in her own home. She has the right to go out with friends. She has the right to pursue personal interests and a career without her husband making claims that she's abandoning him. She has the right to dress as she pleases without being denigrated or criticized for it. She has the right to a profession without her husband trying to degrade or sabotage it. A married woman is not an extension of her husband. Neither partner is the "better half" of the other. They are two individuals cooperating in a partnership. They are not a union of *one*. There is no master of the house.

You, my correspondent, have been damaged by psychosexual abuse from your father. You can get past it. You've gotten as far as realizing that the things he said were wrong. Acknowledging that fact is a huge step. Now it's time to let your beautiful individuality shine with the brilliance of beingness that is the real you. Your mind is your most powerful tool. It can heal. You won't forget the past, but through wisdom and determination, you can use that past to spur you forward into the light of reality. My God, cherish who you are. *Like* who you are. You're a beautiful woman who has a world of options to experience and savor. How you wish to dress is your decision. You have limitless choices out there in the world. Your gender is related to powerful goddesses who are very real . . . even today. And they have returned.

To parents: Take this correspondent's inquiry to heart. Learn from it. Think about it. Think *hard* about it. Little do you realize how impressionable small children are. Little do you understand how powerful your words and statements can be for a small child. If you have negative opinions, keep them to yourselves or don't express them when little ears are within hearing distance. Think. Think about the things that come out of your mouth around small ones. Think about how this comment or that statement may be interpreted by a child. Don't ever cast aspersions on gender. You have no idea how cruelly damaging that can be to his or her psyche and how long it can stay in his or her subconscious and have serious ramifications in the child's adult life. The mind, even a small child's, is like a tape recorder that retains everything heard in life. Everything is automatically sorted into categories and stored. That recorder never erases. It's always there. Remember that the next time you've the urge to say something derogatory to your child or in front of him or her. Everything is recorded in the mind.

► *In my circle of friends, there are some who have been increasingly finding reason to criticize others. It's becoming a regular tendency and it's irritating to have to listen to. Why do they do this?*

The tendency to criticize is ego based. When someone continually points out the faults of others, that critical individual is, in essence, attempting to stroke his or her own ego by contrasting him- or herself with others. Such a person thinks, *Look at that fat person—I'm not fat like that!* or *How can someone be so sloppily dressed? I'm always so neat and presentable!* It's an attempt to emphasize one's own "better" characteristics as contrasted to those of others.

So if you're experiencing increasing irritation with your friends' behavior, what are you going to do about it? If your relationship is one of true friendship, then you should feel as free to express your opinion as your friends do theirs. Ask them why they do this, why they feel a need to criticize others. This question may elicit a look that might give you the impression you've just sprouted a third eye or something, but stick with it and push for an answer. If your friends don't have a logical and reasonable answer, then tell them that perhaps they need to come up with one.

The world is populated by an incredible assortment of folks— big versus petite, tall versus short, and all shades of ethnicity. Clothing, hair color, and hair styles add other dimensions to the variety. But beneath the differences, we are all human. Would your friends prefer everyone to dress exactly as they do? To have the same hairstyle and shape as them—like clones? It's our individual expressiveness that makes us unique and keeps us from being boring. What's to criticize if it's understood that everyone is so different? What's to criticize when there is no norm? Well, perhaps, there is a norm—individuality.

▸ *As much as I'd love to see racism be a thing of the past—an extinct attitude of prehistoric human thought—I don't see how things are ever going to change. Will they?*

In a future time, yes, racism will become a thing of the past because it will be perceived worldwide as an attitude of ignorance and unspirituality, an attitude of an intellectually undeveloped people that caused the near annihilation of the world. Racism, along with intolerance and hatred, will one day be seen as an abhorrent attitude destructive to all enlightened societies. Today, however, people's close-mindedness touches all elements of life and every facet of society. That's why we have the self-righteous preachers of the religious right, and the moral majority, the white supremacists, and those who fit in between. What's it going to take to turn this destructiveness around? Something big. Something really big. Something so big that people's eyes will finally be opened to the shallowness and insignificance of their former attitudes. Something so big that people will perceive others *only* as human beings because all of their prejudicial tendencies will be stripped away within the blink of an owl's eye.

► *It seems as though the world is consumed with paranoia about the future. Fear is ruling lives. Agree?*

As with all attitudes and perspectives, fear is individual. Although some folks have a clear paranoia associated with the future, others are apathetic, in denial, skeptical, worried enough to have taken some measures toward emergency preparedness, or feeling alarmist. You'll find people to fit into each of these attitude categories, so it's inaccurate to be all-inclusive.

No matter what concept or objective fear is related to, it has the bipolar characteristic of being both a positive and a negative force in one's life. The difference between the two effects is perspective—one's individual perspective. Fear, when internalized as paranoia, can be crippling. But when fear is intellectually processed as awareness, it can be life-saving. The difference between how one uses the attitude is monumental.

Because the subject of fear, whether related to the future or to daily life aspects, appears to be on the minds of so many of my readers and because I observe so many ways fear evidences itself in society, I think it clearly deserves a reiteration of a response regarding the issue of fear that I made in my book *Eclipse* when a male correspondent wanted to know "What's up with women these days? Every time I attempt to extend a courtesy like offering help with grocery bags, they respond with rudeness. They all act like Ms. Independent."

My answer:

No, it's more like they're acting like Ms. Wisdom. Don't take offense. Don't take it personal[ly]. You need to read a book

called *The Gift of Fear*, by Gavin de Becker. This man has a
security consulting firm which advises the world's most
prominent media figures, celebrities, corporations, and law
enforcement agencies on the subject of predicting violence
and recognizing potential perpetrators of crime against one's
person. He teaches methods of avoiding abuse through
heightened awareness of another's behavior and informs
women of the importance of strongly attending to the voice
of their inner self (intuitive insights). Carrying a woman's
groceries was one of his prime examples of how men gain
access into a woman's car or apartment. You picked a bad
example to extend your kindness through.

Today's reality presents us with an ugly picture of increasing crimes against women. Every few seconds a woman
gets raped, abused and battered, even murdered. And you
wonder why they prefer to carry their own grocery bags?
Mr. de Becker tries to help women understand that it's far
better and wiser to be rude to a stranger than be hurt or
end up dead. Women, in general, do not wish to be rude to
a stranger; that's not their inherent knee-jerk reaction.
This very fact, though, is what the perpetrator counts on
so he can be as pushy and forward as he likes or needs to be
in order to manipulate his victim into the ideal situation
which perfectly accommodates his intent. Once he gains
entry into her car or apartment he's already manifested half
of his goal.

You need to be aware of society's reality out there. Put
yourself in the woman's place. I know you know she has
nothing to fear from you, but *she* doesn't know that. She's not
merely exercising her independence, she's also behaving in a
manner which will best serve her safety. Get a clue here. Why
do women need to do this? Could it be because men are abus-
ing, raping, and murdering them at a greater rate than ever
before? It's the men who are causing this "rude" behavior
from women. This is no longer the fifties where the ideologies

and behavior of the Cleaver family rule the day. The next time you feel the urge to assist a woman loaded down with grocery bags, reverse perspective. Put yourself in her position and look at you through her eyes. You are a complete stranger. Does she see a gentleman or a potential rapist fronting his ulterior motives with a kind smile and honey-coated voice? Mr. de Becker advises her to [err] on the side of "life" and see the rapist.

The state of our society is not one to be proud of. It's happening because so many men can't control their testosterone and prefer to let it rule their intellect and control their actions. Don't take it personal[ly]; it's just the way it is. This isn't just some cynical, feministic attitude I've taken; it's proven every day on the six-o'clock newscasts. If you're not seeing it, then it's because you don't wish to—you're voluntarily in denial. Sexual crimes have increased a thousandfold and now . . . enter Viagra.

That answer took care of why women have fears for their person, yet it addressed only one cause of that fear—that of violent men. People have all types of fears that invade their lives and prevent them from experiencing a full and expressive life. Some fear the future. This particular fear shouldn't be an all-consuming attitude that negates the beauty of the moment. Fear of the future can turn into an obsession that occupies the center stage of one's consciousness and shoves Today into being a bit player waiting in the shadows of the wings of life's stage. When this happens, life cannot be fully lived—the present cannot be appreciated and daily blessings cannot be recognized and acknowledged. One who lives with an obsessive fear of the future does not live in the moment.

On the other hand, those who recognize the basic reality that disasters can occur—that there can be geological and climatological emergencies—and accept these as being an aspect of

Nature (life) and so are somewhat prepared with some emergency supplies are those who perceive the future with logic and reason. They are the ones who don't necessarily fear the future but rather keep the future in proper perspective by preparing for it with wisdom while also living each day to its fullest.

There are many types of fears. Women's are inherently different from men's. Children's fears are different from adults'. There are career-specific fears. Performance fears. Social and behavioral fears. Fears of heights and fears of flying. People have fears of germs and even fears of going outside their own house. Yet all of these are subject to the mind's ability to adjust one's hold on one's life through analytical thought. We can take rational measures to place our fears in perspective. We can reduce crippling fears to a lower level of anxiety by shifting our focus to other life aspects. Seeking professional help with this is not a sign of incompetence or weakness. It shows that one recognizes a need to reprioritize one's life and acknowledges the fact that one can't always accomplish goals without the assistance of others. That's a big step in itself—recognizing that we all need assistance at one time or another throughout our lives. We were placed here for each other. No one person is an island.

I've seen too many people who allow their fears of tomorrow to steal away the beautiful gift of today. Life is a gift from the Divine. Life is the Divine's present to us—the here and now are meant to be lived to the fullest by recognizing every opportunity life presents to us for fulfillment and growth. Every daybreak is an unopened present placed on the breakfast table. Open it. See what possibilities have been given to you this day.

► *How does one regain a hold on real life priorities? It seems that people's goals are incredibly superficial and shallow.*

Life goals are specific to each individual and are based on a multitude of personal perspectives. Yet I understand your question is related to those goals which are directly generated by greed and the desire for power and status. Yes, such goals are indeed prevalent in the world.

People become caught up in the hectic pace of daily living— the job, making ends meet, the raging traffic, the competition, balancing career with child care, the social scene, the press of the crowds, the nonstop city life. They're jumping through hoops, running on the treadmill of life, juggling responsibilities, looking ahead while watching their backs, and keeping tabs on who's advancing ahead of them and who's falling behind in their race through life. Just when the pace becomes manageable, it quickens again.

People need to dig in their heels every once in a while and come to a screeching halt. They need to jump off the treadmill. Take a breather. Life offers many options to facilitate this breathing time. For some, it's a vacation; for others, it's sitting at home with soft music and a good book. Meditation. Time alone to hear oneself think. Yet the most powerful source for taking a breather that helps one regain one's hold on life's true priorities is Nature. I don't say this because I'm a Nature person and live in a forest either. I say this from experience. Getting out and spending some time reconnecting with Nature's innocent realness puts one back in touch with what's *real*. After one has been immersed in society's hectic environment and among the constant press of people, Nature offers one room to breathe, to take a big breath and exhale a long sigh. It offers peacefulness and quietude. Its innocence is unfettered by the shallow affectations of people. Nature invites you to experience the pureness of simple reality and makes no demands on or judgments of you. It brings reality back into your life and gets you in touch with what's truly important: unconditional goodness and unconditional love.

► *Do you think young children should have idols and heroes?*

Idols, no. Heroines and heroes, possibly. Someone they look up to and respect, definitely. Idols connote adoration. We want to stay away from that. Heroines and heroes can set examples of certain positive traits and qualities such as courage, perseverance, and patience, yet these personalities must be well chosen or else they have the potential of representing an unattainable goal for the child.

What children need is someone they respect as a real person rather than a comic or video game character. Sports personalities, though they may be accomplished athletes, also have private lives that can, depending on their moral behavior, taint their overall value as heroes and heroines. Children need regular people— everyday folks—to respect in their lives, such as neighbors, relatives, and store clerks. These people can be greater heroines and heroes to children than famous people. Children need to see regular folks doing heroic things, so that they learn that heroic and chivalrous behavior is in reach of everyone, not just the Uzi-carrying action hero or the spear-throwing Xena.

Idols? No, we don't want people being adored. We want our children to respect those who take personal responsibility and unconditional goodness seriously . . . every single day. We want our children to understand and appreciate the importance of becoming involved without thinking of oneself first. We want our children to respect life . . . all life.

► *Where has respect for our elders gone? The nursing homes are bursting with unwanted old people. What sort of attitude has taken over here?*

I agree that the nursing homes are filling up at a faster rate than ever before and new ones are being built to accommodate this demand. Some of this is because of the cost of living. Today's cost of daily living is higher than it was a few decades ago. Now many families need both parents to work to make ends meet. This in turn creates a new situation whereby the parents of those in the workforce have no familial home to return to if they reach a stage in life where they need care.

The medical insurance conglomerates are also a prime contributor to this situation because they pay benefits for only professional caregivers. This means that if a family wanted to take Grandma into their home to live out the remainder of her life and she also required round-the-clock care, that family would have to hire a bonafide medical caregiver to receive any financial assistance. This family could not receive monetary aid from a medical insurance's benefits package to pay a friend or family member to care for the elder and be her companion. This fact alone makes familial care for the elderly a difficult goal to achieve for families.

Yet, philosophically speaking, where should one's priorities be? Isn't caring for our elderly parents or grandparents a personal responsibility when the time arrives? Do we become so self-absorbed and entangled in our own lives that we are convinced that we have neither the time nor the energy to give care back to those who cared for us when we were young? Historically, families used to be the hub of home life, where children were nurtured by parents, who in turn gave respect to and received counsel from the grandparents in the home. The home was a lively place, with children running around and their elders receiving joy from watching their high-energy antics and exuberance. Children learned from their grandparents' stories. Everyone was exposed to all life stages, so a natural understanding of the other took hold. But today, the elders are left on their own and are not generally perceived as the hub element of family life. They live somewhere else—in another city, downtown, or out on the country farm. And then, when these same elders reach a stage in life where they can no longer care for themselves and require assistance, the family is thrown into turmoil over a dilemma they really don't want to acknowledge and deal with. Nursing homes are so convenient. "Let someone else take care of Grandma, because I just don't have the time." There are endless excuses backing up this initial knee-jerk idea for a solution, most of them generated by self-absorption. Granted, there are some lifestyle situations that make taking an elder into the home an impossibility, such as when the elder has no surviving child to care for him or her, when the surviving child is a single mother with children of her own and is just barely making ends meet, or when the elder, because of diminished mental faculties, poses a threat to him- or herself or others. On the whole, however, society is apathetic toward its elders. Many people would rather keep elders out of the family unit by putting them in nursing homes than disrupt their own established routines.

This issue really comes down to priorities. People and helping others are more important than possessions, our time schedules, our social life, and so forth. Society has itself locked into a focus on the self. And anything or anyone else is perceived as a disruption or threat to self-fulfillment.

People *think* they make their own reality. They think they have their lives planned and designed according to the wants of self, yet little do they understand the reality of change. Every day presents the potential for one's life to dramatically change. Folks just don't get this. Our paths can change directions unexpectedly. Yet those directions are branches of one's destined trail through life. Instead of denying or fighting these detours, try going with the flow and following them to see what wonders they may reveal, what insights they may bring, what wisdom they instill along the way.

When I bought this modest mountain cabin, I envisioned days and nights of serenity and semisolitude. This remote location provided all I needed to gain inner peace and the quietude of Nature I find so necessary for my work. And it was wonderful, just perfect. Then my companion, Sally, brought her elderly mother into our home to live after we agreed that that was the only right thing to do. Her mother, Mary Belle, could no longer care for herself living alone as she had been. She'd been confusing her medications (taking sleeping pills instead of heart medication) and wouldn't eat because she forgot that she hadn't eaten. Alzheimer's had entered her life. And so it entered ours also. When we initially bought this cabin, the idea of sharing it with an elder never entered our minds, yet when the situation arose, there was no time spent in discussion. The answer was clear right from the start. Sally could not bring herself to even think of a nursing home as a viable consideration for her mother. And though we now experience periods of discord, suspicion, combativeness, and night wandering in the woods that we have to be on the constant watch for, we also have no doubts as to the correctness of our decision. Anyone who has been involved in the daily care of someone with Alzheimer's knows and understands the swift mood swings of the individual. The afflicted person can exhibit deep love and appreciation for others in the home one minute and the very next minute can give you the evil eye and accuse you of all sorts of imagined things. That's just the way of the disease. You understand its progression and work within it. You have compassion. You continue to care about the individual no matter what he or she says or how he or she behaves. To Sally, this person, though mentally nothing like she once was, is still her mother. To me, Mary Belle is an elder who needs someone to care for her and care about her . . . give her love and keep her safe.

Every day, families are confronted with new situations that enter their lives and can change them. New job offers, an unexpected pregnancy, a child's accident, a flood or tornado, and a parent needing assisted care all provide us with opportunities to exercise our free will and practice personal responsibility. What's even more interesting is that not only do these unexpected elements come as disguised opportunities but they also open up a whole new vista of options that never would've presented themselves otherwise. It must be remembered that every new presentation in one's life carries its own set of qualities and values to take advantage of. This is what can alter one's perspective of life events. Does the individual only look at these through the lens of self, of the ego? Or through the clear lens of openness, which allows recognition of chances for new opportunities, opportunities through which the individual can grow and gain priceless insights into life?

When people create their own little world, so to speak, with a comfortable home life, with a circle of hand-picked friends, career, and so on, they attempt to define themselves by these. One is not defined by either friends or career. One is not defined by either home decor or social life. Nor is one defined by clothing or social status. These are all superficial elements that one *adds* to one's inherent beingness—fluff one surrounds oneself with in an attempt to show the world who one is. But it is *behavior* that defines the true inner character of one's beingness. Behavior is the outward expression of one's inner self.

So then, what sort of inner light shines forth from one's inner self when a parent suddenly needs daily care? The answer depends on whether this need is responded to by the ego or the spirit.

▸ *My son worries about everything in life. What should I tell him?*

What you decide to tell him is up to you; you're his mother. But I have a few comments to offer on the issue of worry and perhaps you can use some of them to help him out.

To worry is to not trust. To worry is to have a lack of self-confidence. To worry is to lack an appreciation for life itself. Worry can't change anything. The emotion of worry and the mental energy it consumes cannot cause a positive outcome. Worry is generated by the unknowability of the future. We worry about whether we will pass an exam, whether we will get the results we want on a medical test, how well our children will do in school, and how to help our children when they're ill. But if worrying can't effect a positive outcome, why worry in the first place?

Then there is anxiety. Anxiety is a bit different from worry.

Anxiety is concern. You can have concern for an ill child or about a significant other's sickness. Concern is an expression of caring about another. Concern is a more grounded attitude than worry is. Concern maintains a certain level of rationality, but worry obliterates logic through strong negative attitudes.

Worry negates the moment. What does that mean? It means that while you are worrying about tomorrow—the future—you miss today. A good example of this is those folks who are consumed with worry over the earth's future changes and if the world will end on a certain date, or if the changes will level their house, or if the changes will bring crazed interlopers to their door. Living every day with these negative thoughts and dreads can't do anything but cause someone constant stress. Having these worries over some *possible* future event creates a shadow of depression over one's entire existence. Nobody should have to live that way. Nobody should want to *voluntarily* put themselves through that kind of oppression. Life is far too precious for that. Life is a beautiful gift. Each moment is a surprise to look forward to and relish with excitement and joy. So how can this excitement and joy possibly have a chance if someone is always looking beyond the moment and worrying about the future instead?

The most important aspect to remember and realize about worry is that it can't do a damn thing to effect a positive outcome. Understanding—really understanding—that one sentence can make all the difference.

Some folks think that to worry is to lack faith. I don't agree. Faith is something else altogether and I don't want to let this response drift away into another issue here. Worry is nothing more than a fear of some specific future event. Life takes care of itself. Life is bursting with myriad potentialities that can come to pass at any given moment. Let's not attempt to predetermine future outcomes on the basis of egocentric perspectives. By this I mean to convey that many—most—worries are caused by how an individual specifically wants something to happen or end. And that specific end is not always what is best for the many. That specific result is not always best for the individual, at least not if the big picture of his or her life could be known. We just oftentimes *think* we know what's best. We think we know what a perfect outcome would look like, but we don't. We don't know what the perfect outcome will prove to be, so we take it upon ourselves to create one to force reality into. Nope. Doesn't work that way. Reality marches forward without any help from humans. Reality happens.

► *What's the solution to hate crimes?*

That's a good one.

Love. Oh, isn't that simplistic. Isn't that a cliché.

I'll tell you what it is—it's a worn-out, beaten-to-death word. It's gotten to that point because people use the word without understanding it. It's completely lost its meaning. While shopping in a mall, I hear folks make comments like "Oh, I just love that!" or "I'd just love to have one of those in my house!" or "Don't you just love this?" Phooey! They're talking about stuff! You can *like* stuff, the material objects in life, but you don't *love* stuff. Love is an emotion that is a sense of deep relatedness with another, a bonding that imparts a dynamic sense of interconnectedness. More on this interconnectedness in a later chapter.

Love is the opposite of hate. When respect for all life and love of humanity reside within one's heart, there is no room left for hatred. This love fills one's perspective and emanates out into the world through unconditional goodness and tolerance for people's individuality. This love provides fertile ground for the true understanding that we are all different and, as such, are physical beings created for the prime purpose of having limitless options for the spirit within to express itself. When the spirit is smothered by the ego, the ego takes command and dominates the individual. The ego then seeks things to criticize for the purpose of making the self a pedestal to perch upon. It is the ego that persecutes, not the spirit within. It is the aggrandizement of self that serves as hatred's vile impetus.

Hate crimes are an abomination wreaked upon our society. They are one of the prime examples of how society has not evolved intellectually. Hatred is a sign of Neanderthal thinking. I'd like to say we've gotten a little beyond primitive mental development, but we haven't. In the twenty-first century, our civilization is as backward in demonstrating spiritual development as it was in antediluvian times. We're not here to point out others' differences and persecute because of them; we're here to appreciate them.

We were created with differences so that we'd evolve into an advanced civilization. But if our society was graded on our performance thus far, we'd receive an F— or, more likely, an "incomplete." We have failed miserably to practice tolerance as an intellectually evolved way of life.

What's the solution to hate crimes? Laws that make prejudicial and intolerant behavior of *all* kinds a crime. People in general need to stand up against what they're witnessing in their neighborhoods, cities, and country lanes. It's not just the "other person" who's being persecuted, it's your *own* right to individuality and your freedom to be. Just because you may presently fit into some societally styled norm that defines who is an "acceptable" individual, it doesn't mean that you always will. Perhaps one day, society will shift its myopic view of who and what is the norm and you'll be left outside that circle. What then, my friend? Remember, all actions have effects. You may not be aware of those effects, but they ripple through humanity and vibrate upon the fine strands of reality's Great Web of Life.

As long as hate crimes continue to happen anywhere upon this earth, we are a civilization going nowhere. We are no better than the technologically advanced Atlanteans who lost their understanding of what true power was, who let their ego rule and consequently lost their respect for life.

Not just individual states but also the entire United States need to wake up from deep sleep and recognize the persecutions citizens are suffering because of prejudice. We need to make it a federal offense to commit any kind of hate crime or practice prejudicial behavior. Once this is done, other countries need to follow suit. It won't do much good for just one or two states to pass these laws. It must be done on a national level, and then one nation at a time.

► *I'm fifty-two and my daughter just made me a grandma. I'm a grandma! And I have a ferocious fear of aging. I know it's a ridiculous attitude, but I just can't seem to get over it.*

Congratulations, Grandma!

The fear of aging, especially for women, is mostly due to society's attitude toward aging. Nowhere in world cultures is getting older viewed with such polarity as it is in the United States. Americans perceive aging *men* with their *silver* hair as being *distinguished* but view aging *women* with their *gray* hair as being *old*— just plain old. This attitude, coupled with society's narrow definition of women's sexuality and sensuality, creates the double whammy faced by aging women: They are seen as having lost their sexual attractiveness. Americans' skewed view of aging and sexual appeal results in thousands of women making visits to plastic surgeons' "body shops" each year.

Grandma—what a beautiful sound that word is. It does not mean a decrepit, hunched-over hag; it means a female elder. An elder who has gained a certain measure of wisdom throughout her life, who is respected and cherished for the many years she's lived and learned through experience.

In many of today's cultures, and as far back as ancient times, the aged women of the community were the most respected and revered individuals of the society. They were highly respected because of their age alone; they were revered because of their attained wisdom. The physical appearance of these female elders was perceived as a mark of their status as a wise woman. The silver in their hair and their aged features were indications of their right to be cherished. These women were viewed as being somewhat sacred—the sacred crones of the community who were sought out for advice.

Grandma, how can it be that you do not cherish your own approaching elder stage in this life? How can it be that you think you have no value unless you can hold onto the youthfulness of the less wise life stages? How can it be that you voluntarily buy into and choose society's skewed vision of female beauty and sexuality over the incredible female sensuality of being a respected elder?

Through the last six years of my life, my own physical appearance has made an incredible change. The long, thick black hair has thinned and become half silver. The face looking back at me in the mirror has altered and, though the eyes don't see as well as they once did, there is a particular twinkle in them that reflects back at me as if the crone within is verifying her emergence from my consciousness. And I like what I see. I like it a lot.

People perceive the evidence of aging through the ego rather than by way of the spirit eyes. And that is ignorance. Aging is the process through which we are given the beautiful opportunity to manifest acceptance of our life experience, the wisdom we've gained through years of learning by trial and error, through years of reading and gaining knowledge, through years of practicing acceptance and perseverance.

For society to advance, we must live life through the spirit rather than through the ego. It's the ego that distorts our perception and skews the true meaning of beauty, power, and aging.

▸ *I find myself continually in a state of frustration. Why is this?*

Three words: ego versus acceptance.

Ego generates myriad problems for the individual because seeing with the ego prevents one from seeing *what is*. This means that your own attitudes, emotions, and perceptions are projected onto a situation and over others around you and serve to cloak the purity of reality—the what is—in a surreal shroud made of prejudicial threads. These threads are connected to your own psychological spinning wheel. You are appointing yourself as the rebel weaver of reality, altering it to conform to your perceptual ideals. And when reality refuses to submit to your efforts, you are plunged into a state of frustration.

But acceptance . . . To have acceptance for what is when that *what is* cannot be altered or affected by an outside force is to have the wisdom of patience and tolerance. To accept is to have the inner serenity to let life be, to have the wisdom to flow with the current instead of trying to fight and struggle against it. Acceptance shoves ego out the back door and boots it down the road. Acceptance gifts one with an ability to perceive life in its pure reality without attempting to color it or alter it according to one's attitudes. With acceptance, the frustration level is nearly nil because you're not continually trying to change people's behavior, situations, or relationships into The World According to You.

► *I'm so irritated with my husband. He's constantly trying to live his life to please and impress other people. Isn't there anything I can do or say to change his attitude?*

This is another ego-related situation.

Your husband doesn't understand the concept of individuality, that is, how incredibly beautiful and important it is. He has a need to feel as though everyone accepts and likes him; therefore, he abandons his individual inherent qualities and characteristics to create a false self to present to the world. This false self is made in the image of his peers and possesses their qualities—their hobbies, interests, attitudes, prejudices, world view, and so on. He smothers his own identity for the purpose of becoming a clone of those he perceives as being his judges in life. The thought behind this type of behavior goes something like this: *Get in with the judge, make her like you, and you've got it made.*

You also mentioned that he even changes his clothing style to conform with that of his peers. This behavior would be expected with his perception of himself. You see, if he remained true to himself and wore what he was naturally attracted to, that'd be no good to him because that style of dress might generate criticism from his friends and coworkers. He wants to avoid that criticism at all costs, so he naturally changes his mode of dress so he'll fit in and be accepted.

Your husband needs to understand that he is not one of a group but an individual. He needs to acknowledge his individuality, that being one of a group, class, or school of thought steals away his uniqueness. This behavior creates a false life and makes a sham of living. Nobody needs the acceptance of another to live a fulfilled life. We must each follow the beat of our own inner drumming to have half a chance at accomplishing the goals we each came to achieve. If we don't, we are merely borrowing another's life, attitudes, opinions, mode of dress, and perceptions. We don't make advances in life by limiting ourselves to the framework of others. We don't develop and grow in life by mimicking the behavior of others. We can never even *know* ourselves when we feel the need to emulate those around us.

Your husband's behavior is terribly self-repressive. It smothers the spirit within and its free expression. It's a form of self-denial— a denial of the existence of self and of one's inherent individuality. Continuing this behavior will cause frustration, anxiety, and suppressed anger that will one day have to be released.

It's important to have the wisdom to understand that you can't please everyone. And, once that's understood, why bother trying to please? I'm about as bohemian as you can get and I really don't give a spit what folks think. This is because I relish the idea of free expression and cherish the wonderful feeling of freedom to dress according to my mood and just plain be me. I'm not like anyone else out there in the world—nobody is like everyone else. That fact is important to understand. Why should I dress like you if that style of dress doesn't reflect my unique beingness? Oh, yes, I almost bought into that need for others to like me. Once, because of the perception my readers had of me being some highly spiritual individual, I was embarrassed to be "caught" playing at a video poker machine at a Cripple Creek casino. Shame on me. But I had always said in my books that I'm no spiritual guru, no high-and-mighty spiritual leader, no greater or higher than everyone else. So why should I feel like melting down into a hole in the casino floor when one of my readers came up to me there? After I truly realized that I had to be myself, I never again felt any negative emotions when I met up with my readers in a casino. They were there to have some fun and so was I. End of story. That's the end because being yourself means just that—and having the freedom to *like* being yourself instead of what others think you should be.

To you I suggest sitting your husband down and having a heart-to-heart conversation about individuality and the importance of understanding free expression. Talk about how one smothers that individuality by making the approval of others a priority and how that behavior creates a false perception of self. Most importantly, try to unearth the deep-seated psychological *reasons* for this behavior. Attempt to discover *why* he isn't comfortable or satisfied with his own natural beingness. Why must he have the approbation of others? Why is it so important for his ego and self-esteem?

Many times, just letting someone know that this or that behavior is wrong or self-defeating is not enough; you have to dig down and get to the deep root of the problem. Sometimes these reasons have sent their roots down so deep that it takes considerable time and effort to expose them for what they are. It takes patience, understanding, and love. Don't expect an overnight turnaround. Don't be in expectation at all; just be compassionate and diligent in your efforts to help—because these reasons can stem from incidents as far back as childhood.

Everyone has a right to cherish their beautiful, shining beingness. To do so is so . . . well, so freeing and light. You are who you are on the basis of your own unique composite vibrationary rate. You are a composite of past-life personalities and experiential events that no one on this planet can duplicate. You are an individual. Cherish the wonderful feeling of expressing that individuality without fear of reprisal or criticism. Love that spectacular freedom to . . . be.

► *There is so much ignorance in society that I can hardly stand it.*

This correspondent is referring to the ignorance evinced by prejudice, hatred, intolerance, racism, sexism, and so forth.

Though I would wholeheartedly agree with this reader, what makes ignorance more tolerable for an enlightened individual to live around is having the wisdom to *accept* the fact that there are those who live in ignorance. Now, acceptance doesn't also mean that you're condoning the negative attitudes or that you can't do anything about them; it means merely that you can *deal* with the existence of them on a more intellectual level.

Acceptance of people's ignorance and Neanderthal behavior born of a sense of superiority does not preclude taking active measures to counter such backward thinking. It's past time in humanity's development for those of higher consciousness to become directly involved in raising the consciousness of society as a whole. Hate crimes and prejudicial rallies must be counterbalanced with opposition. People are sick and tired of the fact that hate groups have been allowed to publicly (and secretly) do as they please and boldly run roughshod over everyone. The public has had it up to here with hate-filled violence of these supremacists and self-righteous religious leaders and their intolerance-inciting sermons. The public is finally becoming intolerant of intolerance.

As long as individuality is not free to be openly expressed, as long as individuality is persecuted, this planet's chance for continued survival will continue to decrease as intolerance gets closer to reaching critical mass.

First, people have to accept the existence of intolerant behavior as part of society. With that acceptance comes understanding that they too have a right to express opposition to that negative behavior. Following on that realization comes the active involvement in countering the intolerance with positive intolerance. This implies not "positive violence," for there is no such thing, but to instead participate in "activist demonstrations" that send an antihate message to people caught in an egomaniacal ignorance. If our legal system gives hate groups the right to demonstrate and shout their prejudicial slurs, then antihate groups have equal rights to use countermeasures and express their own strong hatred for hatred.

Yes, it's hard to live among those who make the persecution of others their singular goal in life, yet we as people who are indirectly oppressed and are sickened by that behavior have a duty to stand up and make our disgust known—to join our voices together in a resounding shout around the world that sends the message that the ignorance of hate will no longer be tolerated.

▸ *I seem to have a very optimistic outlook on life and am usually cheery. Why does this irritate people?*

It irritates them because they're jealous of your seemingly carefree perspective. They can't fathom why you don't ever get depressed, get anxious, or worry. You're seen as an oddball who sees life through rose-colored glasses. Yet in your letter to me, you certainly didn't come across as being blind to or in denial of reality. You struck me as a level-headed woman with a strong sense of priorities and a good intellect. You seem to have acceptance and tolerance. You have attained a good measure of wisdom in life, and that accounts for your attitude.

I need to reiterate that as long as you're being yourself and feel free to exercise self-expression, it doesn't matter what others think or how they misperceive you. One day they too may reach the depth of wisdom you've gained and then they'll realize how wrong they were about you. Even if they never do grow to that stage of philosophical understanding, you're still you. And your behavior, your perspectives, aren't contingent on those of others.

▶ *In your Q & A book,* Daybreak, *some of your answers didn't seem to align with your general philosophies on different issues. Why was this? Have you changed perspectives on things?*

No, not at all. Remember though, *Daybreak* was the product of a joint effort between me and the spiritual entities, of No-Eyes, and several advisors. Many of the answers that came from one advisor or another were correspondent specific, meaning that the answers applied to that specific correspondent but not necessarily the general reader. Since the publication of that volume, I've learned that that type of collaboration is not the format of choice because correspondent-specific answers were not general enough to be all-inclusive and, because they were so specific, they oftentimes gave the wrong impression to the general reader. A case in point was the correspondent-specific advisor responses to questions on homosexuality. These ended up causing me great pain and deep regret because they sent the wrong general philosophical message as related to the actual spiritual truths on the subject. Yet . . . it was partly my fault too because I am ultimately responsible for what is written in my books. I felt that I should've asked for a generalized response instead of the correspondent-specific ones that were sometimes provided by the advisors.

Now I've learned the incredible power that words can have and have written all subsequent Q & A books on the basis of my own spiritual philosophy and truths as I've grown to know them to be. In *Eclipse*, I was sure to set the record straight on the issue of sexuality—all forms. The responses to all the readership questions in *Eclipse* and *Beyond Earthway* are solely mine. Through hindsight, I've learned the wisdom of taking personal responsibility for everything I say and write rather than allowing others (spirit entities) to interject their own wording that may not be intended for the general public and therefore may be misinterpreted.

No profession more exemplifies the hard and solid fact that words carry great power than that of writer. Fiction is one thing, but nonfiction is a whole different animal. When writing my own thoughts, I take considerable time to choose the exact wording and terminology that best clarifies my message. I do this not only for clarity but also for simplicity, because I don't believe spiritual philosophy's truths should ever be presented in a complexity that confuses the seeker and causes a conceptual circle dance or knotted braid of intertwined theories and ideologies. Throughout my years of reading correspondents' letters, there proved to be a glaring void in my written material. This void has been acknowledged and filled by writing *Eclipse* and *Beyond Earthway* through which your many questions have been publicly addressed. And because both volumes contain only personal responses from me and no other, they uphold the integrity of the spiritual living message I've come to convey. Both volumes reflect the wide range my personality expresses itself through. Some responses to questions are light and others are quite serious. Some contain humor and others cut to the quick with straightforward wording. Since I've no interest in winning popularity contests, my singular goal is to tell it like it is without extraneous conceptual barnacles attached to a theory. If you strip your reasons for seeking spiritual enlightenment down to the bare naked truth, you'll find that you're really interested not in a teacher but rather in the *Truth*. I'm not a teacher, so my physical self need not be before the public in any way, shape, or form (publicity tours, seminars, lectures, and so forth). What you seek is Truth's message—The Word—not a simple human being. You don't seek an idol; you seek an ideology. You don't need big hundred-dollar words; you need simplicity and clarity. These I've endeavored to bring forth. That is why *Eclipse* and *Beyond Earthway* contain responses that apply to everyone.

THE ANTIDOTE
Dream Interpretation

► *Is there a certain time of night when dreams are more prophetic?*

This question can't be answered the way it was worded unless everyone were to go to bed and fall asleep at the same time. "Time of night" is a subjective factor dependent on the time at which an individual retired and actually fell asleep. Therefore, let's revise the focus to *length of sleep time* rather than time of night.

Generally, the first four hours of one's sleep is when the consciousness is busy processing the day's events. This will be the most fragmented period of dream time where bits and pieces of conversations, things seen during the day, and people you interacted with will make appearances in an ever-changing kaleidoscopic pattern of seeming nonsense. Yet the consciousness recognizes a pattern in this apparent jumble of visuals, and that pattern is its mechanism for sorting out and categorizing all the impressions it received during the day.

After this processing has been completed, the following sleep time will usually consist of a "quiet" nonvisual period in which the consciousness is at rest. It is after this rest period when the dynamic activity begins to occur. This is when there will be vivid dreams, out-of-body experiences, message bringers, activity of one's intuitive faculties, and prophetic insights. This, then, is why so many people experience their most vivid dreams carrying insights and epiphanies that awake them at or around 3 A.M. (if they retired around 10 P.M.). This is when the antidote element enters the picture to give greater clarity to life problems, relationships, and decisions.

▶ *I dreamed that you came to me in a dream and gave me the solution to a major conflict I was having in life. Thank you.*

Before you thank me, we need to analyze this event.

I've received dozens of letters from correspondents who've written to express that they've experienced similar events during their dream time. They've said that I appeared to them in a dream and clarified a problem they were having in life. I need to clarify that this visitation was not *actually* me but rather a *symbolic* representation of my *persona* as created by the dreamer's own subconscious.

During the awake state in life, people choose certain personalities who represent truth or some other commendable quality. For a teenager, it could be a renowned sports figure; for a very devote Catholic woman, it could be the persona of the Blessed Mother; for a computer buff, it could be Bill Gates; for a little girl, it might be her mother, grandmother, or favorite aunt. See what I mean? The consciousness of that person did not visit your dream time. What appeared in the dream was your own subconscious representation of a specific quality personified. Since you stated in your letter that you were searching for the truth to a spiritual philosophic conflict and you also connected that subject matter with my writings, I was the visual your consciousness created to help resolve your dilemma by presenting someone you trusted.

I've noted a widespread belief in the popular concept of night traveling—a lot of it, so much so that you'd think the starlit skies were swarming with dreaming people's spirits flitting here and there into other folks' houses and diving into their dreamscapes. Not so. The actual manifestation of this phenomenon is a rarity. Every time you dream of someone you know talking to you and helping with life problems it does not mean that that individual's spirit entered your dream time. I believe that most people understand that. It's when the dreamscape visitor is a well-known personality that the dreamer tends to mistakenly shift from recognizing his or her own consciousness's created visual for what it is to thinking of it as something more meaningful for the ego—that the visitor's actual spirit visited his or her dream time. This not only gives credence to the information the visitor brought but also increases the dreamer's sense of his or her own importance.

The conceptual realities of dreaming and the subconscious are vast and orderly. We must be discerning and use caution to not interject elements that are not there. Assumptions and extraneously added elements only cloud their integrity for analysis.

► *What does a sea sponge mean in a dream?*

Taken by itself, a sea sponge symbolizes spiritual overabsorption. This represents one's awake-state condition of spiritual redundancy, of voluntarily overwhelming oneself with spiritual—or, more likely, "religious"—dogma, which causes confusion.

I've witnessed this spiritual confusion with people who run from one spiritual philosophy to another, never staying with one long enough to fully comprehend it. I see this happening with folks drawn to the more "psychic" elements of so-called New Age beliefs. They hear of some new guru or foreign teacher and they're off and running with the high goal of gleaning some elevated state of enlightenment from him or her. They're racing here and charging there because they think they're missing out on something monumental if they don't experience it all. What they're really doing is acting like that sea sponge, soaking up all the spiritual waters around them without ever growing into the wisdom of being discerning. You know, sometimes the problem of seeking is in the seeking. Seeking for the sake of seeking indicates a lack of focus. One's centeredness is lost and becomes fragmented among widely scattered concepts, so no singular tenet has the capability of standing out in crystal clarity. The sponge absorbs all spiritual matter floating past and becomes inundated with an amalgamated dilution of concepts that cannot be intellectually clarified. The individual ends up being able to claim having a bit of knowledge on this and that spiritual ideology but having no clear understanding of any particular one. This is what the presentation of a sea sponge in a dreamscape conveys.

I've always encouraged reading—extensive reading. I've been a big proponent of gaining as much knowledge as possible through reading, research, study, and then contemplation. I do this because I've seen the negative effects when folks read on only one subject matter without expanding their knowledge by reading associated material. An example of this would be someone with a high interest in New Age material who, upon entering a bookstore, makes a beeline straight to the Metaphysical section without browsing anywhere else. This habit confines the individual to an extremely narrow viewpoint. He or she needs to expand his or her scope by also visiting the Natural Science, Physics, and Philosophy sections of the store where myriad associated volumes are awaiting to expand the reader's consciousness. After all, I've always said that the definition of New Age material is "the blend of spirit and physics." It's the consciousness within natural science meeting the human consciousness—the living Web of Life. To understand one is to understand the other so that the entire concept can be comprehended in its shimmering totality. So when folks focus only on the spiritual aspects of New Age thought, they're only getting a third of the picture. This is why I advocate extensive reading in all subjects associated with one's interests; to not read widely gives one an extremely myopic view and prevents comprehensive understanding.

The New Age sea sponge will flit here and there like a butterfly to one new channeler after another with an awe-filled expression and a mind searching for greater heights of enlightenment. Phooey. All that's going to get you is more confusion. All you're doing is absorbing, absorbing, absorbing—never filtering your intake through the broad-based knowledge that brings wisdom.

▶ *In dreamscapes, what does the appearance of a snowbird indicate?*

A snowbird symbolizes encouragement.

Snowbirds have distinguished themselves by creating a legend that they appear only when it snows. Curiously, I've witnessed the reality of this at my cabin when they suddenly appear when it's snowing. It makes me wonder where the heck they are when it's not snowing. They're like magical little winged beings who mysteriously exist only during snowfall.

Since in dream symbology snow connotes a strong comprehension and grasp of spiritual truths, the snowbird relates to spiritual encouragement. The presentation of this symbol would indicate the existence of some type of melancholia or inner conflict regarding one's spiritual beliefs. The snowbird presents itself as a sign of encouragement, indicating support for the dreamer's spiritual path and subsequent behavior.

▶ *I dreamed that I owned a rock shop, but I can't figure out what that's supposed to mean for me. Can you help with this interpretation?*

A rock shop represents natural talents and how they're used for humankind's benefit. To dream that you *owned* this shop would indicate that you yourself possess (own) inherent talents that, if used in a manner of unconditional goodness, could greatly benefit your sisters and brothers.

► *What does it mean when you dream that a relative appeared with an animal superimposed over him? My uncle appeared with an overlay of a bear. The bear was more prominent and the man was more like a translucent being beneath it.*

This dreamscape fragment means that your uncle has let his ego dominate his personality. He probably exhibits manipulative and controlling tendencies. He literally hides behind the self-created *hugeness* of the domineering and over*bearing* bear.

There are a few instances where such a visual will represent the opposite. It will signify an individual who is weighted down by some type of overbearing situation or condition in life. Sometimes this can even be a psychological element, such as guilt. There are many psychological defense mechanisms people use in life to hide behind. Some of them are for self-protection and self-preservation; some of them are for the purpose of masking the true character of self or as a shell within which to shield one's sensitivities. Whenever a dreamscape element depicts an individual overshadowed by another, such as an animal, the dreamer needs to know what that animal signifies before proper understanding comes from the analysis.

► *Once in a while I'll be dreaming and something will awaken me; then I'll fall back to sleep only to have something else awaken me. Yet each time I get back asleep, I pick up the same dream where it left off. I've found this experience to be amusing because it seems so unusual. Is this a common occurrence for dreamers?*

Yeah, that's a kick when it happens, isn't it?

What you're referring to is what I call sequential dreaming. Though it isn't very common, it does happen once in a while. What's interesting is that it can also happen during sequential periods of Quantum Meditation too. Some of my recorded experiences were generated from sequential Quantum Meditation sessions.

Generally, when a dreamer is awakened and falls back to sleep, the dreaming sequence will have been interrupted and new visuals will present. There is usually a type of void—an intermission—between dreams that we don't necessarily perceive. This void can be compared to the separation of frames in a movie film that, when the film is running, the eye doesn't catch because it's visually imperceptible.

Sequential dreaming is a rare phenomenon that occurs whenever the dream's content is so powerfully dynamic in intent—message—that its energy is able to maintain itself in an on-hold pattern until the individual's consciousness automatically resumes the action by returning to a state of deep sleep. When sequential dreaming occurs, it's quite interesting and even amusing after the dreamer realizes what transpired. Because it doesn't happen very often, it's quite an event.

▶ *Can dreams be controlled by the consciousness?*

Sure they can, during lucid dreaming. I'm sure you've heard of this. There are many good technical books about it if you want to research it more.

Lucid dreaming is one way of controlling the dreamscape action; there's yet another that sometimes works well. That's the application of *conscious intent* by the individual before falling asleep. Conscious intent is comparable to lying in bed and repeatedly voicing a mantra that is really a short sentence or phrase that encapsulates the subject matter you wish to dream about. And don't tell me you choose the phrase *Lottery numbers, lottery numbers, lottery numbers*—shame on you if you do.

▶ *I can never recall colors in dreams. Do we dream in color?*

Well, I sure can recall some very vivid Technicolor dreams that shimmered with living energy. I think the element of color is not significant in that it may be present but because of the more important intent or message of a dream, the aspect of coloration isn't important enough to be recalled.

► *Most of the flowers in my dreams seem to appear as orchids. Would you know why?*

For the general public, the common interpretation of an *orchid* in a dream is *a fragile talent or benefit that must be carefully maintained.* The not so well known symbology for an orchid comes to us from many ancient matriarchal cultures (especially those in which the Goddess aspect of the Divine was revered), in which the orchid represented the female genitalia.

The repetition of this specific flower is trying to convey a particular message to you that is directly related to your inherent talents associated with your *gender*. Now, of course this isn't pointing to some "nether region" talent; it's indicating that you have some inherent "feminine" talent that should be used. Perhaps you have a gift for counseling women or a talent for organizing women's groups; or maybe it's your destiny to become involved in or establish a women's safe house. This last is what I'm going to do when I'm finished writing books. I'm going to build a women's spiritual sanctuary/safe house called Magdalene Abbey. Anyway, you get the idea about the orchid's symbology.

All this time, your dreams have been attempting to point you in the right direction. You mentioned that you have been on the fence about choosing between several possible paths to travel. Here is a clear marker to aid in making your decision. Whichever one will be more associated with women will be the one indicated as being the better choice.

I realize that the *orchid* entry in my dream symbology book— *Mary Summer Rain's Guide to Dream Symbology*—did not include the interpretation associated with the ancient matriarchal philosophy, and that has me thinking. Perhaps I'll do a women's dream symbology book. That'd be fun. Since I've already amassed at least six hundred new entry words and their symbolic meanings that aren't in the current dream book, I might as well gear a more comprehensive volume toward women. Hmm . . . I'm going to think more about this.

► *Do infants dream?*

Oh, absolutely. Anyone who's ever watched a baby sleep has some sense that babies dream. What adds greater dimension to those baby dreams is the fact that a baby possesses a consciousness that is closer to its recently exited spiritual realm than to its newer physical reality. That alone makes one think on the following puzzlement: Just what *do* babies dream of? Angels? Spiritual friends? Leapfrogging over clouds?

► *I dreamed of my current house and yard. In the garden area, I was planting a redbud tree. I'm not a gardener, so what did the redbud mean and why was I planting it?*

A redbud tree symbolizes personality fragility and/or self-esteem.

You don't have to be a gardener to care about and want to nurture your self-esteem. This dreamscape fragment indicates that you have a sensitive personality that is highly responsive to any life element that could negatively affect your self-esteem. You're planting the redbud for the purpose of nurturing and strengthening your self-confidence and sense of individual beingness.

Having high self-esteem is not the same as being self-absorbed. Everyone should have a solid sense of self-esteem, for this is a natural attachment to one's inherent character and the behavioral aspects that express it. There's nothing wrong with acknowledging such personal characteristics as being a good person, a caring individual, and a trustworthy and faithful mate to your significant other. Acknowledging these characteristics isn't self-aggrandizement or ego stroking but rather giving your character an honest look and recognizing the reality of your behavior and beingness.

We all need to make a routine character self-examination to keep our behavior and motives in check. Honesty—complete honesty—is paramount when analyzing yourself. To make a list of your pros and cons—that is, of your positive and negative aspects—is the only way to effectively get a broad-scope perspective. To list your positive behavioral and character aspects is not being egotistical; it's being realistic.

So this dreamscape fragment of the redbud represents an inner desire to be a good person so that your self-esteem level will remain well within acceptable range on the basis of your own criteria (not those of others). The redbud's being planted indicates a strong desire to continue maintaining that high level of character.

▸ *I can never recall my dreams. Does that mean I don't dream?*

Dreaming is as important as sleep. You don't need me to explain what happens to people's reasoning when they don't get enough sleep. The same thing happens with dream deprivation.

Contrary to popular belief, you don't need to remember your dreams. The mind does all the work for you while you're asleep. It processes the day's activities and experiences by sorting them out and categorizing them. The mind, during sleep, clears away the day's mess of mental impressions and files them in your memory banks. When you awake, you're clear to amass another day's accumulation of impressions. All this is done without your conscious input.

Usually if your dream time has a critical message to convey, you'll recall aspects of it or retain some residual sense of its intent. Otherwise, why worry?

▸ *My dream aquarium, whenever it appears, is always so cloudy I can barely see the many fish inside. Why is this?*

These particular dreamscape elements are attempting to show you that you're dirtying your spiritual integrity by using it as a means to stroke your ego.

An aquarium symbolizes spiritual arrogance, and a *cloudy* aquarium adds another dimension to this by indicating that your spirituality is becoming sullied in some manner because of that arrogance. Arrogance in itself is bad enough, but to exhibit arrogance associated with one's spirituality or spiritual beliefs is an abomination. No one on this planet has the right to be spiritually arrogant. Besides, it's a clear contradiction in terms. The plain fact of the matter is that a spiritually arrogant individual is not a spiritual individual at all.

The fact that your dreamscape aquarium is cloudy denotes that the spiritual beliefs you're holding so dear and sacrosanct are becoming contaminated by your arrogance about them. Your high moral attitude is suffocating them.

▸ *I dreamed that my young son should be an archaeologist. Should I guide him in that direction?*

No, Mom; let your son's own inner promptings be his guide to a career.

A dream of someone's occupation, regardless if that person is a child or some other individual in your life, is not a definitive sign that the career is meant to be the person's destiny. Most times when an occupation is presented as associated with a specific individual, the occupation carries an indirect symbology rather than being represented as a solid aspect of itself. This is the same as following the spirit of the law rather than the letter of the law.

The dream symbology for an archaeologist is one who misuses the past against others. This message most likely came to you as an insight into your son's hidden character traits—that of vindictiveness or arrogance. This may be evinced in a multitude of ways, such as showing selfish attitudes, behaving in ways that make you think he doesn't care about others or their feelings— insensitivity, spontaneous cracks that indicate his real world view, or denigrating others in a somewhat shocking manner. Kids send out all kinds of clues to their developing character. All you have to do is . . . listen.

▶ *What does it mean to dream that you were on the* Titanic*? This has been a recurring dream of mine long before the movie came out.*

Unless someone you know was truly on that ship and survived, I believe that the *Titanic* carries a symbology that would apply to most of the general public—spiritual downfall. The *Titanic* represents spiritual arrogance because that attitude about one's spiritual beliefs or behavior will cause a downfall (or sinking) every time. Don't forget how the people of the time touted the huge vessel: "The ship that even God can't sink!" And I think that says it all.

▶ *Some of my dreams contain such vivid colors that they undulate. Not only that, they are colors that I can't describe because they don't match anything I've ever seen before. What's up with this dream element?*

You're not experiencing a run-of-the-mill dream when this happens. A whole different phenomenon is occurring.

There are times during sleep when the consciousness expands. It expands out through time and space where it experiences different dimensions and vibrational frequencies of reality. It's similar to an out-of-body experience (OOBE), though I choose not to use that New Age-y term because what you experienced encompasses so many more facets of reality than the narrowly confined concept within which most folks have boxed the OOBEs.

You see, technically, both what you experienced and an OOBE manifest through the same means: the consciousness being given its head—given the freedom to explore and experience reality without intellectual reservations or physical constriction. Now, as a caution, don't equate the concept of remote viewing with these. That's something altogether different.

To simplify your experience, your consciousness explored reality with a freedom seldom evidenced in people. Your consciousness experienced the vibrational frequencies of dimensional realities other than the heavy third one our bodies are grounded to.

If you do this often enough in dreams, you'll be able to manage it also in meditation. When you do, you'll be experiencing what I've termed *the Virtual experience of Quantum Meditation.*

▸ *I dreamed that I was in the woods picking basketfuls of mushrooms, and I can't understand the symbology enough to figure out what this means. Comment?*

Mushrooms generally denote a benefit resulting from a seemingly negative factor. Note that I said *generally*; for those who eat the hallucinogenic ones, a mushroom will have an altogether different connotation. So unless you do 'shrooms, your dream was representing many elements in your life that you perceive as being negative ones when, in fact, you derive some benefit from each. The basketfuls mean that you're gathering *many* benefits. And perhaps you're not recognizing those positive aspects which come into your life. This dream fragment suggests that you should be looking at life with a somewhat altered perspective from how you've been currently viewing things—optimism instead of pessimism.

▸ *How come my dream coffee is always brewed from chicory instead of regular coffee beans?*

Because it's telling you that you're not seeing life's alternatives. This dream element is a clear indication that your perception is extremely narrow and myopic, that you're not pulling back to get a broad-scope view that shows all your options and alternatives in life. In dream symbology, chicory denotes alternatives.

▸ *How can one tell if a dream is a regular dream or an out-of-body experience?*

An OOBE, if manifested in *this* dimension, will contain logic and form. By this I mean that everything seen will be as accurately presented as it is in the awake state. Colors will be the same.

Shapes and form will remain duplicated without distortion. Everything you see in the world during the awake state will be likewise seen during an OOBE.

In the dream state, objects may be distorted and logic may be skewed, as in a refrigerator's being in a bathroom or on the house rooftop, or the Pacific Ocean appearing in the middle of New Mexico, and so on. In the dream state, action can also be illogical, like slow-motion running or trying to swim through a peat bog. The singular reason for these irrational scenarios is to present symbology. When the ocean is located in a desert, that denotes a specific message for the dreamer. When a bathtub is in a living room, that signifies another meaning. So the fact that dreams can seem so incredibly silly is because that very silliness, distortion, or lack of reason is the very venue for defining a specific message.

The rule of thumb for the distinction between an OOBE and a regular dream is whether it contains elements of distortion or lacks rational aspects.

► *I dreamed that I became a channeler. Is that dream meant to show me my purpose in life?*

Nope. Nada. What it means is that the dream element is attempting to point out to you that you're listening to advice from everyone but the one person—you—who holds the key to your best advice—that which lies within yourself.

Rarely is an individual's life purpose or personal life career revealed in dreams, because these are life elements born of inherent talents, abilities, and inclinations. In other words, they blossom from the nourished roots that are already within the individual.

In dream symbology, a channeler means one who listens for the guidance of others instead of self. This dream message is attempting to make you aware of your tendency to hand over to others the power to manipulate and direct your life. It's trying to tell you to shoulder your own responsibility for your life and make your own decisions and choices.

Sometimes a channeler appearing as a dreamscape fragment may indicate an individual who is in denial or shuns personal responsibility for actions taken and words voiced. In this manner, the channeler can say with confidence, "I didn't say that; the *entity* did." This is clear indication of a purposeful shift of responsibility, the use of a fabricated scapegoat onto which one can shove one's actions and words.

▶ *I dreamed that you were the returned feminine aspect of the Trinity—the Goddess Sophia. Why would I dream that if it weren't true?*

First, I have to address the premise of your dream. No, I am not this incarnated divine feminine aspect.

Why would you dream that if it weren't true? Probably because you very much desire to identify a currently living woman as this incarnated divine being. Strong desire can initiate all kinds of dreams. One's fantasies (sexual or otherwise) also become creative elements of the dreamscape scenarios. Just because you dream something does not necessarily mean it is a fact, prophecy, or esoteric revelation. Sometimes it's merely a form of wishful thinking or it's generated from a state of frustration caused by a deep-seated need to know something.

It should be fairly evident that not all dreams are true. They can present all sorts of combinations of life elements in patterns directly associated with one's personal and psychological perspective. You want very much to make an identification of this divine feminine aspect because you've read that I've stated She and Her counterpart, the Shekinah (Sophia's Holy Spirit aspect), have incarnated for the purpose of encouraging and strengthening feminine spirituality. And because, over the last few years, my writings have brought forth this ideology of feminine spirituality and have revealed the two feminine aspects of the Trinity, you jumped to an assumed conclusion. This is not wise. No matter who you'd like to connect with what, never make assumptions of relatedness in life.

On the knotty pine wall of my cabin's small office area hangs a framed canvas painting of the Greek poetess Sappho. There appears to be an inexplicable rapport or some form of connectedness we share. Frequently, an aspect of her spirit essence plays the muse and my consciousness is sensitive to her whispered words. Does this phenomenon mean I am Sappho incarnate? Of course not. Yet people have a tendency to take a singular aspect of a concept and push and stretch it until it becomes a full-blown falsehood with no shred of truth remaining to it.

The idea that the Divine Mother Sophia and her spirit aspect, Shekinah, are manifest in the physical world doesn't also mean that They will ever make their identity known and become public figures. Remember, I said that this Second Coming is entirely different this time around, for the return of the Omega will be nothing like the time of the Alpha's appearance two thousand years ago. Prophecy is coming full circle. Now, instead of the emphasis being on a physical being walking among us, it will be on the message. When this is fully understood, there will be no reason to look about in search of the divine feminine aspects among us. Look not with your eyes but with your heart. Discovery comes not from seeing Her person, but from the feel of thunder in your heart when hearing Her message.

I am an author. I write of the spiritual philosophy that it is my destiny to convey. Just because I write of these things does not mean that I am anyone other than a normal human being attending to her purpose. Please don't make more of me than there is to make.

You dreamed this dream because in the awake state, you consciously entertained the idea. During sleep, that idea transferred as a visual. That visual reflected your own theory, nothing more. And because this phenomenon happens so frequently, people need to recognize it for what it is—merely a mirror image of a conscious awake-state thought.

There are folks going around claiming to be the incarnation of Jesus or to be channeling Jesus. There are folks making all sorts of claims. I have never made any such claims or implications and I never will. I would greatly appreciate it if others didn't either. Assumptions are dangerous things.

▸ *How does one differentiate between a truly prophetic dream and one that is based on only the dreamer's fears or hopes?*

The prophetic one will most likely not be precisely aligned with the dreamer's personal perspective or ideology (fears or hopes).

Prophetic concepts that present in the dream state contain various unexpected elements the dreamer hadn't consciously imagined or factored into the specific scenario. This is because a prophetic dream vision will represent reality—a reality replete with all associated aspects that the individual had no way of knowing existed.

A prophetic dream will be more of a revelation than a confirmation.

▸ *It seems so silly that we have to have dream symbology so we can correctly figure out what dreams mean. Why don't their messages just come through loud and clear?*

Because the visuals are recalled far more easily than are worded messages.

You don't need me to tell you that a simple sentence repeatedly passed on to one individual from another ends up nothing like it began. And when you read billboard signs as you're driving down the highway, how often can you recall them verbatim? This last fact in particular exemplifies why worded messages in dreams are pointless. Visuals create a scene, movement, and interaction. The dreamer can recall a story line far better than any exact written or spoken messages given.

Dream symbology is the most effective way to gain understanding from one's dreams. These are not difficult to interpret once the basics are understood. Water symbolizes a spiritual slant to the dream message—the spiritual facet of one's life. Silver refers to spiritual elements, whereas gold indicates the material or physical elements. Marine life relates to spiritual aspects of the self. Birds (air) are associated with thoughts/character/psychological elements of the self. There are strong basic associations on which the additional dream fragments build on as a means of expanding and individualizing the message for the dreamer. People have problems interpreting their dreams when they habitually pick up a dream interpretation reference book and search out only certain recalled elements of the dream instead of spending time actually going through a dream symbology book and studying it. By doing this, people grasp only the basics of how the interpretive meanings relate through logic and reason. To actually read through a dream symbology book is an invaluable intellectual exercise because it results in a deeper understanding of how dream fragments and their representational symbols relate to one another. When people understand the underlying theory, they'll discover that they aren't reaching for the symbology book as frequently as before.

► *Why is it so difficult to pinpoint time frames in dreams?*

It can be difficult to pinpoint time frames in dreams if all the dreamscape's elements aren't noticed or recalled. The key to making some ballpark estimate of a dream's time frame is in the recall of surrounding aspects of a scene, such as season, night or day, and type of clothing people wore. Also, a clock can represent time not only in hours but also as far as time of year. The clock has twelve hours, just as the year has twelve months. A simple clock can designate a particular *month* of year rather than simply pointing to a specific hour. Other dream indicators associated with time are the presence of calendars, open appointment books, a posted train or plane schedule, the performance of such routine activities as having lunch or going home after work, the inclusion of a specific holiday in the dream, and so forth. All of these factors are time references for the dreamer to take note of. Every fragment in a dream carries additional meaning that contributes to the whole.

▶ *What the heck does a spoonbill bird mean in a dream?*

A spoonbill denotes an opportunistic personality. Depending on the surrounding elements of the dream, this factor could be meant to indicate either a positive or a negative message. The characteristic of being opportunistic can be advantageous or detrimental, depending on the individual's intent and the application of it.

▶ *Can you tell me what a chrysoberyl gem means in a dream?*

The chrysoberyl denotes intellectual clarity. The gem's vibrational frequency energy aids in bringing clarity to an individual's comprehension and helps define the finer elements of a puzzlement or situation in which a decision must be made.

▶ *I dreamed that my dog (a mutt) turned into a Lhasa Apso. What did that mean?*

The dream symbology for the Lhasa Apso is supportive force. Now don't forget that a dog connotes a friend. This dream appears to be trying to make you see that one of your friends is effectively providing you with more support than you realize or that this friend has the capability of supporting you more than you're giving her credit for. Since you described your dreamscape dog as a mutt, then that quality alone reveals your nonchalance toward this friend and that you perhaps don't perceive her as being any type of effective force in your life. Better take a closer look at this individual and readjust your perspective of her because this dream element seems to be saying that you're either not cognizant and appreciative of her valuable supportive behavior or that you're not seeing her as a potentially strong ally.

► *In all my dreams, one or more objects are upside down. Why are these appearing like this?*

In dream symbology, upside-down presentations of position connote an inverted or skewed perception of the dreamer. The dreamer's world view is not aligned with reality and there is something amiss about how things are seen.

Sometimes the dreamer can identify what this misperception is associated with by recalling what types of objects make this upside-down appearance. For instance, if one's dog is always lying on its back in a seemingly inverted position, this will denote a misperception of the dreamer's friendships or relations with others. If, on the other hand, the range of inverted objects seems to be myriad and random, then the intent of this dream element would be indicating a *generalized* misperception of life. This would point to an attitude which is serving to alter one's world view. The dreamer is skewing perception by viewing life through a lens distorted by some type of psychological filter.

This situation calls for self-analysis. The dreamer needs to examine attitudes and emotional responses to experiential situations, relationships, and social elements.

► *Frequently I dream of falling asleep beneath a ginkgo tree. Why a ginkgo tree?*

This one's easy—you know what this means. You're going to feel a little silly for not making the obvious connection. Sometimes the dream symbology is so obvious it's overlooked.

If you watch any evening television newscasts or prime-time commercials, you will have been exposed to the growing popularity of the memory-enhancing herb known as *Ginkgo biloba.* The ginkgo dream element will most always be associated with memory (one's experiential past).

The dreamscape aspect of falling asleep beneath a gingko tree denotes a need to give conscious attention to something in your past that requires further consideration, development, or resolution.

▶ *For months on end, some odd little creature has been appearing in my dreams. I'm standing with a group of people and finally, last night, one of them spoke. "Look at the sugar glider!" she said, while pointing up at the creature in the tree. What the heck does that little fellow represent?*

Resourcefulness. A sugar glider corresponds to resourcefulness.

This "little fellow" is attempting to convey to you that you're not taking advantage of all your opportunities in life. These opportunities can be life options, unacknowledged skills, venues for knowledge expansion, creativity, relationship development, and so on. This little fellow knows something about your potential that you have been overlooking or choosing to deny.

Now that you know what this sugar glider is attempting to tell you, you need to pick up the ball and run with it. Perhaps you instinctively know what quality of resourcefulness this dreamscape aspect is pointing to. Or maybe you're going to have to sit down and give this come contemplative thought. Either way, there are one or more elements in your life that are just sitting there waiting for you to recognize their potential.

▶ *I dreamed that I opened my back door and a proboscis monkey ran in. It jumped up on my bathroom sink, stared into the vanity mirror, looked at me, and gave a ridiculously huge smile. Go figure.*

Okay, let's figure this one out. Actually, it's a fairly easy one. Let's say you didn't know a thing about dream interpretation.

Even so, you can still do the symbology work on this. First of all, what does a monkey do? It mimics. The dreamscape monkey ran into your bathroom and looked at herself in the vanity mirror. And according to the content of your letter, you also spend a lot of time in front of that mirror—disliking what you see there.

The proboscis was given that specific name because of its pronounced nose. But you see, that monkey doesn't give a rat's hat about how it looks because she knows that her appearance has nothing to do with her character or inner self. In dream symbology, the proboscis monkey represents self-assuredness. That little monkey snuck in your back door and ran to look at herself in your mirror to emulate your own actions generated from a poor self-image. But then what did it do? It turned to you and gave a huge smile. In essence, the intent of the dream sequence conveyed this monkey's unspoken message to you: *Yes, I look in the mirror and see how I look. My appearance is not what I would've chosen for myself if I were given the choice, but my physical features are not the who of me. The who of me is kind and fun loving. It's open and expressive. No physical feature can change the inherent who of me, and that's the big secret to the wisdom of knowing what defines one's who! Smile! Get a clue— show your who!*

The monkey looked in the mirror and, though she saw her great nose, turned to you and gave a huge grin. Here was a monkey tale to listen to—to take to heart and learn from.

► *What does it mean when one dreams of lighting candles and then the flame always dies out before the wax even begins melting?*

A candle symbolizes that which can ignite our spiritual talents or abilities. The act of lighting a candle exemplifies a desire to actuate some type of personal goodness toward society or another individual. But your flames always die out. How come?

This dreamscape fragment is attempting to make you aware

that although you have the desire to help others (you make an initial overture), you don't follow through. This self-restraint can be caused by any number of psychological aspects. Perhaps you're shy of commitment or you are reluctant to get too involved. Though you want to help, you hold back and end up pulling away.

What you need to do is think about why you have this tendency. If it appeared in a dreamscape, then it was generated from some facet of reality facilitated by your own subconscious functioning. Think about past experiences when you've offered others some type of assistance and then came up with an excuse to cover your deeper reason for backing out. Try to recall the thoughts that spurred your move to retreat. Also try to recall those times when you merely thought about helping another and then never got as far as actually making an expressed offer. What was it that flashed as a caution or warning sign in your mind? Was it fear of involvement? Were you concerned you'd be interfering and then perhaps be perceived as a meddler or interloper into the affairs of another? Are you afraid of ridicule?

Goodness and the expression of it through actions is, of course, good. But *unconditional* goodness is splendorous. We become inspired to help others and we carry through with that inner feeling because the eventual act becomes the fulfillment of the intent. Intent is wonderful, but it cannot blossom unless it is acted on. This dream fragment is reflecting your good intentions (lighting the candle) and lack of follow-through (flame immediately dying out).

You're not alone in this tendency. We all do it to some degree when, during the day, we think about someone and have the thought, "Gosh, I should give her a call just to say hi and let her know I've been thinking about her," and then we continue with what we're doing and, before we realize it, the idea waned away without ever being acted on. The thought lit the candle; the inactivation snuffed it out. Yet because this message is repeatedly being played out in your dream scenes, you most likely have more dynamic psychological elements at work that cause this behavior to be so prevalent that it's reached a problematical point.

▶ *I know that different species of snakes carry different symbologies, but I don't know what a viper means. It wasn't in your dream book.*

Viper is among the hundreds of additional entry words I've been amassing for a future revised and expanded edition. The dream symbology for a viper is vindictiveness. Since you didn't detail your dream, I wasn't provided with the surrounding dream fragment details to accurately interpret the meaning of your viper's presentation. There's no way a correct interpretation can be done unless all associated fragments are known.

Recall the dream. How was this viper related to its surrounding elements? Was it related to another individual, to an object, to yourself? Was the viper curled up on a book that displayed a title? Sometimes this is a major clue in that it will directly point to a specific type of philosophy or subject matter related to this vindictiveness. Did the multiple facets of the dream indicate the vindictiveness was associated with your own behavior? Or another's? Was it in a particular type of building, like a financial institution, a church, or a school? These dream facets help to connect the vindictiveness of the viper to a specific area of society or your personal life. Was the dream viper healthy or did it appear sickly or dying? Was it watchful or ready to strike? All of these questions, when answered, help clarify the symbol's intent.

▶ *I dreamed that I was in a beautiful meadow but was caught in the middle of a patch of purple thistles that were chest high. The valley was so majestically beautiful, yet I couldn't move without getting scratched up. Why the polarity?*

This dream just *seems* to have polarity. It's not at all as incongruous as it appears.

Let's look at the dreamscape elements. The beautiful valley

meadow denotes inner tranquillity. The thistles designate life's lessons. And the color purple relates to one's attained spiritual wisdom and enlightenment.

So then, in this dreamscape, you're in a state of inner tranquillity and are presented with the appearance of spiritual lessons that you interpret as being harmful to your attained state of wisdom or enlightenment. The key to this message is how you *perceive* these thistles. You're interpreting them as being a harmful element that disrupts the status quo of your enlightenment. But, in reality, that's not a correct interpretation at all because those thistles are merely additional aspects that can lead to greater intellectual comprehension and the attainment of even deeper wisdom.

The combination of these dream elements indicate a stern caution for the dreamer to stop being complacent with his current level of spirituality. It reminds him that true spirituality is always raising its quality through continual growth and experience. That to pass through the spiritual thistles is to become wiser for having gained greater experience through the interaction with them.

Spirituality is an ever-developing state of being. It is not a constant. It is not satisfied with mediocrity, nor does it bow to human manipulation or determination. It exists in an ever-changing state, always striving to pull the individual into greater depths of comprehension and higher levels of perceptual wisdom and resultant behavior. Our spiritual beingness is in a constant state of expansion. It fears not the thistles nor the thorns it uses for growth.

▶ *I dreamed my boyfriend gave me an engagement ring with an odd stone in it. He said, "It's morganite." I haven't a clue what this is supposed to mean for me.*

Morganite is the dream symbol for indecision. I don't think this stone in an engagement ring is an encouraging sign. This would indicate that one of you is not altogether sold on the solidness of the relationship and that the strength of commitment may not be there. Just on the basis of these few elements, I'd say that since it was he who chose the type of stone for the ring, he is the one who is sitting on the fence over the idea of marriage. Unless in your heart you feel that you're the one this message is referring to, I suggest you have some long heart-to-heart talks with your intended. The setting for morganite in this dream was very revealing. It shouldn't be ignored and blown off as some type of fear-based dream.

► *I dreamed that my girlfriend had a pet bird. In an elaborately crafted Victorian-style birdcage was a beautiful whippoorwill. I don't know what this means.*

I could give you my immediate intuitive response that directly relates to the secrecy of the relationship with your significant other, but I think you need a more solid explanation.

A birdcage represents restrained thoughts—fear of extending one's thought process into expression. Victorian style of anything means old-fashioned ideologies or unyielding morality. And the whippoorwill denotes melancholia.

So then, let's apply these symbols to the real-life situation of your relationship. Your girlfriend is steeped in hidden melancholy over the fact that society's moral prejudice and your consideration (or fear?) of it is keeping your relationship caged—not free to fly out into the world. You, as an intelligent woman, need to address this with her instead of maintaining a state of denial regarding your friend's emotional distress. She is courageously trying to hold the relationship to your preferred public status while, inside, she can't understand why the opinions of others are even a factor.

Something tells me that this situation is not a revelation to you. There had to have been some outward behavior signs related to her unsettled state of mind regarding this relationship's situation. I don't believe you've been insensitive and not noticed. But I do think that perhaps you've been in denial of what you've observed.

I believe that if you truly love someone, there is no way you can voluntarily choose to be blind to heartache, hidden or otherwise. Clearly, she loves you enough to try to keep her feelings buried for the sake of your desire to present a certain public image. The very least you can do in return is to be sensitive enough to acknowledge her efforts on your behalf. And perhaps you can even love her enough to open that cage door to . . . at least let it fly free around the house. Compromise. Begin with compromise.

▶ *I dreamed that my lawn was covered in bright yellow flowers—all dandelions. I'm thinking this means that I have a lot of weeds in my life. Confirm?*

Confirmation denied.

Dandelions, when presented in dreams, mean hidden qualities. These qualities are those that are not immediately self-evident—they are not inherently identifiable as positive qualities when initially seen. The problem with confirming your interpretation is that it's in error due to your own misperception of what a dandelion is.

Generally, society perceives the dandelion as a simple weed. Just a weed. Yet it is a wonderful addition to salads and an excellent source of vitamin C. So then, the issue of correct interpretation is not with the dandelion itself, but with your idea of its value. You thought it was just a troublesome lawn weed and therefore that's how you made your interpretation. But the dandelion is far more than a common weed. It has hidden value and great worth. This then is the right symbology to apply.

The dream's meaning? You're seeing life yet not comprehending it in terms of its elemental value. The dream is attempting to point out that you're being judgmental and not experiencing or using perceptual clarity. This can be a choice, you know. Many people feel more comfortable when they align themselves with popular opinion because, that way, they preserve their "majority" status.

▶ *Isis appeared in my dream and told me she'd been a real person. She's a fantasy character of Egyptian mythology, so what did she really mean?*

She "really" meant to say that she was . . . *real.* How much clearer could she make it? This type of dream presentation comes to dispel conceptual falsehoods accepted by society and generally perpetuated as myths, folk stories, and old women's tales. Society would do well to start giving more attention to those old women's tales, for the time has arrived for the old men's tales to fall by the wayside.

▶ *Why don't you have an interactive web page to help your readers interpret their dreams? I think that'd be a great idea.*

I don't. The reason I wrote the dream symbology book and have included this explanatory section in *Beyond Earthway* was to help my readers better interpret their dreams. There's a reason why I present only the words of my message to the public instead of including my physical persona as an attachment to the works. I've stated this reason often enough. I'm maintaining my original position. I'm here to write what I came to write. I'm not here to put a face and voice (human personality) to the message. History has proven over and over again that that does not work because people tend to place emphasis on the personality instead of solely to the words given. History speaks for itself.

▶ *What does it mean when objects appear in dreams without their normal color? For example, a purple orange or a blue apple.*

This is usually a symbolic representation of the dreamer's perception being *colored* during the awake-state consciousness. This dreamscape facet may also have a specific intent for the dreamer if the off-color object is meant to be an integral element of a particular message, such as a friend's face or overall skin being blue which could denote a heart/circulatory problem or melancholia/depression.

▶ *I had a dream in which my girlfriend appeared but I awoke with the sense that it wasn't really her. Do strangers manifest behind the face of a friend in dreams?*

Not usually. When the dreamer awakes with the sense that the individuals in his or her dream were not a true presentation of the people they know in the awake state, this most often implies that some hidden aspect of the individual's personality or character is being revealed.

In life, we think we know people. We think we know our friends, relatives, and coworkers fairly well, but do we? Do we really know a lover? Though we would hope we know our significant others well, everyone's psychological makeup is an intricately complex system of attitudes, philosophies, sensitivities, and perspectives. What adds to the equation is the fact that these psychological factors are in a continual state of flux—change—as they develop, shift emphasis, and alter in myriad ways through experiential episodes, intellectual analysis, expanded learning, and so on. One's opinion on a subject matter can alter without being publicly announced. In other words, people's attitudes, emotional sensitivities, and perception change day by day as they journey through life. When familiar people appear in dreams and the dreamer awakes with a sense that some foreign individual was using the physical appearance of the presented person as a mask, then this usually reveals some type of hidden or subconscious aspect of the known person—an aspect the dreamer was unaware of.

▶ *I'm a minister who dreamed I was a psychic. How can that be when I don't believe in that nonsense?*

My suggestion to you would be to give yourself the benefit of honesty by facing your beliefs openly instead of masking them with superficial "religiously correct" opinions on the consciousness's reality, because this dream is telling you that you do believe in the mind's capabilities, which are popularly termed psychic.

Your reticence to voice such a belief comes from a serious lack of understanding regarding the inherent workings of the mind and consciousness. To name but a few of these workings, we'd have to list insight, intuitiveness, inspiration, and the moments of illumined epiphanies that bring clarity to concepts formerly perceived as an impossible complexity or an enigma.

You are in denial of the mind's full reality because of a problem you have with the word *psychic.* You do believe in inspiration, intuitiveness, insight, and epiphanies, but you just refuse to associate them with a term you misperceive as being cult related and, perhaps, of the Devil.

As we begin the twenty-first century, we voluntarily limit our intellectual perception to medieval thought patterns woven of ignorance, prejudice, self-righteousness, and the fanaticism of religious superiority. The intellectual ignorance that brought the historical blight of witch-hunts and the Inquisition are still prevalent today. And until society grows into a clear understanding of the natural physics of consciousness and the simple reality of the mind's potential, dreamers such as this minister will continue to publicly deny belief in reality and perpetrate that belief while secretly acknowledging their own experiential evidence of such reality.

► *In my dream, my neighbor brought me a hand-picked bouquet of milkweed. Your dream book referred to silkweed for the milkweed, yet I still don't get what it means.*

Milkweed denotes emotional sustenance.

This dreamscape fragment is attempting to reveal something that's taking place in your life that you're completely oblivious to—that of your neighbor's empathy for your current problems and her attempts to offer support and comfort. This would imply that perhaps she could be a highly effective influence in your life. She's not being intrusive or a busybody; she's merely making simple unconditional offerings for you to accept with grace.

The silkweed (or milkweed) symbolizes a beneficial element in one's life. To dream that someone brought you these, especially a bouquet of hand-picked ones, is especially significant because it clearly identifies the giver as an individual who is ready and able to offer effective support.

▸ *Aren't dreams a reflection of one's subconscious? Don't they often represent what people consciously hide and deny when they're awake?*

Sure, honesty, by way of an undistorted mirror, is one of the main purposes of dreaming and the presentation of its meaningful symbology. The subconscious forces all the dreamer's daily denials and voluntarily secreted elements to the fore for the dreamer to face. The subconscious doesn't want all that garbage, so it sorts it and sends it back to the dreamer to handle. And this is precisely why dream interpretation is so invaluable and correct symbology is paramount.

▸ *What does it mean to dream that one is speaking without sound or words coming out?*

It means that you're not communicating clearly to others or that you intentionally miscommunicate.

▸ *I dreamed that my sister's face morphed into that of a Manx cat. I don't know what this was supposed to mean.*

In dream symbology, a Manx cat designates unpretentiousness. There was a reason why your sister's face turned into the face of this breed of cat. I suspect the reason came from some misconception you had about your sister. Perhaps you thought she was acting arrogantly or held some type of pretentious attitude. This dreamscape fragment is letting you know that you were mistaken, that your sister is indeed a genuinely unpretentious individual.

Sometimes we think we pick up on another's attitude or get an impression that someone is displaying an attitude that we don't particularly like when in reality our perception is based on only a false assumption made through misinterpretation of that individual's behavior.

► *Can our dead friends and relatives appear to us in dreams?*

Anyone you've ever known can appear in your dreamscape because the awake-state mind has made a visual recording of that individual upon the sensitive recording fabric of the consciousness. Everything you've ever seen, even subliminally, can present itself in a dream. Everything and everyone. This is why I included such entry words in my dream symbology book as *Mickey Mouse, tooth fairy, Isis,* and *Magi.* Anything and anyone known can appear in a dreamscape. Therefore, everything and everyone known would be in the most broad scope and comprehensive dream symbology book.

Now, this correspondent particularly singled out dead friends and relatives. But we don't want to confine this concept to just friends and relatives, either. For the sake of this response, I'm including *all* dead people because a dreamer could have *other* expired individuals enter his or her dreamscape, such as murder victims seen on the evening newscast or a historical figure or even someone like Lady Diana. Thus, the question becomes: Can dead people appear in one's dream?

This answer is going to be important to fully understand. Yes, dead people can appear in one's dream by way of the dreamer's subconscious using that dead person's persona as a means of conveying a specific message. In other words, the dreamer's subconscious only *borrows* the dead individual's *image* to reveal a message. The dead person's living spirit does *not* come to *appear* to the dreamer. The distinction between the two is critical for accurate comprehension of this concept.

► *Are alien abduction dreams evidence of a true event in one's life?*

We need to tread carefully here.

Technically, they can be, because the subconscious holds the recorded history of one's life, and events that the awake-state consciousness blocks, either voluntarily or otherwise, can come to the fore through dreaming. This is not to say that the dreamed abduction actually happened the same night it was dreamed; rather, it might be a subconscious replay of an event which took place in the dreamer's past.

It's important to understand that not all abduction dreams equate to this replay of a real event. Society is inundated by a wide range of alien ideologies, most carrying negative connotations because of people's attraction to violence and the idea that earthlings will fight off and triumph over invading aliens. The mentality of society regarding this subject has reverted back to that of little boys' playacting where they slice their ray gun through the air, hopping from bed to toy chest as they vanquish the invading monsters. From comic books to video games to the film industry, this negative perception of aliens has fostered a fear of the appearance of other planetary intelligences among us. This society has a juvenile and egocentric world view of reality in which violence and might are generally perceived as more powerful attributes than intelligence and wisdom. Though technologically we continue to advance, intellectually we continue to backpedal.

Society inculcates this negative attitude in people, subliminally exposing them to subconscious antialien propaganda. The films *Starman, E.T.—The Extraterrestrial,* and *Close Encounters of the Third Kind* were intelligent portrayals of the concept of other planetary intelligent beings, but for the most part, society has decided that it likes the idea of an alien race it has to conquer.

I'm a little more than confounded over the fact that there is such a great preponderance of abduction stories that far outweigh tales of one-on-one intellectual communication with another intelligence. I don't hear of many people veering away from the popular abduction scenario when recalling and relating their experience. This alone contributes to the possibility (or probability) that many of these dreams are merely stored subconscious impressions gleaned from the media and literature. Young children have been known to have nightmares of the Wicked Witch of the West coming to get them after they've seen the *Wizard of Oz* for the first time. This is not because the witch actually came to them during the night but because their minds were subconsciously imprinted with the visuals and sounds of the film they watched. These imprints become a permanent element of the child's memory base and can come to the fore during sleep. Adults are not immune to the reality of the functioning mind. Though they may not have nightmares of the green-faced witch, they allow other societal impressions to instill fear within them.

We have to be careful what we perceive as reality. We have to be critically discerning and honestly analytical when identifying facts. Most often, a dream of being abducted by aliens is merely a visual reenactment of the subconscious impressions the conscious mind was exposed to during the awake state.

► *I dreamed that I was loading up my belongings into a moving van. Is that a premonition that I'm going to be relocating or is it a message telling me that I should move?*

Not necessarily; in fact, it's not even probable.

You're forgetting that dreamscape fragments come as *symbols*. Though they are sometimes accurate presentations in themselves, most often they're not what they seem because they represent a secondary meaning.

Loading up a moving van will most often mean that you need to move on an issue over which you've either been in denial or procrastinating. This dream action of moving is attempting to give you the visual of getting off your butt and *doing* something . . . *moving* on something. It's telling you that it's time to make that move—not a relocation but a move of some kind.

▸ *Why can't I dream of winning lottery numbers?*

You can't do that because it'd be no different than stealing. If insider trading is illegal, so should be envisioning or dreaming the winning lottery numbers, dreaming of the winning horse in the Kentucky Derby, or dreaming of the final score of a Super Bowl. See? All of these are cheating. Besides, why in heaven's name would you want to come by your money through a less than honest means? Using premonitions and such in an unspiritual manner is a terrible affront to the Divine. It would be better to use such an ability (if you had it) to locate missing children, a serial killer, or some other type of unknown for the purpose of benefiting others . . . instead of self. Spiritual talents and abilities should be used selflessly.

▸ *There is a middle-aged single man living in a rental house down the way from me. His behavior has never given anyone any indication that he's anything but a nice guy, but I dreamed that I got chills every time I saw him. I don't want to make a mountain out of a molehill, so could you help me with a correct interpretation of this?*

Many times, during our awake state, our ego will negate intuitive thoughts. Let me clarify this with your own example.

You have no reason to think ill of this neighbor, yet there has been something in the back of your consciousness that isn't sitting right about him. Consciously, when this something tries to come to the fore, you say to yourself, *Oh c'mon—you're being ridiculous!* So then to avoid letting your ego be injured by ridiculous thoughts about this individual or to save yourself some embarrassment and feelings of paranoia, you brush this thought away with denial. Now you go to sleep and have a dream that this neighbor is causing you the heebie-jeebies. The dream has come to reinforce the fact that you're letting your ego block your intuitive insight.

We have intuitive insight as a natural attribute of our humanness. This inherent attribute is not some hoodoo psychic New

Age thing. It's part of our beingness. It's real. It's there for a reason.

I would advise you to pay heed to your inner sensitivity to this neighbor. This response doesn't need to be an offensive one but should rather be a defensive position; be aware and maintain a wise distance without drawing unwanted attention to yourself.

▸ *Can genders be transposed in dreams? A male coworker of mine appeared as a woman in my dream and I'm not sure how to interpret it. I don't want to jump to the assumption that it means he's gay.*

Good for you. Most folks would make the leap to that conclusion without giving any thought to other options.

Usually a gender transference connotes the yin–yang energy within an individual. We all possess these dual vibrational frequencies and they need to be acknowledged for them to have a chance to be brought into balance.

This dreamscape element is conveying the message that your male coworker, though male, possesses a fine balance of the yin (female) energy. This means that his personality and inherent nature is not geared to the macho perspective his fellow male coworkers share. This individual has a good balance of social and emotional sensitivity. This dreamscape fragment is pointing not to his sexual *inclination* but rather to his perspective of sexual *equality*.

Thanks for giving this guy the benefit of your wisdom by reining in a knee-jerk judgment based on ignorance. Dreams are rarely what they initially seem to be.

▸ *After I read that you live with a woman friend, I dreamed that you were a lesbian. I'd hate to think that that's true, so I won't believe that's the dream's intent. So what did it mean? Am I in denial or are you?*

Good grief. When it comes to this subject matter, the public is beginning to treat me the same way it treats Jodie Foster.

Neither of us is in denial about anything but I would ask you *why* you'd "hate to think that that's true." Clearly you need to analyze your perspective on the issue and come into some sort of spiritual alignment with it. The fact that you'd hate to think that of me evidences a negative perspective toward those who are not heterosexual. I purposely didn't single out the specific sexual inclination of homosexuality because there are other sexual inclinations besides that one and heterosexuality. Some folks have a natural tendency to be asexual, whereby they have no inclination whatever for participating in sexual activity with either gender because they don't appear to have any sort of libido—and that's just fine with them. These folks lead a life without sexual activity and never give it a thought. Some people are bisexual and they can have a meaningful sexual relationship with either sex. How come the religious right doesn't seem to make those folks a target for their self-righteous persecution? And there are individuals who choose to be just plain celibate because they don't care all that much about having a sexual relationship. My question is this: Why is any of this relevant to people anyway? What is in people that makes them feel they have a right to even *know* what another's sexual inclination is? I don't see religious rallies against the celibate folks. I don't see religious groups railing against those who practice bestiality, against pedophiles, or those who practice polygamy. What's so magnetic about homosexuality that it's become such an attractive target for the self-righteous to build their soapboxes on?

Personally, I believe that whom someone loves is a private affair. To persecute someone for whom they love on the basis of some self-styled social mores is to show both intellectual and spiritual ignorance. This applies not only to the heterosexuals who persecute homosexuals but also to homosexuals themselves who hound others to come out into the open and admit to their own homosexuality. My point is that an individual's natural inherent sexual inclination is an extremely private affair. No one must declare him- or herself this or that, because who one lives with is absolutely nobody else's business. This entire issue has gotten way out of hand and become nothing more than another cause of division and discord. It incites hatred, violence, persecution, and even murder. Maybe I'm on the wrong planet, but it seems to me that love is a pure emotion that comes naturally from the heart. To make it into something to persecute and hate others over is so far beyond my understanding that I feel like I'm trying to live in a society of self-absorbed, finger-pointing, name-calling four-year olds.

Love is love, folks. Who we feel deep love for is ingrained in our DNA—a part of our inherent beingness. Those who don't comprehend this are doing nothing but letting their ignorance hang out for all to see.

Okay, on to the second part of your inquiry.

Because the only two significant men in my life (father and husband) felt the draw to greener pastures, they've completely shattered my faith in men and their ability to respect fidelity. No, I'll never have another intimate relationship with a man— because I can no longer trust them. And yes, I share a cabin with someone else—who happens to be a woman—because that woman has been the only close friend who was my sole support during the most emotionally trying upheaval of my life. She gave comfort when I was shattered with hurt and was overcome with hours and hours of crying that I couldn't stop after realizing I was being tossed aside after twenty-nine years of marriage. She gave me understanding space when the anger hit me and I ranted around the cabin to release it. She continued to cook wonderful meals and prompted me to eat when my heartache had wasted me away to ninety-eight pounds. She cared for me when this skeleton of an author contracted double pneumonia and rushed me to the medical clinic when I began bleeding from the ears. The incredible logic she used during one night-long conversation became a powerful counterforce when I'd sunk down into the dark domain where suicidal thoughts lurked. And after I regained some of the weight and perspective and was on my way to physical recovery, she stood tall beside me as I held up my chin despite the awful rumors that began to circulate about me. She was the only person there for me during that terrible time, and I never dwell on where I would've been without her supportive presence. She is now my dearest friend and companion, business assistant, philosophical sounding board, and connection to the outside world. Our relationship is a naturally sequential one that is currently connected to a long line of many, many historical pasts. We've known one another for a long, long time.

Am I a lesbian? To be honest, I don't even know what that is supposed to mean. Am I one if I don't want another relationship with a man? Does that make for a positive ID? Am I one if I live with another woman and her elderly mother? Does three women living together mean that they're all lesbians? If a single woman swears off men and doesn't date, does that mean she's a lesbian . . . or just celibate? What about all those young women living together in college dormitories? Or the guys in frat houses? Are they all gay? What about women in convents? Or what about two women friends who individually aren't drawn to married life but share one dwelling as they manage their separate careers? Or what about two women who live together and also care very much for each other as friends? Is their deep caring a definitive criterion for being labeled lesbians? What? What? I want to know. I want to know because I don't get it. I don't get what criteria the general public is using. How far does society take this? How many innocent situations engender conviction by the morally rigid? In the olden days, women always had female companions and no one ever gave a single prurient thought to the friendship. I have a companion for whom I care very much. Make what you will of it, because I just don't care about gossip born of ignorance. I think the issue is so dominant today because society, especially here in the United States, is so soft. We don't have wars on our land to deal with. We don't have mass starvation and poverty. We've got it made. Therefore, Americans have become soft and, without *real* life priorities to focus on, spend their time trawling the river bottom for the insignificant dregs to feed on. Instead of spending time on practicing unconditional goodness and love to improve the condition of society and raise society to greater heights, we sink down low to point fingers at one another and persecute others' right to express their individuality. What a mess. What a spiritual mess.

To you, my correspondent, I'll respond by saying that I can't be in denial over something I don't even understand the real meaning of when the term itself appears to both include and exclude so many situational gray areas at the same time. I used to love everyone equally, but because I've experienced the infidelity of men and constantly witnessed their overall self-absorption and belief in their own superiority being jokingly called the inherent behavior of good ol' boys, my perception of their integrity (both morally and spiritually) has plummeted. I'm not a stupid woman. I learn from experience. Two infidelities in my life is my absolute limit. Two betrayals of trust is two too many. I've since found deep inner serenity and complete contentment. I like who I am. I like being me. I love my peaceful life surrounded by the innocence of Nature away from the incredible and absurd superficiality of society.

Did I answer the question? If you don't think I answered it pointedly enough, I suggest that you reread it.

Now to the third part of your question.

What did the dream mean, then? It's highly probable that it means that you are equating lesbianism with feminism. Recently, I've observed a tendency for society to make this mistaken association. Even the concept of feminism has been bastardized because nearly every single attempt any woman makes to speak out for herself or for the unfairness of society's treatment of her gender is far too often misidentified as being an example of feministic behavior. Anyone (female or male) who champions gender equality or exposes practices of gender prejudice is not necessarily a dyed-in-the-wool feminist. Again, this is a clear but sad example of how quick society is to slap labels on others without perceiving the behavior or situation with clarity. Every action is viewed through a lens coated with a film of attitude.

You believe that the slant of my writings has turned feministic. But let's examine that premise by going back to the beginning of the beginning and taking a good look. In 1982, my path through life wound through the deep multidimensional woods of personal experience where a wise old woman of wisdom, my mentor, awaited my arrival. The superficial aspects of her persona, such as her social status, physical appearance, and ethnicity, are not revelant because they are merely surface elements unrelated to the dynamic scope of her philosophical knowledge. Though she provided me a name to call her by, it was my instinctive tendency to automatically think of her as the Crone. I can't put my finger on why this was so; I just naturally thought of her in these terms and therefore considered this title as being a highly personal— even sacred—name for her. It was like the second name some cultures have for individuals that no one speaks aloud. So then, from the outset, we have two *women* meeting for the prime purpose of one deepening the philosophical understanding of the other. Is that singular beginning element a feministic premise? Did the entire foundation of my experience start out by being built on a feministic cornerstone?

The Crone's conceptual philosophical analogies were, more often than not, associated with feminine aspects, such as *Grandmother* Earth and *Mother* Nature and *Grandmother* Spider, that latter of which she would frequently interchange with the term *Weaver Woman*. All throughout my conversations with her, she would interject cryptic inferences related to elements of feminine spirituality and the great importance of resurrecting it from the coffin in which patriarchal society had buried it. There would be a sentence here and a phrase there, accompanied by a certain knowing twinkle of her eye that pricked my awareness and warned me to give heed to recognizing the special importance of her implications. These, then, were how she expertly gave lessons beneath the lessons. She had a way of filling in the spaces between the spoken words with even more dynamically meaningful messages. So easily and smoothly did she fill the spaces between her words and her silences that these subliminal lessons would come to represent more important ideologies than those of her spoken words. It was these volume-filled silences and spaces that I kept sacred—that is to say, that I kept to myself. I did this quite naturally, as though these concepts were meant to be buried seeds to remain dormant until it was the appointed time for their nurturing elements to be applied so they could burst into full bloom. And so they remained within me while I wrote of her *spoken* words and held in trust the unspoken ones. During my time with the wise woman, I *heard* her *words* and I *felt* her *unspoken* message. One was immediate and obvious; one was more precious and awaited the passing of time. The former was corporeal, whereas the latter was purely spiritual.

As each book in my series of writings sequentially made its way into physical manifestation, each contained an increasing amount of those unspoken seeds the Crone had passed on to me. In this manner, her secondary message was being carefully and lovingly nurtured along by giving it a great deal of time to gain strength and eventually reveal itself in a beautifully unfurled philosophical blossom.

With the release of *The Visitation*, the idea of the Holy Spirit's actually being a feminine deity (the Shekinah) was introduced. In *Fireside*, the concept was expanded upon. With *Eclipse*, the blossom of feminine deities and feminine spirituality opened in full bloom. And with *Beyond Earthway*, its beauty is further displayed for the public's appreciation. But this feminine deity concept won't stop there. I've written an unpublished personal interpretation of the ancient Gnostic gospel, *The Thunder: Perfect Mind*, that was unearthed in 1945 and is believed by the scholarly translators as being written by Sophia, the Divine Mother aspect of the Trinity.

So you see, my mentor's underlying message of the importance of releasing feminine spirituality from the tight bonds in which patriarchal society has kept it for over two thousand years has been taken to heart and not fallen on deaf ears. I heard her loud and clear. Her timing was precise and serves as an undeniable mark of destiny for, as we begin the new Millennium, patriarchal domination has run its course and feminine spirituality has come full circle to return to its rightful place. As I stated in *Eclipse*, "the slow dance is over and the Sons of Darkness and the Daughters of Light are ready to rock 'n' roll!"

My efforts to return feminine spirituality to its rightful place is not a feministic act. It's an action to resurrect rightful spiritual philosophy whereby women are once again given a spirituality they can relate to rather than being oppressed beneath the heavy yoke of gender-prejudicial and -suppressive patriarchal religions. No religion or spiritual belief should demean a gender. What I'm encouraging is not a "women's religion," because it's not even a religion—it's a freeing of the Divine Mother Sophia from the shroud of masculinity that She's been hidden under for well over two thousand years and letting Her golden light reflect forth from within the hearts and spirits of all women. This isn't about religion; it's about spirituality and a woman's right to it without suppression or persecution.

Is that feministic? Because my work has reached the crossroads where it and the timing for bringing the underlying message of feminine spirituality into full bloom have intersected, does that mean I've turned into a feminist or am displaying lesbian-like philosophy? I don't see it that way, not when this was foreseen as a destined event by even Nostradamus.

I've given you my thoughts on this. Whether they've served to adequately answer your question is up to you. This is the last time I intend to respond to this type of question because to further participate in discussions revolving around prejudice and separatist labels serves only to give ugly energy to society's ongoing love of pettiness.

▶ *What makes you think your dream material more accurate than another's?*

Your wording implies that you think I claim to have interpretations superior to those of others. Watch yourself here because that's just not so.

Dream symbology has always come naturally to me. When young, I would automatically understand what a dream meant without having to closely examine each fragmented element. I'd just have an inexplicable knowing of its bottom-line message. As I grew older and was in grade school, I went through an intense period of insatiable high interest in philosophy. I read everything I could get my hands on. One of those literary volumes was the Edgar Cayce material, and I was pleasantly surprised to notice that his symbology reflected my own. Today I can listen to someone relay his or her dream to me and can respond with a sentence or even a phrase or single word that represents the dream's overall meaning—no need for a long, involved discourse describing each element and its specifically related symbology. Most times, after folks have spent a considerable amount of time relaying every minute detail of a dream, my short and sweet response will first bring a frown to their brow before their eyes light up as they say something like "Oh yeah! That fits! That's it!" It's just been a peculiar knack I've had throughout life—a knack that seems to be right on for people. I never claimed it to be anything more and I've certainly never made a comparison of it with another individual's interpretive symbology. Please, let's carefully watch the tendency to make assumptions. When you *think* someone has made a specific claim, check the facts before you believe that claim or pass an assumption on to others. This world is full of damaged reputations, careers, and relationships because of assumptions and the gossip they engendered. Though the written word is very powerful, the spoken word can be as wounding as a slicing sword or as dangerous as an airborne virus. Once damaging words are spoken, they are uncontrollable and become a deadly contaminant passing from one individual to another. Words carry energy, especially the spoken word. Depending on the words, that energy inherently carries either a positive or a negative force. Each individual is solely responsible for the type of energy he or she contributes to the world.

▶ *In my dream, I kept referring to a thesaurus. In your dream book, that type of book means that I need to choose more appropriate words when communicating with others. I thought I already did that, so what else could it mean?*

With every symbolic interpretation, there can be many associated elements. This one is no different. Though you held to the letter of interpretation, you didn't take it further to reach into the spirit of it. If one dreams of constantly referring to a thesaurus and is convinced that one carefully chooses one's words, then one needs to look beyond the specific words spoken in life to the *manner* and *tone* in which those words are conveyed. Tone of voice can convey meaning more powerfully and explicitly than the words themselves can. Tone of voice can interject personal opinion and attitude into statements, as when one's tone of voice interjects sarcasm or criticism into a statement composed of words that normally wouldn't carry such meaning.

So perhaps you are being advised to attend more carefully to your *manner* of speech and to be more aware of the *tone* of voice you use to verbalize those words. Also, don't forget that body language is a direct attachment to communication that adds the clear dimension of unspoken expression and punctuation to one's words. Body language doesn't even need to attend the spoken word to effectively convey meaning.

In dream symbology, a thesaurus refers to a caution to attend to the manner in which one communicates—choice of words, tone of voice, or expressed body language. So often we don't see our behavior as being a form of communication, but speech, tone, and body language are all integrally related and carry an equal power of conveyance. Even the subconscious act of releasing a simple sigh can transmit a specific attitude, such as frustration, defeat, exasperation, relief, joy, or disgust.

As human beings, we can communicate in many ways. Words are but one of them. So generally, when one is researching the symbology for a specific dreamscape fragment, it's necessary to remember to be all-inclusive by making connections associated with the main or listed interpretation, for the main interpretation serves only as a jumping-off point to discovery.

▶ *I dreamed that my girlfriend showed me a pendant she was wearing and she called it a staurolite. I have no idea what this is supposed to mean. Can you help?*

The staurolite symbolizes density of perception and/or a weighted outlook.

This dream scenario is revealing something about your friend. It appears to be exposing the quality and condition of her perception on a specific issue or subject matter. What that subject matter is may be determined by related dream elements that you didn't convey in your letter. Her perception on this issue is weighted down and caused to be dense through her inclusion of superfluous aspects not relevant to the issue. In other words, she's confusing the issue by involving unrelated aspects with it.

This tendency to confuse the purity of an issue with extraneous elements that contaminate it is a common mistake many people make. This happens all the time and folks rarely realize they're doing it. Yet it's important to not mix concepts or to interject unrelated aspects that compound an issue. This is an important point to remember and, when practiced, is evidence of using wisdom.

To you I would suggest trying to recall all the surrounding details of the dream and attempting to identify the subject matter the pendant was associated with. Then discuss it with your girl-friend.

▸ *I dreamed that it snowed in summer. Is that a premonition of how climatic aspects will be evidenced during The Changes?*

Though the dream could be referring to The Changes, my impression is that it's more accurately associated with yourself—with some element of life in which you're *snowing* yourself. This could be a psychological facet, or some type of past event or current relationship. Only you will have a sense of what this dream is directly related to.

▸ *What does it mean when one's dreamscape moon is always in full lunar eclipse?*

The moon can symbolize spiritual gifts and their application or it can have the stronger feminine application of meaning wisdom. Luna, goddess of wisdom, presides over and ensures the purity of wisdom. She is the keeper of wisdom. This moon in full lunar eclipse symbolizes a dark shadow—a shroud—over wisdom. This dreamscape visual reveals to the dreamer that wisdom is being ignored, forgotten, or smothered with extraneous elements in his or her awake-state life.

▸ *What does it mean if a dream's deciduous trees are bare of leaves in the summertime?*

If you can recall the specific species of trees they were, it'd help to refine the meaning. Generally, wintertime bare trees that appear this way in a dreamscape's summertime season would indicate a lack of fruitful behavior or a situation that is not being fully developed with respect to an individual's use of his or her talents. This can also mean that a situation, condition, or relationship in one's life is being kept from being all that it could be through someone's reluctance to fully express the self. Some element is being withheld.

► *What does a brilliant autumn sugar maple symbolize?*

A healthy sugar maple connotes inner serenity from the attainment of wisdom.

► *I had an odd dream. I dreamed that dogs were smarter than humans. Comment?*

I'll begin by saying that I don't think that was an odd dream at all because after observing the behavior of my own little four-leggeds of the cabin, the same idea has crossed my mind more than once.

The beautiful quality about dogs is that they love unconditionally. They don't look up at you and make judgmental conclusions and they don't see any differentiating characteristics about a human being, such as race, clothing style, social status, level of education, cultural background, and gender. They just love. Now, that perspective alone makes them a whole lot smarter than humans.

Animals also have what's been termed a sixth sense, and they use it openly, whereas humans still don't realize that this sense is a natural aspect of the consciousness. Because this sense is so misunderstood, some humans are so far away from the intelligent end of the scale that they believe this sense is of the Devil. Now you tell me which species has the greater smarts on this subject.

Dogs don't hide their emotions. They're completely open and honest. And I could go on with this for many more pages, but I think it's unnecessary. You get the drift.

This dreamscape fragment is most likely advising you to take a hint or two from the canine species. From the abovementioned clues, you'll probably know exactly what this dream means for you.

► *I dreamed that I was building my house out of balsa wood. What did that mean?*

It meant that you're cutting corners in life. You make attempts to avoid personal responsibility and look for ways to lessen your burdens.

By itself, balsa wood is a positive dream element, but depending both on how it's used in the dream and on other associated aspects, it could have a negative connotation. Generally, balsa wood symbolizes talents and thoughts that lighten burdens. But this dream visual implies that you're trying to build your home life with meager materials—that you're not putting personal effort into making family relationships strong and enduring.

► *What does a meerkat represent in a dream?*

By itself, a meerkat denotes community-mindedness, commitment, and cooperation. Since you didn't include a detailed description of the dream and the surrounding elements related to this animal, there's no way I can make any interpretive connections for you. Try to recall the physical condition of the meerkat and the situation it appeared in. Every dreamscape fragment carries an element contributing to the whole message. Each fragment serves to refine that message by taking it from general obscurity to clarity.

► *I seem to have more vivid dreams during an afternoon power nap than I do from a sound all-nighter. Is that unusual?*

No, and you've hit upon a little-known secret about dreaming.

The nighttime sleep period goes through phases, as I previously explained. During this extended sleep time, the mind begins by sorting out the day's events into memory categories, takes a pause, then begins the playback scenarios composed of symbolically conveyed messages. More pauses of blank void time are interspersed with additional dream sequences. But with a power nap, the individual's consciousness bypasses the sorting-out period and heads straight to the meat of the matter with dreams that come in vivid detail and are usually clearly remembered as being powerful and vivid depictions.

Along with providing vivid dreams, an afternoon nap can serve as a powerful energy boost. This nap doesn't have to necessarily be a long, extended one; it can be for as little as twenty minutes and still be effective.

▶ *What does it mean in a dream when an adult is eating baby food?*

Depending on the associated dreamscape fragments, it could be referring to either physiological (dietary) or psychological (mental) aspects. The dreaming adult could have some hidden physiological condition of which he or she is unaware and the ingestion of baby food may have presented itself as a dietary advisement. If the intent of the message is directed toward a psychological issue, then the adult eating the baby food may need to go back to basics in thought, or the baby food could be reflecting a life situation in which the adult is preferring to stay with elementary concepts rather develop them into a greater scope of knowledge. The scenario of an adult eating baby food can also denote juvenile behavior.

▶ *My friend keeps dreaming that mirrors don't reflect her image. What could that mean?*

This dream phenomenon sends the message that the person has a serious lack of self-image or that his or her self-esteem is so low that it's literally nonexistent. The individual does not have a perception of self. This is not the same as ego. It's related to one's sense of self, which everyone needs to recognize in order to participate in positive interrelated societal behavior. To simplify, one must know oneself before one can know others and exhibit positive behavioral patterns.

An individual who perceives no reflected image of self when looking in dream mirrors needs to begin giving some concentrated time devoted to recognizing the self's qualities and value as an individual, as a human being, and as a member of society who positively affects the lives of others.

▶ *I get a particular recurring dream in which some type of mist or thin fog is present. Nothing appears in absolute clarity, neither people, action, nor locations. Why does this happen?*

It happens for a reason. Every dreamscape element presents for a reason.

The fog or misty shroud covering dreamscapes can mean that the dreamer is not perceiving reality with clarity. If the *same* scenes are repeatedly depicted along with this misty dream, then it definitely means that the cloudy perception is directly related to a specific life situation, relationship, or societal element that appears in the dreamscape. If different scenes and people present themselves through the mist, then it means that the dreamer has some type of *generalized* misperception and he or she is perceiving life though such attitudes as prejudice, jealousy, or greed. Simply put, this dream facet strongly suggests the dreamer should recognize perceptions that are being altered by attitude.

▶ *I dreamed that I was hiking and carried a rucksack full of obsidian rocks. I was out collecting them. Why was I doing this? Why obsidian?*

In dream symbology, obsidian connotes protection. I can't tell you why you feel this need for protection; only you can know the cause for this. It could refer to certain conscious or subconscious fears you're giving energy to. It could be conveying the message that you have all the protection you need within yourself and that there's no reason you can't proceed with confidence through life. Though a dream interpreter can connect the dreamscape elements to their meanings, only the dreamer him- or herself can know how these relate to the self.

► *When we dream of a specific time (a circled calendar date), is this a premonition?*

Calling it an actual premonition is pushing into a gray area and being a bit presumptive. Let's be more accurate and call it a probable possibility.

Reality presents us with a variety of times and outcomes, some of which carry stronger likelihood for manifesting than others. These can present themselves in dreams because they carry more force of energy with them owing to the fact that the interrelated elements that comprise them are already beginning to come together. Therefore, certain outcomes (or specific timings) will evidence as the outstanding probabilities for future events.

A circled calendar date in a dream will most often represent one of these outstanding probabilities for an event to happen; however, this date is not set in stone, because as time progresses toward that date, new elements may enter to affect the probability and cause the date to change. As time gets closer and closer to the date and the same symbol appears without alteration, the probability for it to manifest into reality also becomes stronger.

► *What does a jet stone symbolize in dreams?*

A jet signifies pessimism.

► *Do dreams clarify relationships? I dreamed that my aunt was really my mother.*

This would be a clarification of your *perception* of your aunt as being more like a mother to you than your biological mother is. Sometimes the dream elements represent the dreamer's personal perceptions and psychological bent as shifted realities that are voluntarily or subconsciously superimposed over those of reality.

▸ *Here's a good one for you. I dreamed that the Taco Bell dog wanted to come live with me. So, yo quiero an interpretation!*

   Sí, señorita.

In dream symbology, the Chihuahua exemplifies an advisement to never underestimate the abilities or power of another. This power of another doesn't necessarily refer to strength or power to control but rather to his or her strong qualities and inherent value. The Taco Bell dog is the chosen symbol of your subconscious for presenting this concept. The dog wanted to live with you; therefore, it wanted you to live with this concept, to recognize it and accept it. This dreamscape fragment wouldn't have appeared if there wasn't some need for you to readjust your perception of another (or others).

▸ *I dreamed that my boyfriend's medicine cabinet was overflowing with Viagra. The pills were shoved everywhere—under sofa cushions, in emptied-out cereal boxes, and in coffee cans. They spilled out of the desk drawer when I opened it. We never have any sexual problems, so what's this all about?*

As long as you're sure there are no sexual relation difficulties, then the image isn't about sexual performance at all; it's about your friend's self-perception. There is one or more facets of his life in which he feels highly impotent. Perhaps it's career related, or it could be associated with one or more flaws he thinks he perceives in his personality or social behavior. Does he feel inferior in some way? Less intelligent or knowledgeable than others? Is he uncomfortable with his physique or have some physical characteristic that bothers him? There is something about himself which is causing this deflated self-perception, and he is subconsciously evincing a desire to boost that aspect up to a level he'll feel more satisfied or comfortable with.

► *In many of my dream scenes, little people—such as pixies, gnomes, and fairies—are peeking out at me from hiding places. Does this mean that I have some type of imaginary world view or that my sense of reality is confused by wishful thinking or fantasy?*

Well, no, because that'd mean that you're not applying the correct symbology. In dream symbology, a fairy alludes to the intellect's far conceptual reach through reality. So, as far as your interpretation goes, just the opposite is conveyed in this dream. This dream comes as a confirmation of your clear perception of reality rather than some imaginary viewpoint skewed by fantasy or wishful thought.

Though this fairy symbology may sound quite fantastic and illogical to you, wait until you're out walking in the forest and suddenly spy an actual fairy . . . now that's reality in all its fantastic glory. That's when reality blows logic through the roof, especially when you haven't even been taste-testing the 'shrooms along the way!

Our world is only illogical and seemingly filled with imaginary things when society doesn't have the whole picture, when society holds only a few pieces of reality's puzzle. When all pieces are perfectly placed and precisely fitted together, what an amazing surprise will be revealed! That's when reality will turn all the illogical concepts into logic. That's when reason will replace the current confusion caused by skepticism and ignorance.

► *The landscapes in my recent dreams have been completely barren—there's not even a cactus or a weed of any kind. Even a moonscape would feel more alive than my dreamscapes do. Comment?*

This is a common dream scene signifying a sense of uselessness (the barrenness) of the life you find yourself surrounded by. This may represent not your awake-state reality but rather how you *perceive* that reality to be. This indicates a lack of acceptance in life and signifies a state of voluntary blindness in which you choose not to recognize life's gifts and blessings existing within your immediate realm of experience. This barren landscape reflects your barren thoughts and self-perspective. It's egocentric and self-serving in that it mirrors a misguided and misperceived state of self-pity. If that barren landscape could talk, it would echo the dreamer's words, "Oh dear. Look at poor me. There's nothing in my life to live for . . . nothing." But then that landscape would like to have a voice of its own and speak back: "Oh dear. Look at lucky you. There's so much to live for in your life. Just open your eyes to it all!" And the hidden sprouts would suddenly break through the cracked earth and rise tall to bear colorful blossoms, and waterfalls would begin to fill in the land depression to form a crystal clear lake full of swimming life, and trees would grow forth bearing fruit of every kind, and birdsong would fill the air. This dream element comes as a strong warning to open one's eyes and recognize what is then seen. Too often we think our lives are without meaning or hold no joyful aspects to cherish, yet in each person's life, something wonderful can be found to treasure . . . usually there are many somethings.

► *The pickup truck I was driving in my dream only had three wheels, yet it was perfectly balanced and drove just fine. What did this mean?*

This is a dream element that is associated with the dreamer's perspective regarding what's necessary in life. That dream pickup ran just fine on three wheels. This correlates to some aspect of your awake-state life in which you tend to think you don't have all the necessary elements gathered for something to work out right . . . yet it appears that you really do. Are you getting the meaning here?

The general dream symbology for any vehicle is usually associated with the physical body and its condition (state of health). If we equate these tires to the "feet" one uses to progress through life and the truck to personal efforts, we come up with a situation involving the dreamer's efforts applied to life progression. This, then, is the subject matter of the dream's message. Now, this truck ran perfectly fine on three tires and it was also perfectly balanced. So then this dream fragment is trying to convey to you that the current efforts applied to a specific goal are more than sufficient to attain success without the additional elements you believe you need.

Dream interpretation is like adding two and two. It's similar to working out a completed puzzle from all the pieces supplied in the dreamscape's visuals. Every element is a valuable, integral piece. Together they make the message. This is why it's so important to try to recall every single element presented within a dreamscape. Color plays a role as one piece of the puzzle. Odd shapes in dreams, such as designs or patterns, give another puzzle-piece clue. Action, how people are presented, and what they're wearing are other pieces. Vehicles and their condition are another. And so on. The more elements of a dream that can be remembered, the sharper the dream's definition will be and the clearer its message becomes.

▶ *Your dream symbology for salmon was "going against a spiritual current." I thought everyone was supposed to follow his or her own spiritual inclinations. Will you clarify this?*

The only clarification needed is that you made an assumption when reading my symbolic interpretation for *salmon*. You assumed I meant "traditional" religious concepts of the general populace, and that is not what it says in my dream symbology book.

Owing to each person's own mean vibrational rate and the composite rate, to which each person is continually making

ments, everyone has certain philosophical
spiritual matters and concepts. This indi-
s what the symbology refers to. In other
symbology says, *Don't fight against your own current
spiritual inclination by ignoring it and following that which societal
tradition determines most popular.* Your own inherent spiritual inclinations will be pulling you along in a natural flow of conceptual perception, yet you fight against that current in an
attempt to fit in with traditional belief systems. That's not being
true to yourself. And when one isn't true to his or her spiritual
self, the inner beingness remains in a constant state of flux and
turmoil.

▶ *I dreamed that for my birthday, I received four beautiful
flower arrangements that within an hour were all wilted or dead.
Is that an omen of my impending death?*

No, this is a typical fear-based dream. Your fear of dying is not
even a subconscious element; it's a conscious one that came to the
fore by way of dreamscape visuals. Those beautiful flowers might
as well be dead because the perception of your life span is just as
negatively depressive and fatalistic. You're not appreciating the
beauty that surrounds you on a daily basis for the fear of dying
that you allow to consume your awake-state hours. Four bouquets were delivered to you. This in itself is a number element
related to this important message. The number four signifies a
direct reference to the physical body. The four bouquets were
beautiful (your body is in a beautiful healthy state), yet they all
wilted and died (your fear of your dying to the physical world).
You've got to get past this because it's ruining your life and your
ability to appreciate the blessings you have by way of health, relationships, career, financial stability, and so on. You're handicap-
ping yourself with a voluntarily debilitating affliction of the mind
that cloaks your life in a shrouded pall and chokes out all chances
for joy and optimism.

Fearing death is a self-centered attitude that, all by itself, kills the life within Life—its shimmering vitality and exuberance of beingness. Don't do that to yourself. Please, don't do that. Your life is so full, if only you'd recognize and acknowledge that fact. If you have only one good, loyal friend in life, you are blessed beyond words. People today just do not realize all they have to be grateful for. They let the little blessings pass before their eyes in a continual stream of nonexistence, unrecognized and so sadly taken for granted. Most times it's life's most simple things that are blessings in disguise because society makes them invisible beneath a perceptual cloak of triviality. Folks seem to think that some blessings are merely the fundamental elements of life that they deserve, yet few recognize those things as blessings, and even fewer acknowledge them as such. Shelter is a blessing. It's a rarity for people in the United States to think of having a permanent dwelling as a blessing because most Americans have the money to go out and rent an apartment or buy a house. Yet there are literally thousands of homeless people around the world—and even in the United States. This is just one glaring example of how society takes its multitude of blessings for granted.

Dear lady, you have so much to live for and so much to take real inner joy from in your life. Don't ignore the beauty that surrounds you by being blind to all you have been given, by choosing to view life through a self-woven death veil.

► *What did it mean when I dreamed that I was walking down my church steps wearing a medieval costume?*

The *church* denotes one's *spiritual belief or spiritual concepts*. The *Middle Ages* or *medieval period* signifies a *time when one will begin to become more aware*. Pulling these two dreamscape elements together, one can see the theme of spiritual awareness. Also, since you were *leaving* this church instead of entering it, this would indicate that this new spiritual awareness is going to come from some source other than the church.

► *In my dream, I was adding more memory to my computer. My real computer already has more memory than most people have on theirs, so what did this mean?*

The intent of this dream aspect was not a message about your real-life computer but rather about your own mind. It is making a suggestion to recall or retain memory of something that you're either consciously or subconsciously locking away or in denial over. This dream is telling you to give more "thought energy" to your memory bank.

When people lock memories away or choose denial they only postpone the necessity of bringing these out, examining them, and airing them. Most of these types of memories are locked away in a state of entanglement, as a braided mess that one day must be unraveled and dealt with. Just because they're out of view doesn't mean they don't still exist, and they certainly haven't gone away.

► *I dreamed that the Ku Klux Klan was burning a cross in my front yard. I'm English and white, so what was up with that weird one?*

This dream aspect, the Ku Klux Klan, stands for prejudice. Since you're neither black nor Jewish, this dream fragment suggests that you subconsciously (or consciously) have some type of fear of discovery. There is something about your behavior or philosophy that you feel you need to keep under wraps and don't wish to have publicly acknowledged. Your fear is not of the Klan per se but of someone discovering your secret and exposing you to ridicule, humiliation, or other types of character-harming reactions.

► *In real life I have a picture of my grown daughter on the dining room breakfront. What did it mean when I dreamed that the picture frame was covered with fast-growing mold?*

It means that your relationship with her leaves something to be desired. The message can't be more clear. You're letting your relationship with her get moldy! I know nothing about what could be causing this, but you probably do. This dream fragment is telling you to get going and freshen up that relationship before it's beyond repair.

▸ *I dreamed that I was having an estate sale. I had price tags on everything I owned. But I'm not moving. Does this mean that I'm going to be moving soon? And if so, why would I sell all my things instead of taking them with me?*

You're taking this dream literally instead of symbolically, as it was meant to be interpreted.

This dream is making an attempt to visually show you your tendency to perceive life through dollar signs. It's trying to make you see that you're placing a price tag on everything and every-one. That your criterion for worth is measured monetarily instead of spiritually. The dream had nothing at all to do with relo-cating unless it's strongly suggesting that you relocate your world view out of the socially judgmental category in which you tend to place it.

▸ *I dreamed that I was a fortuneteller. Did that mean that I have this ability without knowing it? Is this pointing to my future career?*

Nope. It means that not only do you have an obsession with the future but you also want to be able to predict it. This ability may appear to be a glamorous or fame-generating one, but it's not all it's cracked up to be. Knowing the future demands a highly stable mind to go along with it because living the mo-ment can then become extremely difficult to maintain. Knowing the future has its place; so does living the moment. A fine bal-ance is necessary, and not everyone—few—can manage to pull it off with grace. Knowing the future must be accompanied by a certain level of wisdom. The major portion of that wisdom is understanding that The Knowing can never be a self-serving gift, in that the gift freely given to you cannot be turned into a gift one charges others for. And your thought about its being a career makes me think this is what you're envisioning doing with a gift of foresight. Divine gifts are tarnished when received with an eye to make money from them. Divine gifts should be perceived as being Divine *blessings* comparable to those of empathy and compassion, which we utilize to help our sisters and brothers in life. Do we put a price tag on giving compassion? Comfort? Giving someone a lift or helping an elderly woman across the street? Well, I know that sounds simplistically silly to you, but it's the same thing when individuals gifted with foresight charge for their advice or knowledge. It's exactly the same thing and nobody seems to see it. Nobody seems to get it. Foresight is not to be used in a career . . . it's a Divine gift to be freely shared for the benefit of humankind.

▸ *I dreamed that I ran a foster care home for children. I don't even like children all that much. Why would I dream this? What could it possibly mean?*

This is another instance when the dreamer is interpreting the message literally instead of perceiving the spirit of it.

This dream is not intending to show you a future of caring for foster children. It's clearly pointing out a philosophical concept that evidently you're not grasping. In dream symbology, foster care alludes to a reminder that we must have brotherly/sisterly love and take personal responsibility to care for anyone needing it. Therefore, this dream element comes to you because there must be aspects of your personality or social perception that don't include this ideology of unconditional love. If you do think you have unconditional love, then it clearly doesn't extend beyond the familial circle that you've drawn around the concept. The dream is urging you to widen your view of this concept and make adjustments in your resulting behavior toward others.

▸ *Quite frequently I dream that I'm out rock hounding and I dig up a large peridot gemstone. I'm not sure how to interpret that.*

Although a peridot can denote a sunny disposition that serves as an uplifting and healing force for others, it also signifies a gentle healing, a long-term healing process. Since you were the one who found the stone, the intent of the message is for you. The healing can be associated with a physical or a psychological (emotional) issue in your life.

From other information supplied in your letter, this dreamscape fragment would indicate a psychological issue and that perhaps you've been disappointed that you've not yet fully recovered from the emotional residuals left over from a past event. Some healings cannot be complete unless they're accomplished in a slow and gentle manner. A scab that forms over a festering infection does not indicate a healing. All it indicates is a surface covering that hides the illness beneath, so some healings take longer because they have to heal from the inside out, not the other way around.

▸ *What does a sand lily mean in a dream? I dreamed that my yard was covered with them and I had them around inside the house too.*

A sand lily connotes life's smaller blessings, those which are easily taken for granted and so are frequently overlooked. Clearly these floral visuals presented with the intent to help you see the many blessings that surround you. You are blessed in many ways, and this dream element is attempting to bring that to the fore of your consciousness.

▸ *I dreamed that my friend gifted me with a watermelon tourmaline stone that was made into a pendant to wear around my neck. What does that stone symbolize and why was I gifted with it?*

In dream symbology, the watermelon tourmaline connotes the healing benefits from an attitude of optimism and joyfulness.

So often people don't realize the healthful benefits that naturally come from a lighter life perspective. Joyfulness and optimism are two prime examples of attitudes that actually help one's physiological system heal itself. The saying "as above, so below" is not a shallow cliché; it's a concept of reality that's highly accurate. One's state of mind is as important—sometimes more so—as the prescription medications one takes for an illness. This also has dynamic application for such psychological conditions as melancholia, fear-based perceptions, and attitudes generated from low self-esteem and feelings of inadequacy. This dreamscape fragment is attempting to point out the above concepts so that perhaps you'll learn something important from it, something so important it could change your entire outlook for the better.

► *In my dream I visited a friend who had a houseful of bitterns. I've no clue what this is supposed to mean regarding my friend. Comment?*

Sometimes the dreams we have of friends are, in reality, subtly directed toward us. In dream symbology, the bittern bird signifies spiritual serenity. Clearly your friend has attained this much-desired state within herself, but have you? Could this dreamscape element be sending you a personal message regarding your own spiritual state? Is it in confusion or does it vacillate between conflicting tenets? Do you ever feel any twinge of embarrassment over your spiritual beliefs? All of these questions help to identify a less than serene spiritual belief system. This particular dream aspect is suggesting that you take a closer look at your own spiritual beliefs and analyze how you truly feel about them.

► *What does a catalpa tree represent in dreams?*

Priorities, high priorities. If you know anything about a catalpa tree, if you've ever had one, you know how fast and strong they can grow. Determination, inner strength, perseverance, and resiliency are their qualities. These attributes, associated with priorities, make for goals from which one rarely veers.

THE
S·P·I·R·I·T

The Blossom of
Eternal Life

THE CRYSTAL STREAM
Quantum Consciousness and Virtual Meditation

▶ *Meditation isn't as popular as it was in the 1960s, so how come you've taken the subject matter even further to coin the terms* Virtual Meditation *and* Quantum Meditation? *Aren't you addressing an outdated process?*

Perhaps that could be true if the idea of meditation were confined to the singular decade of the 1960s; however, meditation was in style long before the time of Christ. You're missing the whole point of the matter when you make these types of statements, because meditation is ageless. It's been practiced by most all ancient cultures in some form or another. I'm sad to say the 1960s was when the Western world finally caught on to the idea after it'd been an accepted concept the world over for many millennia. Meditation is not a fad or some New Age idea or cultish practice. Meditation is a means of attaining inner serenity and, if practiced often enough, can lead to an expansion of consciousness into the myriad quantum realms of reality.

I've coined the phrases *Quantum Consciousness, Virtual Meditation,* and *Quantum Meditation* because my own journeys into meditation have led to regions far beyond the generalized and simplistic popular conception of meditation, and I discovered no written record of corresponding ideas or terms related to these far-reaching elements of reality. Though there exist volumes upon volumes of books, both cultish and technical, on the subject of meditation, they all seemed to be constrictive and to confine the consciousness to a box defined by "the common rules" of meditation. My experiences proved beyond the shadow of doubt that meditation has no rules of behavior and certainly has no commonality whatsoever associated with it. It is expansively boundless. It is limitless in scope and depth. It is absolute freedom for one's consciousness to explore the microcosm, macrocosm, and infinity facets of reality. It allows one to experience all the dimensional frequencies of life. It isn't some little ten-minute event of closing one's eyes and chanting a mantra . . . it is traveling out into *quantum* reality and experiencing *virtual* events! The difference between meditation and Quantum Meditation is the contrast between walking in your yard and walking on the moon . . . in *another* galaxy!

You and many others have missed the boat entirely when it comes to the issue of meditation.

► *Is meditation a religious thing? This is confusing for me because I'm an atheist and I'm not sure I should be looking into doing it.*

I've often said this: "Meditation is nonthought. It's listening for the Divine message." Yet that's extremely simplistic, a broad-scope generality. Meditation truly is nonthought because the consciousness takes the lead so it can be free of the tether of thought and journey out into the realities of reality during Quantum Meditation.

More than a religious practice, meditation is an effective method of calming one's physical and psychological beingness. Far more than a religious practice, meditation is associated with the mind's consciousness—not the awake-state consciousness but the entire nature of consciousness. Our consciousness is that which survives the physical death of our bodies; it's that which lives on and is the core of our inner eternal beingness. Therefore, during simple meditation, the consciousness has the capability to calm and settle the inner forces that operate the physical and mental; during Quantum Meditation, the consciousness has the potential to journey into the far-reaching realities of reality to discover the intricate interrelatedness of all life. This, then, associates meditation with the more natural functioning of human vision or sense of touch and smell than it relates to the issue of religion. It's an inherent aspect of the human consciousness, nothing more and nothing less.

For an atheist, it would certainly not be a religious offense to participate in meditation.

▶ *There are so many meditation books available. How does one know which one is best?*

My first reaction to this question was to ask a return question. Why would you think only one should be best? I agree that there are a multitude of meditation books available; many are wonderfully informative. I always suggest broad-scope reading for those researching a new subject matter. The more one reads, the broader one's understanding becomes. Even if some of the material appears conflicting, the researching individual will begin to sort these out in his or her own head as comprehension deepens. Never read just one or two books on any given subject matter. Doing this will instill a myopic perspective of the issue rather than providing the wide-angle lens that extensive reading provides.

After doing the reading research, practice on your own through trial and error with the various methodologies suggested. Eventually you'll come into your own comfortable method of meditation. Never try to force an uncomfortable position or create distractions such as mantras if these only serve to keep your consciousness focused on them. These then will defeat the sole purpose of meditation by keeping your mind energized with thought instead of allowing it to drift into nonthought. A book is good. Many books are better. Finding your own methodology is best.

► *Is it good to meditate on a saying or a visual?*

Impossible. That's focusing thought. Meditation is non-thought. What you're asking is directly related to *contemplation*. Remember, contemplation is thought, whereas meditation is non-thought. You cannot meditate on a saying or visual or your navel. The very idea is a clear contradiction in terms.

► *My sister told me that one must meditate in the dark for it to work. Is that true?*

Perhaps it's true for her. I can meditate out in the woods with a bright sunbeam spearing down through the pines on me or on a hillside in full moonlight. Each individual has different criteria for successful meditation. Everyone discovers his or her own.

► *Is incense or certain music necessary for meditation?*

For beginners, these types of aids seem to be helpful to put them in the mood, yet experienced folks don't need any extraneous aids to achieve successful meditative states.

► *I've read that different cultures use specific methodologies for meditating. Should I choose one of these or just go with the flow?*

I think you've answered your own question here. The fact that you included the "go with the flow" alternative indicates that you think that your own style is an option. Sure it is; in fact, it's the best option for success. Because we are all unique individuals, what works best for one person may not work at all for another. Sitting cross-legged absolutely distracts me, so I don't use that positioning. Music can also distract me unless it's perfectly soothing. I use incense only because I always have it burning in the cabin anyway and it is not an item reserved solely for meditation times. I can achieve quantum meditative states while lying down or sitting relaxed in my high-back reading chair or sitting out in the woods leaning against a tree. The key here is not the precise body position but body *relaxation*. Chants, temple bells, drums, incense, music, and so forth are not imperative elements to achieving successful meditation; they are merely personal aids if one requires them. My suggestion to you would be to go with that flow. After trial and error, stick with whatever works best for you. Remember, the whole idea of meditation is to set the consciousness free. You do not want to do anything to tether it by way of third-dimensional distractions and active thought.

► *Is it best to meditate naked? Don't clothes hamper the process? That's what my guru tells us.*

Jeez Louise. Us? He's telling your whole group that?

Listen, the *mind* cannot be hampered by a hat! It's the *consciousness* that is involved with meditation, not the skin surface or even one's aura. The consciousness doesn't have clothing! It's pure energy. Do atoms wear Anne Klein dress pants? When was the last time you spied a surge of energy zap past you in Levi's jeans? I'm not being sarcastic, either; I'm being rational—which your so-called guru is not being. Obviously he has a hidden agenda to his meditative technique. You're too smart to be falling for this kind of trickery. While all you women close your eyes in meditation, even if you've snuck a peek to see if your guru was doing the same, you could very well be on his private little hidden video camera. Please, ladies, use discernment. Although it's wise to wear loose clothing, that's only because any binding or tight areas could be a distraction to meditation. It's certainly never necessary to be naked. Your aura flows freely with or without clothing. Your mind functions with or without clothing. Your consciousness is free and unencumbered when you're within nonthought. Thoughts are the only possible constriction or tether that will keep you from attaining nonthought.

► *Sometimes when I meditate, I get frightened because I'll feel an unexplainable breeze cross my face or my hair will feel as though it moved. I stop myself whenever things like this happen and am reluctant to try again.*

This type of phenomenon usually occurs in the second stage of meditation when the consciousness is approaching the threshold of absolute nonthought. These events happen because the consciousness is then more aware of the finer elements of reality, such as slight breezes you don't normally take note of during the day or the little tingles of the scalp that naturally occur. During the awake state of daily activity, our minds are focused and centered on material matters. Yet when the mind is stilled for any significant amount of time, it becomes highly sensitized to the more subtle aspects of your world, including the human physiological system. These are aspects of reality and nothing to be fearful of. They should cause no more fear than watching a shadow move with the sun across your living room floor. We aren't normally aware of this movement either, unless we're purposely sitting down watching it shift past us.

Our daily awake-state consciousness is just that—an awake-state of awareness in which we purposely focus our minds on the elements of daily living. We voluntarily control what we think about and that which we choose to sense. During meditation, we are voluntarily shifting that focused control over to a control in which the consciousness itself is given the freedom to choose its own focus. In the awake state, we control what our consciousness centers on. In the meditative state, particularly the quantum meditative state, the consciousness itself freely moves about the limitless frequencies of reality. That's the difference.

So to experience a sensation of breeze, a scalp tingle, or hair movement is simply to have approached that mental state threshold where the consciousness is beginning to take the reins from your own voluntary control—nothing more.

► *I have no place quiet to go to meditate, so I never meditate.*

Have you tried putting headphones on and listening to one of those nature tapes? Have you ever thought that you could use your car as a sanctuary for meditation by driving somewhere less noisy? How about checking out some local house of worship to discover a time of day when no one is around? You don't even have to be a member to go inside and sit there awhile. How about a library reading room? Or during the night when everyone's asleep? Usually, where there's a will, there's a way.

► *My minister says that meditation is of the Devil and we shouldn't be doing it.*

Though meditation is not a religious exercise at all, it has been practiced by religious ascetics throughout history. Saints, mystics, martyrs, popes, and so on have all meditated and spent a great deal of time in thoughtful contemplation. Meditation has nothing to do with religion, the Divine, or the Devil. That idea is evidence of medieval, primitive thought. Meditation is directly associated with the expansion of the human consciousness. Nothing else. To see the Devil in everything is to give the concept energy and aggrandize it. It's a way people, especially religious leaders, use a concept to control and manipulate others through fear. It exhibits a clear lack of understanding of reality and the natural functioning of the human consciousness. Such ignorance has no place in the beautiful practice of meditation.

► *In* Earthway, *why did you refer to meditation as the crystal stream?*

In the technological sense, it has to do with the body's energy—the *chi*—that flows through the body. The central focus of this energy during meditation can be up through the trunk of the body and is sometimes referred to as the kundalini energy. Yet this is only a fraction of what comprises the crystal stream.

Since successful meditation, especially Quantum Meditation,

is not solely contingent on the flow of this energy up through the body, the crystal stream therefore refers more to the stream of consciousness within us. Every cell has consciousness. Every cell has a form of memory. This is evidenced through cells' amazing capacity to regenerate themselves. Skin cells will grow more skin cells, liver cells will regenerate themselves, and blood cells do the same—all because our cellular structure has a basic memory pattern unique to each type of cell. So our bodies have consciousness within them and so too do our minds have an eternal living consciousness independent of the body. Though housed within the brain, this consciousness is not dependent upon the brain's physiology. This is evidenced when the body expires and the consciousness (which some call spirit) continues to experience reality in other dimensional frequencies. So the crystal stream is the body's energy *chi* plus its living consciousness.

▶ *Why did you coin the term* Virtual Meditation? *What is there about it that makes it virtual?*

The aliveness of reality is what makes it virtual.

First, I need to differentiate the two terms I coined. *Quantum Meditation* references the place or location of the consciousness's meditative-state destination. And *Virtual Meditation* denotes the experience or activity that takes place in Quantum Meditation. One is associated with place and the other represents the experiences while there.

You want to know why I termed these experiences that happen during Quantum Meditation "virtual." I did this because there was no other term available within the English language with which to equate them. *Virtual* is the word we use to mean "real" or "literal." When the consciousness experiences other dimensional realms and frequencies of reality, that consciousness is actually *there*. It's there because it has no tether to the physical body to keep it held within the third-dimensional realm. And while there, all the senses are in a dynamic state of heightened sensitivity. Every olfactory, auditory, tactile, visual, and emotional response is exquisitely perceived. Colors vibrate with incredible energy; they actually shimmer with undulating energy. The people one's consciousness encounters are as real in their dimension as we are within ours. It's consciousness experiencing the virtual reality of other dimensional fields comprising the totality of reality.

We sit here in the simplistic third dimension and think we reign supreme, yet we are as ants believing our little system of anthills and tunnels is all there is to reality. We've no conception of what's out there beyond our touchable world, a world only touchable through the senses. We've no idea what's out there (in quantum reality) and so touchably accessible through the experiences of our consciousness (Virtual Meditation). Because of this minuscule view we have of reality's totality, we've no adequate words to encompass reality's incredible hugeness. I could use such terms as *infinity, endlessness, expansiveness, limitlessness, fullness,* and *never-endingness,* yet they still seem quite inadequate after experiencing the virtual realness of reality's totality.

When the consciousness passes from the superficial levels of meditation, crosses the threshold into Quantum Meditation, and begins to experience the virtual meditative events of reality, there are few words to choose from to describe what occurs, what is felt, and what is comprehended while there. Every experience and individual the consciousness encounters there is as real and alive as they are here in this heavily weighted third dimension. Yet I realize that many people can't understand this. They can't fathom the vast expansiveness of reality because their minds are too centered on the self and its immediate touchable surroundings.

I would love it if everyone could journey out and through quantum reality and have beautifully exquisite virtual experiences there because, once they did so, they would see society's behavior as incredibly petty and savage. Experiencing the extent of reality and the undescribable beauty of it exposes the attitudes of human prejudice, intolerance for one another, hatred, sexism, and so on as being from the mentality of primitive savages. The contrast between the intellectual behavior within this dimension and that of others is like night and day. Here there is religion and the hatred it generates between the separatist believers; there there is only pure spirituality. Here there is deceit and subterfuge, whereas there there is only the open honesty of what is. How much more real can you get? How much more "virtual" can reality be when the consciousness experiences its pure totality?

This earth of ours and the people upon it are but a minuscule dot among the millions of others that join to comprise the big picture we so misunderstandingly call reality. Humans have no idea . . . no idea whatsoever.

▶ *Can dead relatives communicate with someone who's meditating? Is meditation a venue for that kind of communication?*

This is not the venue for such communication. Remember, unless this relative has very recently passed over, the spirit will most likely already have made another transition into a physical life.

▶ *If meditation is nonthought, how can one experience Virtual Meditation if the consciousness isn't supposed to have a thought?*

You're missing the point that there's the awake-state consciousness and then there's the true consciousness. The former is dependent upon a mechanized brain function; the latter is dependent on nothing. You're confusing the two meanings of consciousness.

When beginning the practice period of meditation, you want to avoid having any awake-state conscious thoughts. The goal is to allow these to float through your mind without giving them any energy by looking at them. Successful meditation comes after the mind is clear of all awake-state thought and has reached a state of *awake-state* nonthought. It is after this period of awake-state nonthought that the true consciousness takes over to have its natural experiences within reality. See the difference? It's a major one to understand if you expect to comprehend these important concepts of Quantum Meditation and Virtual Meditation.

The awake-state consciousness is most frequently addressed and referred to when someone is in a poor state of health, as when in a hospital. The staff will say, "He's semiconscious" or "He's not conscious." This refers to the individual's awake-state of consciousness. This is also associated with being in a coma because the patient's consciousness is not awake. Yet that patient's true consciousness is always viable and alive. Though the awake-state aspect of consciousness may not be awake and aware, the true consciousness *is* and can be out of the body watching all the action or anywhere else within the limitless realms of quantum reality.

▸ *Can I attain spiritual enlightenment without practicing meditation?*

Well, sure you can. I don't think anyone ever equated spiritual enlightenment with the necessity of having achieved meditative success. Spiritual enlightenment isn't what most folks think it is either. I'll address this issue in the next chapter of the book, which is on spiritual philosophy.

Meditation is an aid to inner relaxation and serenity. If one manages to expand the meditative state of consciousness into Quantum Meditation, then a certain knowing of reality's totality dramatically and irrevocably alters one's world view and imparts spiritual priorities related to using wisdom in one's behavior; that behavior becomes more spiritual as it rejects intolerance, prejudice, and other negative societal attitudes. That new world view is what allows one to see the aforementioned negative attitudes as being incredibly petty and those who evince them as being primitive savages. These may sound like harsh terms, but the beauty and hugeness of reality clearly show that this earthly reality is but a single cell of reality's magnificent wholeness. In this sense,

Quantum Meditation can hasten one's comprehension of what is and clarify the pettiness of prejudice, hatred, and intolerance between the quarrelsome siblings of this earthly human family. But, in general, meditation is not germane to the attainment of spiritual enlightenment. Even common sense tells us that we shouldn't put labels on others, that we shouldn't point fingers and engage in gossip (substantiated or otherwise), that we shouldn't hate one another or despise our differences. Common sense and logic tell us that religious leaders are wrong to incite hatred and intolerance for sisters and brothers. We inherently know that right spiritual behavior and attitude is loving one another and practicing unconditional goodness whenever and wherever the opportunity presents itself. We don't need meditation to convey these beautiful spiritual tenets. All we need is common sense and love within our hearts. Spiritual enlightenment grows and thrives through the practice of spiritual behavior.

▶ *My guide told me that you will teach me how to meditate.*

Your guide is mistaken. Please, be careful how you use spiritual concepts in your life. Don't ever use them for self-serving ends. They are not means to appeasement of personal wants and desires.

I am confounded by this idea that a teacher must be involved in meditation. Do you need a teacher to teach you how to sleep? Or to breathe? Or to pray? Meditation is not some highly esoteric process. It doesn't involve some mysterious methodology. There is no right or wrong way to it. It's natural—as natural as lying down and taking an afternoon nap.

Meditation is merely quieting the mind. To do that, you naturally need a reasonably quiet place. Meditation is letting all your awake-state conscious thoughts float through your mind without giving them staying power. Once the mind is reasonably void of thought, the body and mind relaxes and may drift into a state of total tranquillity. That's meditation. If in meditating you accomplish nothing more than total relaxation for body and mind, then you can still claim success. To accomplish that is a great achievement because society is so overexposed to all types of intense stress. If in your meditative state you journey beyond this total relaxation stage and pass into Quantum Meditation where virtual experiences take place, that's an added plus. But to think you need some kind of teacher for this is just ridiculous. Meditation, with all its varied techniques, is as individualized as the people who practice it.

▸ *Some people say that meditation is dangerous because one could open oneself up to negative forces while under the influence.*

Under the influence of what? Your consciousness? You made it sound as though meditation equated to a drunken stupor. In meditation, you're still in full awareness of your own true consciousness. Though your *awake-state* consciousness is set aside, your true consciousness is active and perceptive. That's the difference that folks aren't getting.

▸ *Should one be a certain age or reach a certain level of intellectual understanding before the practice of meditation is attempted?*

Age or intellectual capacity has no relationship to an ability to meditate. Anyone can. For children, for the aged, and for everyone in between, meditation is a wonderful form of physical and emotional relaxation. Meditation need not pass beyond this purpose. The relaxation stage in and of itself is highly beneficial for every individual.

▸ *Should children be taught to meditate?*

In a sense, they do it quite naturally without realizing it's called meditation. They can have periods during the day in which their consciousness is in between the awake-state consciousness and the meditative state. It's not daydreaming and it's not napping, but rather somewhere in between the two.

▶ *My minister says that meditation is a New Age thing and that New Age ideas are evil.*

Now that you've told me what your minister thinks, what do *you* think?

U.S. society is too eager to live its lives and think its thoughts according to the dictates of others. Individuality—especially individual thought—has degraded to such a state that people actually fear to think for themselves. Popular opinion, political correctness, or the religious right, the moral majority, and other movements and groups have come to control the actions and thoughts of others by playing on our fear of thinking for ourselves.

We've witnessed this over and over again throughout history. England's populace and religious beliefs were once controlled by those of the ruling king or queen. If the monarch was aligned with the pope, the country was considered to be papist (Catholic); if the king or queen was aligned with John Knox, it was Protestant. All those with other beliefs were persecuted on the whim of the monarch, according to his or her personal belief system. No alternative individual beliefs were abided. It was believe or off with your head. Today, the Inquisition still lives . . . in the self-righteous, the supremacists, the racists, the self-appointed religious soldiers of God, and the separatists—those who claim their religion is the only true faith.

Get a clue, girl. You have a mind that the Divine Essence gave to you. You are slapping the Creatrix in the face if you don't use it yourself instead of letting others steal it away.

▶ *I can't manage meditation. I can't manage to get past falling asleep. What's the matter with me?*

Nothing's the matter with you. You just don't realize how many folks can't even get that far with it. Instead of focusing on the negative of not getting further, you need to realize that you get far enough to accomplish the feat of letting all your awake-state conscious thoughts drift by so that you reach the stage of complete nonthought and total relaxation. That's great! There are literally thousands of people out there who can't get to that stage because they can't stop giving their thoughts energy by looking at each of them.

If you're falling asleep, that's fine; there's absolutely nothing wrong with that. At least you've given your mind and body some invaluable relaxation time. Don't despair. Keep up the good work. You'll eventually get past that falling-asleep pattern. You're doing just fine.

► *When I meditate, I can never manage to stop looking at the thoughts that come to mind. I just cannot do it.*

With that mind-set, you've set yourself up for failure because you've programmed yourself to not do it. You're entering the process with negativity and the expectation for failure.

What may help is to envision your mind and the incoming rush of thoughts as being separate entities. Envision the mind as sitting on the right side of your brain (or head) and the incoming thoughts arriving on your left. In this way there is a separation between the two so that the thoughts can pass *before* the mind instead of *through* it. See where I'm going with this? This would be somewhat like the mind sitting on a park bench, minding its own peaceful business while the busy thoughts parade along the sidewalk in front. Have you ever sat on a bench in a park or in a mall and had your mind so completely consumed with whatever that you watched the passersby without really watching them? This is what my example is similar to. After getting in a comfortable physical position, imagine your mind on that park bench. The mind is completely consumed in nonthought while the incoming thoughts parade by you without your giving them any attention or awareness of any kind. It's just

like sitting on that bench and subconsciously being aware of passing pigeons waddling by but never really looking at them. It's
the same as when you drive home from work and all the time
your mind is so consumed by thoughts that you later exclaim,
"I don't even remember driving!" By putting your mind aside (on
the bench), you voluntarily make a shift of consciousness that
allows the incoming thoughts to more easily proceed without
your giving them the energy of attention. This suggestion has
helped others get past the block that the incoming thoughts can
cause. Perhaps it'll help you too. But . . . you have to get rid of that
negative mind-set first. Every meditative period is a new one, just
like each day is a spanking new gift from the Creatrix. Every outcome does not have to be a repetitive echo of the one before it. It
can change with attitude—attitude and a slight shift of mental
focus.

► *I think meditation is so beneficial that it should be taught in
schools. Maybe not as a part of the mandatory curriculum, but
as an alternative course.*

Not a great idea. Not a good idea at all. Well, it's a wonderful
idea in and of itself if we wouldn't have to factor in the religious
right, which has a medieval perception of meditation. Lady, you
have no idea of the Pandora's box you'd be opening if you ever
made that suggestion to your school board.

I've witnessed a similar situation in our mountain town
school. The Woodland Park school offered a course in mythology.
Oh, sister, you just wouldn't believe the ignorance that that
course brought out in people. It was so pitiful to see. A great hue
and cry was sent up from a fundamentalist minister who thought
the mythology course was teaching our young people about
pagan goddesses and gods. His false logic was this: "If you're going
to teach about pagan religion, you need to counter it with
Christian religion and the Bible." He was demanding that
either the Bible be taught also or the mythology course be

withdrawn. Maybe I'm mistaken (I don't really think so), but mythology is more ancient cultural history than religion. The ancients' beliefs in deities were an integral and inseparable aspect of historical cultures, as evidenced by their literature, art, social structure, and architecture style. Also, studying mythology in public schools expands children's understanding of the world. How else would they know where the word *lunar* came from? They'd be completely ignorant of the meaning of the phrase *Achilles' heel.* They would wonder why Venus and Aphrodite represent love and why Cupid is depicted on Valentine's Day cards. "What's with the bow and arrow?" they'd ask. So much of our phraseology comes from various ancient cultures' beliefs in many goddesses and gods that to not educate our children about them would be a great disservice and create a glaring void within their comprehension of the world. From astrology to astronomy to the naming of our celestial bodies and space program projects, the myriad facets of ancient mythology have become so intertwined in our society that it'd be an impossibility to cull them.

So your idea to include meditation in the public school curriculum, though a good one, would cause far too many problems. Meditation is a personal means of relaxation. And many less knowledgeable people would begin a witch-hunt in trying to eradicate it. When folks don't have a thorough understanding of something, they have a tendency to attribute it to the Devil. Sounds rather archaic, doesn't it?

► *Historically, when did the concept of meditation first appear?*
That's a question I can't answer because I don't think anyone knows. Meditation has been around for a long, long while. It's been practiced in some form or another in most cultures throughout the world since before recorded history. In every age, indigenous peoples around the world have used some meditation-like practice. Mystics, popes, hermits in the woods, Taoists in caves,

nuns in abbeys, and Druids among the standing stones have all meditated in some way of their own.

Don't forget, meditation—and the process by which it is practiced—is unique to each individual. There is no set-in-stone technique. Meditation is stilling the mind, and that can be accomplished in limitless ways. Various cultures may have different terms for the practice.

Asking when meditation was born is like asking when thought began. I suspect that even the first *Homo sapiens* experienced some type of meditative state. If one can think, one can experience a period of nonthinking.

► *Does concentration play a role in successful meditation?*

How can the application of thought energy contribute to achieving a state of nonthought? Your answer lies within your question. Meditation is managed through *avoiding* any form of concentration (concentrated thought).

► *Is group meditation okay to participate in?*

This idea of group meditation is being confused with group prayer or group healing gatherings. Meditation is a personal and extremely private practice. It loses its potential for purity when practiced with others. When others are present, they provide greater chances of one's meditative state being interrupted by distracting noise, and their simple presence can also present a distraction. Someone's breathing, throat clearing, or coughing can interrupt a meditative state.

Simple meditation—that is, the first stage of meditation—could be accomplished through group participation if the individuals didn't mind being disturbed. However, the deeper state of Quantum Meditation cannot be accomplished in the presence of another.

► *I've tried meditating on holy pictures and I just can't seem to be successful. Why?*

It's because you're *looking* at something and *thinking*. That's not even meditation; it's *contemplation*. You're contemplating an image. You're thinking about what it represents and what that representation means for you. Please separate the two concepts. Studying something, looking at it, thinking about it—this is contemplation. Nonthought is meditation. One is active; the other is inactive. *Contemplation* is active. *Meditation* is inactive. Therefore, you couldn't achieve a state of meditation while actively looking at and thinking about a picture before you. What you were doing was contemplating it. You can stare at your navel all you want and contemplate it, but you sure can't meditate on it.

► *Does one specific incense fragrance serve as a greater meditative impetus than another?*

It can, but read my explanation carefully. Meditation is the achievement of a completely relaxed state in mind and body. Now that we've noted that basic definition, let's elaborate. Each individual, because of his or her unique mean and composite vibratory rate, has equally unique sets of criteria for what soothes and relaxes him or her. In this manner alone can specific fragrances of incense aid personal relaxation. See what I'm saying? The incense alone is not a *key* to successful meditation, but it can be a key *aid* in relaxing the individual.

► *Is meditation a gift from God?*

The Creatrix gave us a mind. With that mind we have intelligence to develop and common sense to use. What the Divine Essence created was our *consciousness* (the spirit). Meditation is a method by which to expand that consciousness to a full understanding and experiential comprehension of creation's total reality.

▸ *I'm not into meditation, but I'm amazed at the wisdom that comes to me when I'm totally relaxed.*

You don't have to be "into" meditation to be doing it naturally.

Should a family meditate together? You know, like praying together?

No, because this is still group meditation. Whether the members of that group are strangers or immediate family members makes no discernible difference; the premise remains the same. Some activities (or nonactivities, such as meditation) are better done individually. Just because a family prays together doesn't also mean it bathes together. The type of activity itself determines whether it should be done as a group, family, or individually.

▸ *Does the practice of meditation help the world?*

No, because meditation is nonthought. What can help the world is energy applied through positive thought, prayer, and the continual practice of unconditional love and goodness. This means practicing acceptance and tolerance. It means avoiding prejudicial attitudes. It means encouraging unity with others by one's behavior. What can help the world more than anything else is having this behavioral priority: Do no harm. And you must mean it. Preface every thought, word, and action by silently asking yourself: *Will I cause any harm by saying or doing this?* If you do this, your behavior is going to really surprise you—maybe even embarrass you—because throughout the day, we do so many little automatic things that are in reality absolutely thoughtless in regard to others.

▸ *Will you be writing a meditation book?*

Absolutely not. Everyone has his or her own way of achieving a personal state of relaxation. It's up to each individual to write his or her own book, so to speak.

► *In Quantum Meditation, can one's consciousness relate to that of a discarnate entity?*

In Quantum Meditation, yes, but not in the generalized form that the public thinks of as meditation. The latter is simply a state of complete relaxation and doesn't extend further into the deeper state of quantum realities where Virtual Meditation can occur. In the Quantum Meditation stage, the meditator's consciousness is literally unbounded by the physical and can expand into any one of the thousands of other dimensional frequencies of reality where other consciousnesses can be present. To think that the meditator's consciousness is the only one within a dimensional realm is simply as arrogant and egocentric as thinking earth is the only celestial body with an intelligent humanoid life form.

► *When I meditate, I get a sensation that my whole body's expanding. Why does that happen?*

The expansion sensation comes from your sensing the fact that your entire body contains consciousness—each and every cellular structure—and your being made aware of that condition. It's not your body expanding—it's your consciousness. Once you get past the idea that the expansion is connected to only the physical body, your consciousness will expand further . . . much further.

► *Some authors who write about meditation strongly suggest that one begin the process with a positive affirmation for the purpose of self-protection. Is that necessary?*

Though it's not a mandatory prelude to meditation, it's not altogether a bad idea, either. Voicing a positive affirmation can be compared to whispering a prayer for a safe journey. It surrounds the self with an aura of good intent. There's nothing wrong with that, and it makes some folks more comfortable.

▶ *I don't try to meditate anymore because I once got into it and felt fear come over me. I didn't want any part of spookiness, so I avoid trying again.*

There's not a thing spooky about meditation. What you experienced was a fear of the unknown. Now, I won't deny that that in itself can frighten folks, but isn't it all a matter of one's particular perspective? If one is adventurous and inquisitive, if one is an explorer at heart, then one will welcome the thrill of discovery. On the other hand, if one has to peek beneath the bed before getting in, then that one will shy away from sending one's consciousness out into the vast expanse of reality to see what's there to experience. Meditation is not spooky. Meditation has the potential of being a highly unusual experience—a journey into the known, which is unknown only until we experience it.

▶ *I just don't get what the big hoopla is over meditation. I do fine without it. What's your opinion?*

First off, I hadn't realized that there was a big hoopla over meditation. It's merely a practice that some folks follow and some don't.

My opinion is that if you think you do fine without it, then that's great. That's your opinion and you seem to be comfortable with it. That's fine too. I'm not sure what you want me to address other than the "hoopla" bit.

Perhaps this perceived hoopla comes from your friends and acquaintances who practice meditation and talk about it. But again, because we're each unique, our preferences for relaxation vary greatly. Although some find sitting zombielike in front of a blaring TV a form of relaxation, others will find reading a book or meditation equally enjoyable. "To each his/her own" is not a cliché—it is just as meaningful today as it ever was.

If you have the impression that too much is made over the issue of meditation, then perhaps you might let those others know it's a subject you don't want to hear about constantly. I'm sure they could find other subject matters to talk about around you if they're made aware of the fact that it's become somewhat of an irritation to you.

► *My parents think I'm weird because I meditate, and that perception bothers me. How can I change their minds?*

The solution isn't in changing anyone's mind but in how you perceive yourself and accept your own individuality.

Your question shows that you're not accepting your uniqueness and enjoying the wonderful sense of freedom that comes from self-expression. You're depending on the acceptance and positive acknowledgments of others. You feel that your behavior has to fit into the confinements prescribed by others. Rather than striving for the acceptance of others (even parents or peers), strive to accept and treasure the inherent beingness of *yourself* and be proud of that beautiful individuality.

Everyone has an opinion on everything under the sun and moon. To strive to live your life according to those myriad opinions will, in the end, drive you crazy with continual vacillation as you try to align yourself with this one and that one. What's *your* opinion? That's the one to which you need to be true. What's your perception on issues? On life? On meditation?

I've had plenty of experience with this subject matter. Being an author of twenty books containing extremely personal life experiences and philosophy has put me out there on that proverbial limb. But is it a limb? Is it a limb if you're true to yourself and feel free to express your honest opinion and share what you've learned of life? Honesty is never a limb unless you don't possess a pure sense of self. Honesty is never a limb unless you feel a need to defer to the opinions of others. Peer pressure and public opinion (or anyone's opinion) should never color or fragment your inherent qualities. Others' opinions should never be a shroud that smothers your individuality and its free expression. How can you

celebrate the who of you and all that who entails if you hide it
beneath a damp and musty blanket of public opinion?

You'll be much happier and have a more optimistic view of life
if you simply realize that everyone will have a different opinion
and perspective than you do. That fact doesn't mean that any one
is better or more correct or truer than yours; it just means that
we're all different and opinions are a very real facet of that differentness.

▸ *During meditation, I frequently hear voices talking to me. Is*
that an indication that I'm being chosen and groomed to be a
channeler?

Absolutely not. That conclusion is self-serving and delusion-
ary. In the deeper stage of meditation, insights can come to one.
Intuitive thoughts and mental visuals can present themselves, but
never are actual *voices* heard in a physically *audible* manner.

Now, some readers might recall the times when I heard voices
and think I'm contradicting myself, but I'm not. I'm definitely not
contradicting myself. I've never, ever heard audible voices while
meditating. In fact, the only times I heard audible physical voices
were the two or three times that my life was saved by hearing
someone loudly whisper my name close to my ear, causing me to
pause or stop walking and look about me. That pause was always
just long enough to hold back my forward motion and save me
from being hit by a passing bus or other vehicle. Even when I
transmitted communications from spiritual advisors, I never
heard actual voices with my ears or in my head. The messages
came as inspirational thoughts and a natural Knowing.

If you're actually hearing audible voices during meditation (or
any other time), I suggest you consult a neurosurgeon or a psy-
chiatrist. I'm not being flip here. I'm offering a sincere suggestion
because it's not normal to hear audible voices talking to you when
no one else is around speaking the words—it's not a normal
aspect of meditation.

▸ *Is it better to meditate out in Nature or outside somewhere rather than in an enclosed space like a building?*

Thoughts cannot be confined by physical means; nor can the consciousness. In Quantum Meditation, the consciousness is not confined to even the brain or the physical body. It doesn't matter where the meditating is performed, as long as it's quiet and the individual can reach a state of total relaxation without the potential for interruption or distraction.

Technically, whether meditation is performed out in the open air or within a building doesn't matter. But again, I have to address the element of one's individuality and personal preference. Some people will attain total relaxation better if they're outside, and others need to feel more secure by doing it within a room. There are still others who don't really have a preference and can successfully accomplish a satisfactory meditative state in either place. It's up to the individual.

It's a personal technicality, not a universal one. I've known people who can meditate only out in Nature and I've known folks who can feel safe enough to manage it only in their home at night after everyone's asleep. Whatever works best for you is best for you.

▸ *My routine practice of meditation is causing problems between my husband and me. He thinks it's hoodoo and makes fun of me. What should I do?*

I can't tell you this. You have to make your own decision. Your mate isn't respecting your individuality. He's attempting to humiliate you by denigrating your beliefs. Perhaps you could suggest to him that he needs to analyze why he feels such a need to do this. Sometimes when people think about the reasons they behave the way they do, they see themselves in a whole different light and make adjustments to their behavior. Oftentimes, denigration and humiliation are generated from attempts to raise one's own self-image. There are other reasons too, so you might try having him explain his need to do this. Perhaps he simply doesn't understand what meditation is all about. Maybe he's secretly tried it and makes fun of your doing it because he didn't get anywhere. Talk about it—talk.

▶ *Sometimes when I come out of a meditative state I have tears rolling down my cheeks. I never remember anything happening to cause this. Can you shed some light on this?*

Frequently the meditative state brings us to a perceptual point of crystal clarity whereby we are emotionally sensitive and in touch with reality. That touch can generate natural and highly emotional responses. Sometimes it's empathy, which, during our busy awake state, we keep hardened so we can endure society's inhumanity. Sometimes it's compassion or sympathetic responses. Other times it's just plain sorrow for the suffering people endure around the world. The specific cause doesn't have to be recalled for the spiritual beingness within us to evince an honest and natural reaction.

We pass through the hours of our days in a self-created shell. This is for self-preservation, a meager means of creating a distance from the negative elements that invade our world view. This shell is a subconscious attempt to insulate our sensitivities and protect them from injury. Meditation, because it frees one's true consciousness, exposes the core self to reality . . . to all facets of that reality. And the true consciousness, without the insulating hardened shell, responds.

▶ *Can meditation reveal solutions to one's personal life problems?*

Rather than revealing specific, detailed solutions, it has the potential for providing a variety of insights that in turn can lead to those desired resolutions. Meditation can bring clarity to situations or relationships that are, in one's awake state, muddled with complexity. The clarity doesn't come as definitive answers but rather insightful generalities we interpret as sparks of enlightenment or wisdom or epiphanies. One of the beautiful benefits of meditation is that it has the capability of bringing clarity of thought.

► *Meditation doesn't ever give me any sparks of enlightenment. What am I doing wrong?*

The most obvious thing you're doing wrong is being in expectation when going into meditation—in expectation of being given great bits of high wisdom and esoteric pieces of enlightenment. Meditation is most successful when one goes into it without any kind of specified purpose other than simple relaxation. If it's meant to be more than that, everything else will follow quite naturally on its own. First and foremost, meditation is a means of complete relaxation. To expect more is to invite failure.

► *I'm an overweight person and can't sit up with my spine erect for meditation. Does this mean that I'll never be able to do it?*

Absolutely not. What's the matter with lying down on your bed with your back straight? You don't have to sit up to meditate.

► *Should meditation be done every day for it to be successful and advance to deeper levels?*

No, not at all. Meditation is most successful when the conditions are right for the individual to perform it. The idea of keeping to a time schedule is forcing it. Relaxation cannot be forced into a time slot that cannot be naturally accommodated. To attempt this causes stress; the meditator will sit there thinking about all the other things he or she needs to attend to. And to think meditation needs to be done every single day is just as illogical. Meditation is most effective and successful when it's done whenever the individual is most comfortable performing it.

► *I found myself meditating during some of the church services I attended. I felt so disrespectful and couldn't believe I'd done that. How could I?*

My opinion is that you in no way showed disrespect. The meditative state you slipped into during church service showed that the atmosphere caused you to be spiritually relaxed. Church is a great place to seek solace, and solace is a wonderful relaxer. I think it was more of a compliment to the Divine than being an act of disrespectful behavior. It's all in the perspective.

► *Can dark forces get you while you're meditating?*

This is a fear-generated idea used as an excuse by many people who don't want to put out the effort to meditate. A spirit entity (light or dark) has no interest in those who are meditating. Since the meditator's consciousness is being used (as opposed to what happens in the case of a drunken or drug-induced state), there is no viable opportunity for another entity to gain entrance. This explanation is a clarification of and refinement of previous misconceptions on this issue.

► *Should one be in a particular frame of mind when beginning meditation?*

Contrary to popular belief, being in a particular frame of mind when beginning meditation is not necessary. Most folks naturally think that one has to be in an upbeat frame of mind or have a positive or optimistic attitude, but that's just not so because it's not relevant to attaining success. Sometimes when we're down, meditation can have an uplifting effect on our mood and better our perspective on life. Meditation is extremely therapeutic not only as a relaxant for the physiological system and a respite from daily stress but also as an impetus for rearranging priorities into a more spiritually proper alignment.

▸ *Why would I come out of a good meditative state in a bad mood? That's just so illogical.*

It does seem illogical but it's really not. After spending time in an exceptionally good and successful meditation, you can feel let down upon returning to the awake state of consciousness. It'd be much like taking a visit to heaven and then having to come back home or dreaming that you had more money than you knew what to do with and then waking up to find you still had your same old money crunch. Still, you should have a residual feeling of elation and wonder that you carry through the rest of the day. This helps to balance the mundane elements of the daily grind. There are little tricks to avoiding this common letdown after a particularly good meditative period. For example, rather than focusing your mental energy on the dreariness of being back to your third-dimensional reality, carry the remembrance of your meditative state with you like a perfume scent that goes wherever you go. That's just one trick; I'm sure you can come up with others more specifically designed for you.

▸ *While trying to meditate, I find myself opening my eyes to look about the room as though to spot someone who might have suddenly appeared. I can't seem to break this interfering habit. Suggestions?*

You do this because when reaching a certain phase of your meditation—a certain depth—your sensual perception is intensified. This intensified sense of perception can frequently intuit the finer alteration of surrounding vibrations, which, in turn, you misinterpret as a presence of some type. Suddenly your eyes whip open to check who's there or, more accurately, to make sure who's not there. But there's no need to do this—the sensation is simply a slight shift in vibrational frequency of which you became aware. There's nothing to fear. Nothing has really changed. Your room is just the same as it was before you began meditation. It's you who's altered. It's your consciousness that's shifted, that's all. You're perfectly safe within your own consciousness. It's certainly not going to let anything untoward happen to you or around you. What it is going to do is give you the ride of your life . . . if you can keep those eyelids closed.

▸ *My cousin keeps telling me that the Devil will take my soul away when I meditate. He's so sure of this that his conviction scares me.*

You have an opportunity to counter his conviction with one of your own. Is yours not as dynamic and full of energy as his is? The next time you meditate, begin with an affirmation. Do you know what that is? An affirmation is a statement of intent. It doesn't have to be long and complex. It doesn't have to be a litany, just one simple phrase or sentence before you begin. You might want to work on the specific wording that you feel will be most effective, but make it a message of telling the Devil to go back to hell where he belongs and stay away from you. You may want to make the statement one that tells the Devil that you're surrounded with the Divine protective shield of white light. There are all sorts of ways to make yourself feel much more comfortable in the face of your cousin's belief.

Personal conviction is the strength of one's faith. Conviction cannot be forced or false. It has to have the power of strength behind it to reinforce its viability and effectiveness. Your own faith and trust in the practice of meditation can far outweigh that of your cousin's. It's up to you whether it does. If your belief in something is true and heartfelt, never let other people lessen its beauty by their ignorance. So many times in life we allow our beliefs or even our innate personal characteristics to be sullied by the rude and unkindly expressed opinions of those around us. Another's opinion, even if it's that of a relative, should never lessen the intensity of the light shimmering within yourself. Try to remember that the next time your cousin begins his tirade about your meditative practices. Cherish your unique beingness. Treasure your beliefs.

► *You may think I'm absolutely bonkers when I tell you this. I once meditated with my boyfriend while we held hands and, suddenly, some powerful energy surged through both of us and it was just like we simultaneously had an orgasm. We were shocked because it was nearly better than the real thing! Have you ever heard of that happening?*

Ahh, yes, I have.

I've not written of this before because, well, the way people can be, they'd want to meditate for the express purpose of experiencing orgasms. They wouldn't care to admit that such an experience is a rarity that manifests only when an individual is in a specific stage of spiritual development. That stage is when the lower Energy Gate (the gonads) has just opened up. Evidently you and your boyfriend both were at the same stage of development and your united hands served as the connection point to vector the tandem energy between you.

Yes, this can happen, but meditation is not for this purpose. It's to relax the body, yes, but not *that* much. One normally doesn't have the urge to reach for a cigarette after meditation.

If you want to avoid future disappointment, don't go into it again expecting the same result. Expectation is a form of thought, and meditation is nonthought.

► *Do spiritual people such as priests experience a different type of meditation than that of common folk?*

Priests *are* common folk. No, they're no different than you when it comes to meditation. In fact, they could have more difficulties with it than you do because oftentimes, they have a spiritually elevated perception of themselves and are in expectation regarding how spectacularly religious their meditations should be.

► *When I try to meditate, really weird visuals appear. Is this normal? Why does this happen?*

When you first settle in to meditate, thoughts come unbidden and visuals pass before your mind's eye. These are common and quite normal. Thoughts can come in the form of words or as visuals, as in dreams. This latter is what you're experiencing.

Our days are chock-full of subliminal impressions to which we give little conscious attention. The beginning stage of meditation is much like the initial stage of night sleep. The awake-state consciousness is being laid to rest and the subconscious takes the helm for a time. During this time, the mind begins its playback of recorded impressions and they come as thoughts and symbolic visuals. The important thing to remember is to just let them pass by without giving them any energy of applied thought. Allow the visuals to pass just as you do the thoughts. Eventually they'll play out to the end of the tape and you'll reach the second stage of nonthought. Visuals are not unusual during meditation; they're an alternative means of thought presentation.

► *Most of the books I've read on meditation stress the importance of the straight-back position, but I've a medical condition that prevents my using that position. I've found that I can meditate best in a half-sitting, half-lying position on a chaise longue. Am I hampering success by this positioning?*

No, not at all.

The reason for the straight-back position is to provide a straight shot for the body's energy (the *chi* or kundalini) to rise up through the six main Gates located along the spine. However, I've personally found that it makes no difference what position one meditates in because the energy will still freely flow upward unencumbered by any chosen position. The energy flow is not hampered or held by gravity because it follows a singular pathway through the body. It's like one road leading from here to there, so that "traffic" cannot be detoured or directed elsewhere by a curve in that road or a dip or rise. The energy still follows the same course no matter how that course is configured. Oftentimes I find myself slouching down in my reading chair with my feet up on the ottoman and slipping into a state of semimeditation that flows into a full-blown meditative event. I've never experienced a bit of trouble because of my positioning. You're fine.

► *I've had my thyroid removed. Does that mean the kundalini can't flow past that region and will consequently prevent me from achieving successful meditation?*

Successful meditation is not contingent on the body's central glands or Gates. These merely open up when one's meditation advances the energy up through them. If one or more glands are absent, that only speeds up the process rather than hampers or negates it. You should have no trouble meditating without these centralized glands.

► *When I meditate, I feel as though someone is touching me, and this always distracts me. I open my eyes, brush the spot, and then have to begin all over again. Who's doing this and how do I stop it?*

As explained in my response to an earlier question, the consciousness has reached a highly perceptive stage where bodily sensations and intuitive perceptions are intensely heightened. This heightened perception to sensation and vibrations makes one more aware of the little innocuous physiological occurrences (skin tingles, hair movements, nerve twinges) that go unnoticed during one's busy awake state. Frequently these sensations can come by way of seemingly tactile skin surface prickles or touches. They're really not anomalies at all, because they're occurring all the time during one's day, but since one's consciousness is so perceptive during meditation, they're experienced as anomalies or odd sensations. Because of this perception, the meditator can easily interpret them as being generated by an outside force.

The next time this happens, I suggest that you try to restrain yourself from moving to brush at the spot. Usually, once one understands the cause of such perceptions, the urge to make responsive movements dissipates and one can progress beyond them.

▶ *I used to meditate every single day, but then somehow I got away from it. If I begin again, will it be like starting all over again or will my development continue where it left off?*

Regarding meditation, one's attained level of advancement doesn't wane with absence or time away from meditation. It's like riding a bike. You may have to get into the swing of it again, but you certainly won't have to start from scratch because your level of attainment is still the same.

▶ *Does meditation have to be done every day for one to achieve an advanced or more developed stage?*

As I stated earlier, to think it has to be practiced every single day is, in a way, detrimental. I say this because generally, if one feels that one must do a certain task or activity every single day, then that activity can easily shift from being one of enjoyment and pleasure to being one of drudgery. One's perspective about it can dramatically alter. Instead of its being an enjoyable activity to look forward to, it becomes just another routine job that demands one's time. No, meditation does not have to be practiced every day for one to achieve an advanced or more developed stage.

▶ *If meditation is so great and so many people believe in it, why is society's behavior still so ugly and hateful?*

Though meditation relaxes mind and body, it can't work the miracle of changing an intolerant attitude into unconditional acceptance. It can't turn a skeptic into a believer. It can't make a philanthropist out of a wealthy tightwad. Understanding the concept of meditation also allows one to fully comprehend its scope of functionality, including its benefits and limitations. To expect the practice of meditation to be a cure-all isn't rational. To think of it as being the magic bullet for all of society's behavioral ills is not only unreasonable but downright delusional.

I believe that this world of ours would indeed be a much better place if every person did practice meditation, because it's so effective at relieving daily stress. Many of society's problems are generated by people's increased stress levels, so anything that eases that stress would naturally result in altered behavior. Yet everyone does not practice meditation, so we don't see an overall change.

► *Meditation doesn't seem to do for me what it does for others. How come?*

Since you didn't clarify exactly what meditation's doing for these other people you're talking about, I can't directly comment about that aspect of your question. My first inclination is to ask you if you're sure these other individuals aren't exaggerating their results or attendant experiences.

Hearing about others' experiences during their meditation can sometimes increase one's expectations of meditation. There should never be expectation with meditation. For each individual, it is what it is. It's the type of activity for which results and benefits are specifically geared to the specific requirements and particular characteristics of the individual meditator. What one person experiences won't necessarily be beneficial for another person to experience. What's so intriguing about meditation is its fundamental individuality. It's never the same for everyone. The experiences are usually something you can truly call your own. It's like one's fingerprint or voiceprint—uniquely personal.

► *I'm sick of hearing about meditation. I've tried and tried and it just doesn't work, so I tell my friends that I never seem to have time for it.*

You really don't want to do it, do you? You've tried and tried only because your friends and other peers have been practicing it.

Feeling you can be accepted by your peers only by involving yourself in their activities is no way to celebrate your individuality.

Oftentimes comment such as yours are a means of escapism that extricates one from having to participate in socially acceptable activities. I've found that many folks really have a poor opinion of meditation, much less have a desire to practice it, and that's okay. It really is. And if that's your perspective, then you should feel free to be honest and straightforward about it rather than make excuses to friends why you don't do it. Why the need for excuses? You have just as much right to your own opinion as they do, even if you feel you don't or even if you feel that you'll be ridiculed for it. Fear of ridicule shouldn't ever stop you from being honest and expressing an alternative opinion on something. Cherish your own integrity. Fear of ridicule never stopped me, and as everyone knows, I've certainly had my share of detractors who love their right to free expression. But listen, you tarnish your integrity if you think you need to make excuses for yourself or your beliefs. Don't do that to yourself. If you continue to make excuses to cover your real opinion, then deep down, your convictions aren't solid and your actions do not verify them. Never be embarrassed about what you believe. If meditation isn't for you, then fine, it isn't for you. End of story, no excuses or explanations required. Be honest about it with your friends. If they don't understand, then they don't understand. They don't need to put their seal of understanding and acceptance on your opinion. One's personal opinions and perspectives need no approval from others. They stand tall on their own.

► *Can meditation be a form of prayer?*

Any thought or behavior that affects benevolent or peaceful perspectives can be seen as a form of prayer. Any type of activity that improves one's world view through the reduction of stress can be perceived as a form of prayer. Anything that serves to uplift humankind is seen in the eyes of the Creatrix as a form of prayer.

Generally, just as a matter of course, society has become so conditioned regarding its perspective on prayer that people view it exclusively as the reciting of prescribed words or as the active asking of some favor from the Divine Essence. But this view is so myopic that it literally excludes all other forms of prayer, such as those generated by positive behavior like unconditional love and acts of unconditional goodness, the expression of empathy and compassion, and exercising tolerance and acceptance. Our spiritual *behavior* is far more an act of prayer than are all the other types of prayer combined, including meditation, which is a form of prayer because it has the potential to reduce the psychological stress that causes unkind and thoughtless behavior. Any voluntary attempt made to reduce the unspiritual behavior in our lives is perceived as a prayer in the eyes of the Divine. Even a kind thought can be a prayer. Stopping along the roadside to help someone with his or her impaired vehicle can be a prayer; likewise, shoveling snow from a neighbor's walk, visiting a sick friend, running an errand for another, and just giving a warm smile can be acts of prayer.

▶ *Is there a particular time of day (or night) that's best for meditation?*

The best time to meditate is whatever time is best for the meditator. Depending on the individual's schedule, meditation times will vary greatly from one person to the next. Choose a time when you can be relatively assured of quiet time and the chance of interruptions will be at a minimum. Women with families seem to have the most difficulty finding the time to meditate, especially those with small children at home all day and a husband around in the evenings. When my own daughters were wee babies, I'd put them down for a nap, turn the phone ringer off, and run the vacuum outside their door. The droning sound put them to sleep and I could meditate at the same time because the sound was no more distracting to me than having a window air conditioner running.

Now there are those Nature sound machines that a mom could place in the baby's room to lull the child to sleep.

The point of all this is that since everyone's daily lifestyle is different, each person has to determine his or her own best time when a reasonable span of peaceful time is available for them because, technically, there is no best prescribed time for practicing meditation.

THE KNOWING AND THE GREAT ALONE

Wisdom and Spiritual Philosophy

▶ *This planet is filled with such hatred that I often feel as though I don't belong here, that I made a reentry mistake and landed on the wrong planet. I'm often asking myself, "What am I doing here?" Since I feel like such a misfit among all this hate-filled behavior, could it be possible that I really did come to the wrong place?*

No, those types of errors don't happen. You came to the exact place your spirit consciousness wanted to be. Your spirit marked an X on the spot it wanted to be and you landed smack dab in the middle of the crosshairs.

There are many who share your same feelings, though knowing this may not help to soothe your dismay over feeling like a misfit here. For those who love unconditionally with no taint of intolerance or prejudice, living here with the continual hatred going on can be extremely difficult. Yet what better place for one such as yourself and all those others to be? A place filled with hatred needs the counterforce of unconditional love and goodness to nullify it and bring the social behavior and perspective back into spiritual balance. Without folks like you, there'd be nothing different for the hatred to come up against. See what I mean? You and those like you can make an incredible difference. If those filled with prejudice and intolerance can form hate groups, you and yours can form unconditional love groups. You and yours can organize walks against hate, work to establish legislation against hate crimes, connect with others through networking and . . . make a difference! That's why you're here among the hate-filled ones. That's why you came. You came to *do* something constructive and be an effective counterforce to the hatred.

Isn't it time for society to raise its consciousness up to the advanced level it should be at this time in history? Isn't hatred reminiscent of primitive humankind's savage mentality? Those who understand this and have unconditional love and goodness in their hearts should not just give up in the face of primeval behavior. They need to take a stand together and make their voices heard as one. As one, those voices can make an earth-shattering sound that overpowers the shouts of the hatemongers. Goodness is just as powerful as hatred. Use it. Use it as a counterforce in as many ways as possible.

▸ *I like going to my church, but I feel so left out and somewhat demeaned because I'm a woman.*

Guess what? The time for patriarchal domination is waning. The time for women to walk into their churches with bowed and covered heads is over. It's time for all women to walk into their places of worship with raised chins so they can proudly look straight into the sacred eyes of the Divine Feminine Aspect who lovingly acknowledges their presence.

Ever since men gathered two thousand years ago to mandate the official canonical gospels, women's spirituality was deemed satanic and banned. Womanhood itself was degraded and all aspects of femininity were declared sinful. Women were shoved out of their ancient and long-standing matriarchal position and into one of patriarchal subjugation and servitude. They were declared to be unclean and to have no intellect. Their feminine worship was banned and their goddesses were degraded. Only one god was allowed to be recognized and worshiped, and that god was male. He was called the Father. His aspects were the Son and Holy Ghost. For two thousand years, women underwent indoctrination about that male perspective.

As introduced in my book, *The Visitation,* the reality of the Trinity is not all male. The reality of the Trinity is Mother, Father, Daughter . . . *two* feminine aspects. It is the Mother *Sophia* aspect that is reflected in terms such as *Mother* Nature, the Earth *Mother, Grandmother* Spider, and the *Grandmother* Crone (representing the high wisdom of the feminine elder). The Mother Sophia aspect of the Trinity was the Creatrix of all things spiritual. She is the life force behind all the physical creations that emitted from the God/Father aspect. She is the breath of life. Sophia is life.

Mother Sophia has a lower Sophia aspect that is called Shekinah. Shekinah is the Holy Spirit Aspect of Sophia. Shekinah is the spirit of the Divine at work in the world. And Their spirits have both returned to the physical to raise feminine spirituality back to its rightful place. They have come to cast off the shroud patriarchal religion has smothered them with.

Among the ancient hidden scrolls and codices discovered in the Najᶜ Hammādī desert in December of 1945 was one called *The Thunder: Perfect Mind.* It was written in the first person, and the scholarly translators propose that this text was authored by the dual aspects of the higher and lower Sophias.

Several years ago, I experienced continual promptings to research these ancient gnostic gospels and, after doing so, was inexplicably drawn to this specific one. So strong was the draw that it plagued my waking hours and invaded my sleep time with visuals of it. Finally, to still the thoughts of this writing that continually intruded into my life, I decided I had to address it in a physical manner. When the words *Song of Sophia* speared into my mind, I knew that they were meant to be one of my book titles, done as a personal interpretation of *The Thunder: Perfect Mind.*

After I decided to go through with this, the nagging thoughts subsided. It was as if they breathed a collective sigh of relief and could now rest . . . the message had gotten through. Though I've given my attention to *Song of Sophia,* it's time for publication has not yet been determined and it may end up being an 'unpublished' work.

▸ *Are hatred and intolerance evidence of influential dark spirit forces?*

Your question caused me to think you're implying actual dark spirit entities similar to demons and such. If this was your intent, my response is this: not necessarily.

If we look at the opposite behavioral quality—that of unconditional goodness—we wouldn't necessarily say that is evidence of a light spirit or an angel sitting on our shoulder influencing that good behavior. The same applies to unspiritual behavior. There is spiritual behavior and there is unspiritual behavior. Both are not necessarily directly inspired by light and dark spirit entities. People have to realize that they have *personal* responsibility for their free-will choice regarding the type of behavior they exhibit.

Behavior is a choice. Babies aren't born racists, they're psychologically conditioned to be so through life experiences and choices. Inherently, a racist or individual exhibiting any other type of prejudicial attitude knows that the perspective is wrong. They know it's wrong to hate, yet because of a strongly focused ego, they manage, through the psychological mechanism of rationalization, to skew that knowing into a belief that prejudice is acceptable. In effect, they move the lines delineating good behavior from bad so their own self-styled perspective fits within what they then perceive as a framework of acceptable attitudes and behavior. This is not necessarily the work of demons or entities of a dark force whispering nasty thoughts in their ears; it's the work of the human mind's ability to rationalize behavior according to egomaniacal elements.

Oftentimes bad behavior is attributed to dark forces because folks don't want to admit personal responsibility for their thoughts and actions. It's so easy and convenient to make a scapegoat out of anyone who's within reach. Who's handier than the Devil and his minions? Yeah, let's blame our bad behavior on them! The reality is that every one of us has a free will and the ability to make rational choices in life. The reality is that even if a little arrow-tailed imp told you to do it, you have a mind and mouth with which to say no. The final choice is still yours to make and be accountable for. People need to stop making excuses and creating scapegoats for their own behavior.

► *Why does God call back babies and children before they've had a chance to live?*

The Creatrix created spirits. God created all things physical and the Creatrix breathed life into those physical creations. The end.

The rest is all the functionings and manifestations of reality. Sickness, accidents, climatological and geological catastrophes, disease, murder, and so on are all inherent elements of reality. A premature infant born without the strength to persevere is a situational aspect of reality. An earthquake or avalanche that devastates an entire town or village is an element of reality. A drive-by shooting is a facet of reality. These are not the work of God. What kind of God do you believe in if you think any of the divine aspects of the Trinity would look down (or about) and randomly point a holy finger at this baby or that town and shout, "Die!"? The Divine does not create human grief or sorrow. The divine aspects do not wish to cause sorrow and human pain. Reality does it all quite naturally . . . all by itself. And what reality leaves undone, human cruelty finishes.

▸ *My sister has strong religious beliefs, yet her behavior rarely reflects them. I can't understand how that type of situation exists.*

There are people who use religion as a means of gaining acceptance, especially those beliefs to which are attached the label of *traditional.* These are the safe ones, the ones accepted by conservatives, thus supposedly providing the least opportunity for ridicule.

Religious beliefs can be directly expressed through public worship and they can be indirectly expressed through behavioral patterns. The public elements are those such as regularly showing up at worship services, participating in religious group socials, volunteering for religious group committees, and so forth. Those are the direct, obvious elements. The more subtle inner behavioral elements of one's spiritual belief include the exhibition of tolerance, acceptance, unconditional goodness and love, a desire to go out of one's way for others, compassion, and assistance of those who need help. These are the qualities of spirituality your sister is lacking because she is into *religion* instead of *spirituality.* There's a wide chasm of difference between religion and spirituality. I'm not a religious person, because I associate myself with no form of established, traditional tenets; instead, I'm a *spiritual* person. I recognize the necessity of having a personal relationship with the Divine, not a relationship confined by dogma devised by a group of sexist men. My connection with the Divine Sophia and Shekinah is never rigid or composed of recited preformed prayers and written traditional ritual. It's expressed from within the soft core of my beingness—spontaneous, tender, and spiritually sensual. I don't approach the feminine Divine Essences with fear or any sense of submission but rather with a heart overflowing with love. In return, I am blessed—blessed with tears of fulfillment and deep serenity. The Divine Feminine Aspects of the Trinity shun ritual, for they perceive them as self-serving human elements. They demand no ceremony or prescribed prayers. They turn Their heads at the sight of golden vestments and walk away from any sign of physical offerings. They rejoice and lovingly accept behavioral gifts of unconditional love and goodness. Their hearts are gladdened when people understand the true meaning of power and wisdom. They shed tears of joy when people comprehend the true scope and depth of love. And solitude is Their abode. It is only the serenity of solitude—the sanctuary within—that They've chosen as Their touchable connection to us.

I didn't go into all of the above to shift the focus of this question to myself but to offer my own strong sense of spirituality as an example to clarify my reply.

Today's idea of spirituality is religion, consisting of personal exhibitions of one's holiness that in reality are incredibly self-aggrandizing. It's become egocentric. Show yourself at your house of worship to advertise how devoted you are, all the while avoiding spiritual behavior within your daily life. Volunteer for religious group socials and projects but spread rumors over the fence and shake your head over those who are different. Give generously to your religious group's new building fund while doing nothing to keep the local homeless shelter's coffers full. Pray during worship for your more "unfortunate" sisters and brothers but then sign a petition to keep a home for abused women out of your neighborhood. Religion—it's become a venue for public display of one's goodness while hiding one's true spirituality. Religion and spirituality have nothing in common. One is external; the other is internal. One says, "*Look* at me, God. See how many ways I help your religious body!" The other says, "Look not upon me, Goddess, but rather *feel* my love for humanity." Religion and churches versus pure spirituality and sanctuaries—that's the faceoff we'll all soon witness.

These are my thoughts; perhaps you'd like to pass some of them on to your sister. Perhaps it will open her eyes a little. Whatever divine concepts you profess to believe in, if your behavior doesn't reflect them in daily life, then neither religion nor spirituality is truly a living presence in your life. Then those concepts have no more substance than a movie-set building with a false front. If this situation is one you identify with, then you need to sit down and seriously analyze your behavior. Why are you using religion as a front? Is it for acceptance? You need to realize that the outward profession of religion is nothing but a shallow, empty shell unless you live the essence of it daily. You have to acknowledge that such behavior is hypocritical and means you are not being true to yourself.

▶ *I've lost all faith in religion after seeing how these self-righteous fundamentalist leaders incite intolerance and prejudice within their congregations.*

Religion is manmade to begin with. It is better to place your trust and faith in personal spirituality, within which there are no leaders. Religious leaders oftentimes use their falsely perceived elevated position to manipulate public opinion and incite negative behavior. They support their opinions by citing biblical passages. But the Bible has been changed each time men have translated it—and it began as written hearsay and recorded recollections of ordinary people. They cite the Bible without understanding that the book is full of glaring contradictions. Yet they claim that it's the absolute word of God.

Many religious leaders misuse the power they believe they have by inciting their followers with fire-and-brimstone tirades fueled by prejudice. They love repeating such words as *sinners* and *pagans* in their rants. They liberally pepper their sermons with *infidels* and *abominations* like they're trying to win a Texas chili contest and then they have the audacity to slip in the word *looove* at the end of the sentence. Religious leaders have incited and perpetrated ongoing prejudice and hatred because of their staunch intolerance for the differentness of human beings. They've started entire land wars over their beliefs. They've gathered "holy" armies of fighting men to kill others for the preservation of their faiths. And when there are no religious-related land grabbers against whom to incite their followers to fight, these leaders fire up their followers to hate individuality and uniqueness in others.

Putting faith in religion or religious leaders is like putting all your resources into building on swamp land. Disappointment is never a side effect of spirituality. It is better that you discover your spiritual source as the One living in the sacred temple within yourself rather than placing all your faith in men and their ever-shifting delusions of power.

► *I'm so ashamed. My minister said that I was a bad person. I don't know what to do.*

You can start by dumping your minister. I'm serious. No religious figure has the right to tell anyone that he or she is a bad person. That's a prime example of why so many people are currently questioning their faith, their religion, their spiritual direction, and their ministers. That, coupled with the recent increase in reports of pedophilic behavior by priests and ministers, is making people take a hard look at whom they look to for religious leadership.

I just can't fathom a religious person telling someone that he or she is a bad person. Everyone alive has skeletons in his or her closet. No one is perfect, for perfection can be attributed to only the Divine Essences. We all have failings. Not a one of us is without fault and not a one of us has the right to claim or imply that we're as pure as the driven snow. Even Jesus cursed, got enraged, gambled, and so forth. To the straight-laced religious leaders of today, Jesus' real-life behavior would be seen as an abomination, but because those religious leaders have whitewashed over all of that, he's presented as the epitome of Godhood. For any official religious personality to outright say that a person is bad is poor counseling generated by a lack of understanding of human psychology and the reality of life. It's inexcusable, and I feel so much empathy for you over this travesty.

You're a good person. You're no more bad than the rest of us. As per the information provided in the rest of your letter, just because you firmly disagree with your church's stance on allowing women to be ministers or hold any official position certainly does not make you a bad person. This is just another method by which the patriarchy-based religions uphold their women-excluding tenets—they humiliate women by attempting to make them feel shame over their attitude and disrespect for the "laws of God." If you must feel that you need a physical church to attend, try another one—one that teaches gender equality, not male superiority.

► *Do spirits have to reincarnate?*

Lifetimes spent in the physical are the means for providing opportunities to learn and to rectify past mistakes. Because of this, physical experiences for the spirit are important. However, there are also these same opportunities within other dimensions of reality, and many entities opt to experience those between lifetimes spent in the third dimension. Many times people naturally perceive earth as being the only three-dimensional place where spirits can reincarnate, yet there are a multitude of others.

► *Your spiritual philosophy has shifted to the feminine from your former male God–focused concept. Though I find this somehow enlightening, I was wondering how come the change.*

It's not actually a change or shift at all but rather a final blossoming of the flower I've always nurtured. I'm nearing the end of the message (writing) phase of my work, so it would naturally follow that those later messages represent the full bloom of final development. Rather than my work's actually being more feministic, I think it is perceived that way because of society's conditioning to "think male." People have been conditioned to always use the male gender for terminology; they are used to seeing *brotherhood,* so when I use *sisterhood* in the term's general sense, I'm perceived as being feministic. If I write *she/he* instead of the more accustomed presentation of *he/she*, I'm viewed as being feministic. Yet all I'm doing is attempting to balance gender in my writing by not making it so male focused. Most folks don't even realize how male focused society has been. And when an author tries to balance that focus, she or he is seen as being a feminist.

For two thousand years, women have lived with society's male focus in language. Even the God they believed in was presented as male—in fact, all the aspects of the Trinity were presented as being male, after their ancient beliefs in the many benevolent goddesses were banned by the male forefathers of the Christian religion. So now comes someone who wants to bring a bit of balance back into the language and not shut out the female gender, and that individual is perceived as a feminist. The time has come for the reality of the Trinity's true nature to be reestablished and brought back into focus. This concept of the Mother Sophia, God the Father, and the Shekinah (Holy Spirit) is not even a revelation because it's an age-old concept that even Jesus spoke about when he told Mary Magdalene that she was blessed because she fully understood the concept of the Sophia as being the Divine Mother. This last was recorded in some of the discovered Naj‘ Ḥammādī scrolls that were hidden two thousand years ago from the Christian forefathers who planned to redesign the persona of Jesus and his teachings according to their own patriarchal strictures. In the forefathers' attempt to accomplish this, they banned all opposing records and written transcripts of Jesus' teachings. Therefore, many had to be hidden away and buried to preserve the truth. The year the truth came to light was 1945.

So now as my series of books nears its time of conclusion and the final messages blossom forth in them, I really don't care what people misperceive or what label they slap on my back as a result, because when all is written and done, there will be nothing presented that wasn't already there, not only two thousand years ago but since the beginning of time. All I'm doing is releasing it from the dark grave men have buried it in and raising it back up into the glorious sunlight.

I never paid much attention to labels. They're such a separatist kind of thing and always seemed so petty, as if people didn't have anything more productive to do with their lives than to look for things to criticize about people and then call each other names. What an incredible waste of good energy and intellect.

▸ *Do you foresee the Second Coming happening in this lifetime?*

This event is not going to be what people are expecting. People have the same misperception about the Second Coming as they do about the book of Revelation and Armageddon. They're taking the literal letter of them rather than the more subtle spirit of them. If I were to suggest to you that all of those events were happening right now, you wouldn't believe me, so I prefer to leave the matter up to each individual's contemplation.

▸ *I understand about quantum realities and other dimensional planes of existence, but is there really such a place as heaven?*

That's difficult to answer because of the wide variety of conceptions people have of the place. Are there pearly gates with Saint Peter standing there as official gatekeeper? No, not really, but then I have to qualify that answer to include the possibility that that image is created by the minds of those believing in that visual at the time of their death. Because our true consciousness is what survives the demise of the physical body, that consciousness is what has the after-death experience, and within that consciousness are impressions and philosophies imposed on it during life. If these impressions *aren't* viable elements of reality, then they will be present upon physical death but then wane away as reality is experienced by the consciousness and the true state of affairs becomes evident.

The consciousness never dies. After physical death, it lives on.

The consciousness is one's spirit essence. If that essence has been brought into a state of spiritual alignment that is pleasing to the Divine Beings, then that's as close to heaven as one can get. This gets us back to labels and terminology. Heaven is a conceptual term, not a descriptive one.

► *I have such a hard time holding my tongue. In* Fireside, *you outlined the qualities of wisdom that are the main elements of power, but I still have trouble applying it in life.*

I never said it was easy.

What you're referring to is wisdom's quality of silence, and what an incredibly powerful tool it can be. Silence is indeed power. Knee-jerk reactive responses are the most difficult to control and contain. Knowing the wisdom of using silence isn't the same as actually practicing it. For you, what this comes down to is self-control—you need to control that knee-jerk, quick-draw comment that wants to fire out of your mouth. You need to remember that words are powerful things; they can be used as a weapon or a soothing balm. Nonwords are the same. Silence can be just as powerful as the words you want to fire off—perhaps more so. Think about that one. *Silence can be more powerful than the words you want to fire off.* Here's something else to consider: When you fire your words back at someone, you could be allowing yourself to be the willing victim of manipulation. Ever think that some people might be inciting you? Goading you on? This type of behavior can be a subtle form of manipulation few recognize. Silence foils it completely. By keeping silent, you prevent the situation from gaining negative energy. Silence can prevent a situation from turning ugly or keep you from saying something you may greatly regret.

We all have moments when the urge to spout a comeback is strong, yet holding your tongue shows you have the wisdom of self-control. The more times you can manage to keep silent, the easier it becomes. You may be surprised at the responses your silence elicits when folks are expecting you to make a sharp-tongued retort and nothing happens. Make it a game of sorts. Turn it into a study of human behavior.

► *Is being psychic an indication of one's spiritual advancement?*

No, it's a skill or talent like being an artist or having a knack for architectural design. The psychic qualities some folks exhibit have nothing at all to do with their level of spirituality. This is a common misconception. One is not directly associated with the other.

► *Why are some people so fascinated with the Devil? I know a fundamentalist and he's always saying that Satan is causing this or that.*

It's a form of religious prurient interest. By attaching religious connotations to Satan, such people can have a bona fide reason to talk about the dark side of Nature and people's behavior. They do appear to have an unhealthy fascination with dark forces. It's as if they attribute more power to the Devil than to God because I've frequently heard some people make claims of personal "satanic attacks" upon their person. They're obsessed with satanic attacks and see them happening everywhere. It's delusional and using religion as a means of self-serving attention getting.

► *I don't understand why people fight over religion. If you're comfortable in your own personal belief system, why should you care what others believe?*

Got me on that one. I would have to suggest that the reason they do this is to try to convince others that their belief is the only true one and all others are false. This is why religion is so problematic and why simple spirituality is so much better. Religion is composed of manmade dogma and ceremonial elements over which folks argue. Spirituality is purely the behavior of unconditional love and goodness—nothing to argue over.

► *Can you suggest some good spiritual reading material?*

I prefer to let people's reading choices be prompted by their own inner guidance, but there are a few good general ones I usually suggest:

- *The Gnostic Gospels,* by Elaine Pagels, published by Vintage Books, ISBN 0-394-74043-3
- *Pope Joan: A Novel,* by Donna Woolfolk Cross, published by Crown, ISBN 0-517-59365-3
- *She Who Dwells Within: A Feminist Vision of a Renewed Judaism,* by Rabbi Lynn Gottlieb, published by HarperSanFrancisco, ISBN 0-060-63292-5
- *Nostradamus: Prophecies for Women,* by Manuela Dunn Mascetti and Peter Lorie, published by Simon & Schuster, ISBN 0-671-89656-3
- *The Nag Hammadi Library in English,* edited by James M. Robinson, published by Harper & Row, ISBN 0-060-66934-9

► *Why do people's personal prayers always seem to be asking for something?*

Personal prayers always seem to be asking for something because people don't understand reality and personal responsibility. It's the same with the thank-you prayers—most of the situations they think they need to thank God for were obtained or attained through their own efforts.

These two types of prayers come from the general misperception that God has a constant hand in every individual's life, when in fact the Divine Essences leave it up to the reality of free will and personal choices folks make in life. If someone holds the winning lottery ticket, he or she thanks God, but in actuality, God wouldn't be so selective as to choose one individual to be the winner. God doesn't care a whit about the lottery. It was just a matter of that winner's good happenstance to have bought the chosen ticket. Nothing more. Same with sports. You ever see a receiver in a football game make the catch and run for the touchdown, then go down on bended knee and make the sign of the cross? Why's he thanking God? Did he think God was personally rooting for his team? What?

Prayers have become as diluted as the idea of love. Both terms are used indiscriminately, sullying the purity of their meanings. People continually ask God for things and call that prayer. I call it greed. I call it wanting reality to be aligned with personal desires rather than using the wisdom of acceptance of What Is and What Is Meant To Be. Prayer is often misperceived and used as an alternative to personal responsibility. If someone wants something, then he or she works for it—but then that person thanks God for it when God had no hand in its manifestation. In some ways, prayer can be evidence of spiritual arrogance and an expression of the ego's self-importance because it clearly gives the message that the petitioner believes God will grant her/his wishes despite that individual's destiny, life path, or ultimate purpose. This is why I keep stressing the importance for folks to make acceptance a priority in their lives. With acceptance, life doesn't become consumed with personal wants; it is full of recognized blessings and the attainment of greater tolerance. The petitioning prayers can indicate a bucking of life's current, whereas acceptance implies an attitude of destiny acknowledgment.

I explained in the response to an earlier question, prayer is not for the purpose of asking, but rather for expressing spiritual behavior. Unconditional love and unconditional goodness are all the prayer the Divine Essences hope for. These two negate intolerance, hatred, prejudice, persecution, sexism, racism, and all the other negative behavior society can come up with. These two say it all.

Do a small experiment. Put yourself in the Di[...] places for a moment and listen to all the prayers [...] earth. What kind would most please you? Those which a[...] edly recited by rote and no longer hold meaning for the one mouthing them? Or those that are composed from the heart of the individual and come across more like a personal communion than a one-way conversation? Those begging for stuff in return for shallow promises to be good? Or those expressing a desire to be more accepting of What Is? Those blaming you for bad happenings or missed opportunities? Or those expressing understanding that the responsibility to recognize opportunities belongs to each person? Those soldiers praying for a successful battle? Or those soldiers who refuse to be a killing machine? Being in the position of the Divine Essences, wouldn't you much rather see someone hold her or his tongue and practice the powerful wisdom of silence than see that person spout off without giving thought to the hurt the comment would cause? Wouldn't you rather see someone shouldering personal responsibility rather than shoving that responsibility for outcomes on you—making you the scapegoat for all the negatives in that person's life?

Prayer is good; don't misinterpret my message here. But prayer is not what most folks think it is. It's not asking for anything. It's not thanking, either. It's a personal communion with the Divine in the form of private conversation and, more important, it's the active expression of spiritual *behavior* toward others (unconditional love and unconditional goodness). That is what the pure meaning of true prayer is.

▶ *Do you think that women should have a religion geared more toward them and have women priests and officials?*

Though I know it's not the case, this feels like a "setup" question.

No, I do not think this women's religion would be a good thing because things would be no better than they are now under male-oriented religions. I have a problem with religion itself as a means to replace pure spirituality. I don't believe there should be any type of leader or priest (or priestess) connected to a religion. The idea of formatting services confines religion's practitioners to a specific type of worship rather than one coming directly from the heart and expressing one's personal relationship with the Divine. Turning religion into a matriarchal one as an attempt to counter the patriarchal domination of two thousand years is not the answer. Rather, women should cherish their right to a feminine spirituality whereby they recognize the existence of the Mother Sophia and Her Holy Spirit aspect, the Shekinah, and make their communion with these Divine Essences a personal one in a sanctuary provided for that purpose.

I agree that the time has arrived for women to recognize their own spirituality and their own unique relationship with the Divine Feminine Aspects, but we cannot make the same mistakes that men did, turning that sacred spirituality into a manipulative venue by appointing priestesses and formatting worship ceremonies. Pure spirituality, which is the very nature of Sophia and Shekinah, shuns ceremony and leadership in deference to a personal and individualized relationship. Men created patriarchal religion because they have a need to dominate, and their nature is associated with the *letter* of conceptual spirituality. Women, on the other hand, have a need to experience a personal relationship with the Divine, and their nature is more closely associated with the *spirit* of conceptual spirituality. A women's spirituality would fail if it conformed to the male model of religion—because it would end up being a contradiction in concepts. Women have no need to emulate men; they have to follow their nature to be true to their own inherent inner beingness.

No, a women's religion is not a good idea. Let us instead look toward the ancient feminine *spirituality* that is now rising up from the ashes.

▶ *Is the pope infallible?*

Infallible as related to what?

As I understand it, the pope's infallibility is associated with God's mind or Divine intent. Do you concur that it was the intent of the Divine Essences to kill all those who didn't believe in the Catholic faith, as was the purpose of the Spanish Inquisition sanctioned by the pope of the time? Are Sophia, God, and Shekinah Catholic? Jesus was Jewish, so at what point in time did he himself establish a separate faith called Catholicism? Where are His words in Scriptures stating that? Do you see where I'm going with this?

Another element for close scrutiny regarding this infallibility idea is the following gender-related concept: Would the Divine Essences show gender preference? If all human beings are supposed to be God's children, then where does this subjugation of women enter in? This doesn't come from any spiritual concept from the Divine Minds; it comes from those men who wrote the official canonical Scriptures for their own purposes. If two of the divine aspects of the Trinity are feminine, how can religions be made into predominantly male-oriented systems that place women far below the status of men? Could this be because most religions are *man*made? I don't think I need to offer any more examples on why the pope's infallibility is a concept devised by men because, if you want documented illustrations, all you have to do is study the church's history, preferably those volumes not slanted by the opinions of a Catholic author or historian. You'll want a totally unbiased account.

▶ *Is homosexuality a sin?*

The term *sin* is far too religiously selective. Let's use the conceptually related term *wrong* instead.

Let me begin by asking if you realize that, when the biblical Scriptures were originally put together to form the official version, much of Jesus' daily activities were deleted? Why did the Christian forefathers feel the need to do this? Why did they feel they needed to sanitize the official accounting according to their own idea of what Jesus needed to represent? Why not just tell it the way it really was? If they had done so, society wouldn't have the self-righteous finger-pointers that we witness today.

Jesus loved everyone. Everyone. He laughed with gay men and danced with lesbians. Is that a shocker? Why? *Everyone means every one. Everyone* is not exclusive or prejudicial. *Everyone* is unconditional. And those religious founding fathers had a big problem with that—a really huge problem with that—and also with Jesus' perspective toward women, whom he greatly cherished. His real relationship with Mary Magdalene has been completely deleted from official records. But I don't want to get into another subject matter here, so I'll stay focused on the issue of homosexuality.

As I said, the Scriptures ended up with a completely sanitized version of Jesus' life and philosophy, so throughout history right up to today, people have been believing the words that the Scriptures' designers put in Jesus' mouth instead of what really came out of it. Let's get rational here. If Jesus loved everyone, why would humans take it upon themselves to exclude anyone from that concept? If Jesus laughed and joked with homosexuals, why do humans point prejudicial fingers at them? I thought Christians were supposed to emulate Jesus' life and philosophy. One of Jesus' most important messages was that of unconditional love. Yet society, in its self-righteous religious arrogance, places conditions on that tenet and restricts it to heterosexuals. Does not the human mind comprehend the meaning of *unconditional*? Must religious leaders point their fingers at others so they can elevate themselves with righteousness? False righteousness?

I addressed the issue of love in a former question, so I'll only summarize that here. Love is love, folks. Homosexual love is no more wrong than the love you feel for your pet. No one has the right to persecute another individual because of who he or she feels love for. No one. If Jesus were here walking among you right now, he'd demonstrate the same idea. And he'd also set the world straight about the scriptures' being a highly selective and manipulated record of history.

Please, let's stop the fault-finding tendency. Isn't life hard enough just getting through each day and handling our own affairs without inciting intolerance and hatred? One of the most important spiritual concepts to live and one most pleasing to the Divine Minds is this: *Do no harm.* At some point in time, this vile and savage penchant for hatred has got to stop. Let it begin with you.

► *If the Bible isn't accurate, what do we have to model our behavior and beliefs on?*

Contrary to what you may think, one doesn't have to have religious beliefs—any religious beliefs—to live a spiritual life. An atheist can live a model spiritual life. Religious beliefs only add another element for society to fight over, but with spirituality there are no dogma, tenets, gods, land, or ceremony to cause disputes. With the principle of pure spirituality, there's only the behavior of unconditional love and goodness.

Even a half-intelligent individual needs no model for spiritual behavior. People inherently know it's not right to kill another, to steal something that isn't theirs, to lie and cheat, to spread ill will about another, and so forth. Human beings don't need a *Right Behavior 101* textbook to teach them the difference between right and wrong.

The deal with this is that as long as we live a reasonable spiritual life by thinking of the feelings and needs of others instead of letting the ego interfere, thus living according to the philosophy of doing no harm, then our lives will automatically be spiritual ones even if we have no specific religious beliefs whatsoever.

Let's look at a single comparable example of this. Catholics' claim that their faith is the one true faith is a bit arrogant, but regardless, they feel strongly guided by that faith. The Protestants feel equally strongly about their own. So you'd think it'd naturally follow that both these groups would devote themselves to spiritual behavior through the guidance of their individual faiths . . . instead of killing each other over them, as in Ireland. Same with the Israelis and the Palestinians. Jews and Gentiles. Muslims and Christians.

When you label a religious belief, you bind it with humanmade rules and tenets instead of allowing it to just flow freely from one's inner beingness. Spirituality is neither dogma nor tenets nor ceremony. It is not any kind of separatist belief. Spirituality just is. So for you, who think that spiritual behavior must be spelled out in a manual, I would suggest taking a closer look at your own guidance of common sense and your knowledge of what types of behavior define acts of goodness.

► *How come society's spiritual behavior hasn't kept up with its technological advancements?*

Because of the isms. Religious separatism. Racism. Sexism. The prejudicial attitudes generated from the ego's sense of superiority are evident in social behavior.

► *I'm so disgusted with the religious right. Recently they threw a public fit over a cartoon character who wears a triangle on its head—one leader said it stood for a gay/lesbian symbol. I thought the triangle also stood for the Holy Trinity. Where'd that symbology go?*

Great point.

I have a gold ring with a garnet triangle on it. I was attracted to it not because the triangle had a gay/lesbian or Holy Trinity symbology but because the triangle, in ancient times, symbolized feminine spirituality—the goddesses.

Two thousand years ago, when the Christian forefathers were banning all matriarchal spiritual beliefs, the men stole the triangle from the women's belief system and made it their own symbol for the Holy Trinity. Since then, paintings, holy pictures, and biblical illustrations have depicted the triangle as a sign of the Holy Spirit, who in actuality is the feminine Shekinah.

Your example of how the religious right infringes on one's personal individualism and integrity with their wildly negative assumptions is something society must rally against because if it is left unchecked, it will only get worse. We cannot allow prejudicial and presumptive persecution to gain an upper hand by manipulating society's thoughts. To incite finger-pointing because of some specific design one chooses to wear or use is highly reminiscent of the mentality exhibited during the Salem witch-hunts. Back then, if a woman had a birthmark, she was a witch; if she had a black cat, she was a witch; if her broom was left outside, she was a witch. C'mon, people—we're brighter than that. I know we are. Let's not sit back and let one or two twisted religious leaders destroy all our sacred symbology or our right to be individuals.

▶ *Does society's level of spiritual development affect the earth?*
The earth (Nature) is affected by the vibrations emitted by all living energy. So then if our spiritual development hasn't risen to the point where we live by the philosophy of *"do no harm,"* then society does harm to the earth in myriad ways: manufacturing plants that dump and emit pollutants from their smokestacks, emissions, mechanics who dump oil and other chemicals into the dirt behind their shops, homeowners who change their car oil and pour the old dirty oil out in the alley, lovers who carve their initials in a forest or park tree, those who fish and leave tangles of line on the shore for wildlife to get caught and strangled in, and so on.

Spiritual behavior is considering the needs of others. Going fishing without thinking about the ramifications of the trash we leave by the shore is but one simple example of how we clumsily trudge our noisy way through life without respecting it. When we do this, the earth ends up paying the price for society's thought-lessness.

▸ *Is having statues of holy images in one's house idolatry?*

Idolatry is not an object but a behavior.

For example, in my cabin, I have a bronze statue of a woman by the name of Kuan Yin, who is the Asian goddess of empathy and compassion. I have a brass statue of Parvati, who, in India, is believed to be the daughter of heaven, the Mother Earth goddess. I have a small white marble statue of the Three Graces and an ebony wood carving of an African mother goddess. On the book-shelf stands a statue of Selket, female guardian of the tomb, and above a cabinet stands an image of Maat, the Egyptian goddess of justice. In differing cultures, these statues represent a holy image. But I don't worship or adore them. I haven't built an altar around them. They're merely symbols of different cultures' feminine deities.

So what we're talking about here is not the images or statues themselves but how they're used when associated with the owner's behavior or attitude toward them. We don't worship stat-ues and images themselves; they serve only as a representation of a spiritual concept. We hold a spiritual concept within our philo-sophical belief system and the images serve as *reminders* of that representational spiritual behavior.

Sometimes folks have statues in their homes for reasons other than serving as reminders of spiritual concepts—perhaps for the sake of pure art appreciation. Think of a statue based on the *Birth of Venus*, or Michelangelo's *David*. I've had a *Pietà* statue for years. It was the first statue I purchased; a bust of Tutankhamun soon followed. But these are not images of idolatry; they're simply works of cultural art one is specifically attracted to. They turn into objects of idolatry only if one actually perceives them as an object of worship and prayer.

Again, we must not make assumptions about what folks have

in their homes, especially about the *purpose* of such items.
I have a statue of a lady holding a pendulum clock on t.
table, I don't worship it. I have it because I was attracted
uniqueness. My tastes are very eclectic and I am drawn to the
more unusual items. Statues and such in one's home do not mean
one practices idolatry.

▶ *Do I need to expose my sins to a confessor so I can be forgiven?*

This depends on whom you think you need to seek forgiveness
from. God forgives automatically if one expresses remorse or sorrow for having offended. God forgives unconditionally without
making demands for or exacting retribution for such sins. Your
whispered contrition in the form of a personal prayer is enough.
Your behavior is between you and the Divine, Who needs no one
to forgive in Her stead.

The idea of a human confessor came from men's minds, not
from the Divines' Minds. If you must confess to a human being to
feel relieved of the sin's emotional burden, then do so; it's up to
each individual what soothes his or her conscience. However, it's
not necessary for forgiveness.

My perspective on this issue is that religions devised confession
and human confessors to whom one reveals one's sins as a means
of controlling the faithful. Religion says: *You will be doomed if you
do not confess your sins to the church's priest or minister.* This then
keeps the faithful faithful because they'll keep returning to church
officials to absolve them of their sins. But who better to provide
absolution than the Divine for this purpose? Isn't your relationship with the Divine an extremely personal and private affair? So
why make that relationship once removed by confessing to a
human being instead of talking directly to the One above—the
One Who forgives unconditionally without attaching any form of
penance as a condition of absolution?

I'm sure no perfect person. I lose my temper, have moments of
frustration and depression, and experience periods of doubting

my effectiveness as messenger, but I do know that the Divine understands my human failings and forgives all transgressions related to them because She's all-forgiving because of Her incredible depth of unconditional love. I need no human confessor to tell me that after performing a self-styled go-between ceremony. I'm perfectly capable of telling the Divine my own sins. She can look into my heart and see the contriteness residing there. You can do the same. If you don't need a priest or minister to transmit your prayers for you, why do you need one to transmit your sins? If you expect a priest or minister to answer your private prayers, why do you expect him or her to absolve your sins? Why *pray* to the Divine and then think it's necessary to go to a religious official when it comes to asking the Divine Essences' *forgiveness?* Why are people making the distinction? Aren't both things a private communion? Absolute forgiveness is a quality of the Divine, not of humans. It's a private affair between you and the Divine.

► *I don't understand why religions are so separatist. I mean, if they truly believe in their faith, why do they go out and cause dissension because of it?*

Oh my, that's a good one. You're asking an outsider to look inside to figure why this happens.

From what I've observed, people aren't content in their faith unless they're attempting to convert everyone else and win them over to their cubbyhole. It's religious arrogance to make claims of being the one and only true religion here on earth. It's religious self-righteousness to inhibit the freedom of others to believe as they choose. It's not even necessary to be on the inside to see that this is why it's happening. The fundamentalists who denigrate others for their different beliefs or persecute them for their inherent lifestyle differences, the born-agains who don't understand that the definition of *New Age* is "a blend of spirituality and natural physics," the Jehovah's Witnesses who continually attempt to push their beliefs into your home, and all the other groups who perceive themselves as the spiritual elites of the world appoint themselves as soldiers of God and devote their days to converting all others or persecuting those who refuse. That, my friend, is religious arrogance. It's evidence of religion gone amok. It's been prophesied. It's coming to pass and it's going to get worse before it gets better.

What I can't figure is that if religion is supposed to reflect the ideals of the Divine, why can't these folks see how counterspiritual their behavior is? Criticism is not "doing no harm." Prejudice and persecution are not "doing no harm." Like you, I cannot figure why these people, if they truly are content with their own spiritual beliefs, feel such a desperate need to use it as a prejudicial right of "spiritual" passage. If they're doing anyone any kind of harm, whether physical, emotional, psychological, or any other kind of discriminatory invasion of privacy or interference with one's right to individuality, they're using their religion as a wounding sword rather than as a cup of love that flows forth with refreshing droplets of acceptance, tolerance, and unconditional goodness.

▸ *Aren't some famous religious organizations using the issue of family solidarity as a cover for the continued subjugation of women?*

Oh, to be sure. I won't list them, but they're out there and they're gaining strength because people have a tendency to only see what's on the surface rather than look any deeper.

▸ *My minister says that it's paganistic to see God in Nature because Nature is not God. Comment?*

There is an aspect of the Divine Consciousness in all living things. Nature just happens to contain the highest population of living innocence. Nature is reality in its purest form and, because of that, is the best mirror that reflects the Divine Essences. Nature teaches us endless spiritual philosophies to live by: innocence, nonjudgment, individuality, freedom to openly express one's inherent beingness, total honesty (no masks), self-reliance, inter-relatedness, awareness, caution, interdependence, and so on. Through the observance of Nature, we can develop a more com-prehensive spiritual philosophy than all the theologians could teach us, the most important tenet of which would be that it's spir-itual behavior that counts, not dogma.

What is paganism, anyway? Perhaps the easier way to define it is to address what it is not. It is not within the circle that men call "traditional religion"; therefore, men reason, it must be a vile ungodly belief system. Yet the Australian Aborigines and the indigenous peoples of many cultures have pagan beliefs. They're not Christianized beliefs; they're purely *spiritual* beliefs. How can it be that their idea of a supreme being or goddess/god should be deemed unacceptable or pagan? They had these beliefs long before Jesus, Buddha, John Knox, Joseph Smith, or Martin Luther appeared on the historical scene. What now makes the ancient spiritual beliefs something to be thrown away? Could it be because that ugly old cobra called religious arrogance is spreading its hood?

Most all spiritual beliefs society categorizes as pagan are nature-centered. Perceiving the hand of God in Nature is what the Divine wants us to do—to recognize the beautifully shimmering interconnectedness in all of life rather than reserve it for an offi-cial worship service on Saturday or Sunday.

The next time you hear the word *pagan,* think instead of react-ing from ignorance; think *Nature* —the Divine in Nature.

► *Will religious persecution ever stop?*
Only when religious arrogance does.

▶ *What makes your spiritual philosophy more true than traditional religious beliefs?*

I never said or implied that it was more true, yet I've observed the hand of humankind in all religious belief systems and wonder why that human input is required. When I observe so much hatred and prejudice in the world that is religion generated, it doesn't take an astrophysicist to see that something is gravely amiss. When I see women being subjugated and demeaned by religious dogma, I see a great effort by patriarchy to maintain control. When I see organized religions squeezing the poor faithful's pocketbooks, I see greed. When I witness the opulence of the Vatican and the papal robes and jewels, I see materialism. I could give hundreds more examples, but these few are enough to quite literally turn my stomach.

I see the spiritual behavior as pointing to one's spirituality. Our spiritual behavior toward each other is what is most pleasing to the Divine. The rituals and religious ceremonies are but shallow and extraneous elements for people to use as a means of building up self-importance, not for God. The Divine Essences care not a whit for ceremonies, dogma, rituals, and jewel-encrusted vestments. It's our behavior that reflects unconditional love and goodness that counts, not the puny manmade religions that serve only as a means to separate us from each other. Spiritual behavior is the grand-scale philosophy, whereas religion is a set of rules that in the end will prove insubstantial.

▶ *If and when you establish your Magdalene Abbey, will you be the abbess?*

You haven't been listening. If I did that, then I'd be contradicting all my messages and everything I hold spiritually dear. The abbey is intended to be an open women's sanctuary for spiritual solitude and respite. No leaders, no priestesses, no ceremony, no ritual. Just a quiet place providing a few minutes' (or hours') worth of personal spiritual connectedness with the Divine.

Please don't make assumptions like this.

► *Will the Magdalene Abbey have a women's choir?*

The abbey will not have an established type of anything. It's intended to be purely for personal meditation or contemplation, a women's temporary sanctuary from worldly stress and concerns. There will be no membership. No one will reside there, with the possibile exception of women needing to escape domestic abuse who stay in some area on the property set aside as a safe house. This last is a secondary purpose planned for the abbey. But don't forget, this project is still in the idea stage, and it will take me some years to accumulate the funds to build the abbey. It's the second phase of my purpose for being here, and I feel I have the full responsibility for its manifestation.

► *I don't think God would create such a place as hell. Do you?*

Hell, like heaven, is a place created within the human mind. Since I've already spoken extensively on this subject in *Eclipse*, I'll just recap here. The concept of hell is a favorite of religious leaders because it keeps fear of punishment in the minds of the faithful. It's a tool for manipulation and control. The revivalist ministers in particular use the concepts of hell and Satan to fill tents and stadiums with people to hear and experience their fire-and-brimstone dramatics. People aren't getting it. They aren't getting the message that the Divine Minds don't want humans to fear Their essences. They want to be loved, not feared. They want to be loved because people *love* Them, not because people *fear* Them. And this is exactly what these fundamentalists and other religious leaders are doing: They're instilling good behavior through fear of hellish punishment instead of through love of the Divine. Therefore, people are "getting religion" for all the wrong reasons.

► *How can religions change their long-standing dogmatic rules? For example, demoting the canonized saints.*

I suppose this happens because—to use your example—saint-hood is a humanmade concept, not one of the Divine's. If people make the rules or dogma, people can unmake them just as easily. A church appoints itself as the prime determiner of who's a saint and who isn't. It also makes up the rules—the determining criteria—by which these dead folks are judged. It would seem to me, though, if a church determined that an individual met the criteria at one time, then there wouldn't be any way that that canonized saint could lose her or his status. That'd be a bit fishy to me and make me look a bit closer at what's going on. You know, faith is a wonderful attribute, but it can also come with intellectual blinders if one isn't discriminating enough.

► *Does the second half of your mission involve journeying about the country teaching?*

Teaching what? I'm not a teacher. I'm not a lecturer or any kind of public person. I didn't come to be a public figure. I never have been and never intend to be. What more is there to teach than a repetition of what I've already written down? You can have access to those same messages by holding them in your hands. You don't even have to buy the books; borrow them from the local library or a friend. Once you've read them, you have the concepts in your head. Seeing the physical me won't make them any more valid for you. The message is not the messenger. The message is not a person . . . it's the words.

► *In one of your books, you commented that you're going to be attending some annual women's gatherings. Will you be speaking at these or signing books?*

No. If and when I have the time for this activity, I'll be attending anonymously. Right now, as I write this, I'm homebound with the constant care of my companion's elderly mother who has

Alzheimer's. As anyone in the same situation knows, this type of job is an hour-by-hour experience with unexpected surprises. One minute you can be dealing with a sweet and loving personality, and then within the blink of an eye, you're being suddenly confronted by an argumentative and combative person full of imagined suspicions and false accusations. More than once while working on this book, when I was deep in concentration while transferring my thoughts onto the screen of my computer, a movement out the window behind the monitor caught my attention. It was Grandma walking out in the woods. My companion had been gone doing errands and her mother had taken advantage of my concentration to quietly sneak out the back door and take a wandering walk. I had to rush outside and bring her back. No, it'll be a while before I can take off to attend those women's gatherings, but when I can, I will definitely try to be anonymous.

▶ *I can't seem to pray. Reciting the words from a prayer book doesn't work. I get only halfway through reading them before I get to feeling insincere. What's wrong with me?*

Nothing's wrong with you. You just want a more personal communion with the Divine. I suggest you make up your own prayers or, even better, just start talking to the Divine as though you both were having a heart-to-heart conversation. Believe me, that method is so much more meaningful to both of you. It's so much more satisfying.

▶ *Is penance a necessary aspect to forgiveness for one's transgressions?*

No, not at all. The idea of penance was conceived by men. The Divine forgives unconditionally. If you express remorse to the Divine, then what more do you think is expected of you? Only religions claim that one must do penance for one's sins.

▸ *Why do spiritual beliefs have to have a label?*

They don't. It appears that way only because men have deemed it necessary to have a name for their specific sects. Labels are separatist. Anything that's separatist defeats the goal of humanity's becoming a united family. I don't have a label for what I believe because it's pure spirituality, and you can't put a name on that. The problem is that folks think they have to belong to something. They think they need some kind of religious camaraderie. Yet when one's relationship with the Divine is so personal, private, and individually sacred, why this camaraderie is perceived as a necessity isn't really reasonable. It becomes an ego thing—a need to know that others believe as you do rather than cherishing your own close relationship with the Divine. The need for *religious peers* becomes more important than the *personal* relationship. Also, being one of the "faithful" gives the ego an excellent boost—one is "religious" if one shows up at one's house of worship regularly, if one is the first to volunteer for social programs, and so forth. It becomes a means of publicly showing off one's goodness, but it's really religious vanity. On the other hand, doing *anonymous* spiritual works of goodness is far more pleasing in the eyes of the Divine. Why? Because it isn't self-serving—it doesn't stroke one's religious ego.

Having labels for individual religious sects highlights the alterations that have been made to the initially organized set of concepts and thus highlights division. For example, the Catholic church was once a solid organization until people like John Knox, Henry VIII, Elizabeth I, and Martin Luther decided that its beliefs constituted worship of the pope and that they would make their own "true" religion. Eventually, the spinoffs from Catholicism began to gain a foothold. Since then, as men decided to alter this and change that, new terms and labels had to be devised. The religious labels have become so numerous that differentiation between religions has become nearly impossible.

▶ *Without belonging to a specific religion, how does one keep the Sabbath holy each week?*

Who ever said that attending church each week was the only way to keep the Sabbath holy? The *spirit* of that commandment was what was meant, not the letter. The spirit of the commandment says: *Remember to not get so busy you forget about the Divine.* The term *Sabbath* was meant to indicate the Divine, that we should give thoughts to the *Divine*, not attend organized religious services. And you can give these thoughts to the Divine each day! Several times a day. Nobody ever meant *just* on Sunday or Saturday. Good grief! Get a clue here. Religions love this belief that the commandment means one must attend religious services each week to be able to give thoughts and attention to the Divine. After all, this misconception is what they teach, isn't it? But it's wrong! The commandment is about not *forgetting* about the Divine, not requiring one church day a week. It's reminding us to have thoughts directed toward holy and sacred issues (the Sabbath). Keeping the Sabbath holy means remembering to make your life a *continual living* spiritual experience, not reserving spirituality for only one day of the week.

▶ *Don't we need religious organizations for the purpose of garnering the faithful's donations to the poor and hungry?*

No, that's what all the nonprofit organizations are for. Churches aren't needed as a once-removed donation depository for the poor, the hungry, wildlife, or any other type of recipient, because these have their own organizations to which people can donate directly.

▶ *Don't you think that society has a twisted perception of what power is?*

Sure I do. Men think it's muscle, male superiority, and gun firepower. Women think it's a beautiful face and an hourglass body.

And both think that money is power. Some think intelligence is power. Few recognize the fact that the real power is having wisdom, that real power is the spiritual behaviors of acceptance, tolerance, unconditional love and goodness, and silence.

► *I don't belong to any organized religion. What are the main spiritual points you think young children should be taught?*

- First of all, I want to point out that children learn more by example than by words. So my first suggestion is to show them by example.
- Teach them to commune personally with the Divine, to come to an intimate relationship like they're talking to a best friend.
- Help them feel free to openly express their emotions and their individuality. Never apply negative language associated with their natural inclinations or interests.
- By example, have them help gather and distribute unwanted household and personal goods so they can experience the wonderful feeling that comes from giving.
- Stress the importance of intangible possessions such as the attitudes of love, generosity, unity, individuality, expressiveness, honesty, sharing, and fair play, instead of physical possessions and material *stuff*. This helps them be less materialistic in adulthood.
- Instill a knowledge and realization of what true power is. Help them see that it doesn't come from wielding an Uzi but rather from using one's own quiet wisdom.
- Show them productive means of releasing pent-up emotions, such as frustration, anger, and hurt.
- Reinforce the idea that their relationship with the Divine is not a religious one but a personalized spiritual one.
- By example, show them that unconditional love is more powerful than hatred.

These suggestions are but a few ways to encourage spiritual behavior in children. I'm sure that if you think on it a bit, you can come up with many more.

► *You've been using the term* Goddess *throughout your recent books. Aren't you afraid that the word has a paganistic connotation and you'll lose readership?*

Afraid? Afraid to use correct terminology? Since the Holy Spirit and the Mother Aspect of the Trinity are feminine, what other word would be correct to use for them other than the feminine form of the term *God?* The only reason any type of problem arises from using this word is the skewed perspective patriarchal society has attached to it for so many centuries. That's not Sophia's or Shekinah's fault; that's humans' fault. And it's become such a faulty perception that the term *Goddess* is automatically equated with some type of paganistic religion. This just is absolutely unfair and incredibly disrespectful to the feminine Aspects of the Trinity.

Afraid I'll lose readership? By now, my readers have come to count on my message as being one that doesn't pull any punches, one that's never designed for the public's ever-changing philosophical fads or concept of the moment. I present the reality of spiritual aspects as I've come to understand them through my own experiential validations. These I pass on in a straightforward manner, avoiding complexities and making the message as clear and simple as I can regardless of current New Age popular opinion or criticism from the public. What would be the purpose of being wishy-washy and presenting vacillating spiritual philosophies that align to oft-opposing public philosophies? Where would the wisdom be in that?

I could see the reasoning behind your point if I had a secondary goal or agenda geared toward myself. By this I mean personal popularity, a personal desire to be *the* spiritual teacher of the century. But that's silly. That's not why I'm here. I don't care if some of my messages are unpopular. If fear of how the concepts I write about will be received means I don't call reality as I see and experience it, then I am gravely compromising my reason for being here. I mean, why bother writing at all then? To reshape and mold one's experiences within multidimensional realities and what one has learned from these events into a milder form the general public might think more palatable is not my idea of how a valid messenger behaves. A true messenger doesn't rehash popular ideas just to gain popularity. Who needs that? Who needs another messenger saying the same old things? Sure, some of my concepts have incited controversy, but so what? Some of them are completely new, and there are folks who don't want to look at anything new because they're comfortable with the philosophical status quo. And there are others who have recently decided to slap a lesbian label on my work just because I came out and stated the reality of the Trinity's true identities. They want to hear that the Trinity is all male, so therefore, because I say otherwise, I'm a lesbian attempting to encourage Goddess worship. There are innumerable reasons and rationalizations people use to disagree with some of my works, but they're entitled to their reasons and rationalizations. Those people will stop reading my material and stay with what they want to hear instead. Yet there are those who want to know the reality of spiritual philosophy, and whether my words underscore their basic beliefs or gift them with new and inspiring ideas makes no difference because they read my work knowing that I don't and won't compromise the message for the sake of personal popularity or public opinion. This latter group is the one I've come to write for. These are the people meant to hear the message.

I'm not in competition with other authors for the greatest readership base. I pass on what I've learned through the personal experiences in quantum meditation, contemplation, inspiration, insight, and study without expecting anything by way of public response. I just put it out there. That's the sole purpose of the first phase of my mission—the message phase. Now that it's conclud-

ing as I focus my attention on my final books, folks will begin looking for some other author at whom to aim their prejudicial barbs.
Just remember that real is real. What one's consciousness experiences in all the many other dimensional frequency realities is just
as real as those experienced in this third-dimensional one. Losing
readers is not a consideration for me. Getting the reality of spiritual philosophy and wisdom out into the world is. The word has
always been the priority and taken precedence over the persona
or feelings of the messenger.

So again, the feminine term for *God* is none other than . . . *Goddess.* Don't be afraid to let the word pass over your lips. The time
has come for society's primitive and patriarchal attitude toward
the word to rise up into the light of its beautiful reality because the
two feminine aspects of the Trinity have had quite enough—the
goddesses are back. You don't even have to take my word for it.
Read some of the Naj^c Ḥammādī gospels that Christianity's founding fathers didn't want people to see. I'm not introducing anything new here, folks. It had just been buried from you until
December 1945, when the words were rediscovered and reborn
into the light of day. Even the most important aspect of my mentor was overshadowed by prejudicial separatist attitudes when her
ethnicity was focused on instead of her main message . . . that of
being a woman.

We must elevate our perspectives, which are currently confined within and bound to the tactile world of the human self—
the ego. We must free our consciousness to experience the realness and vastness of reality without insisting on keeping it teth-
ered to our tiny world of perceptual separatistic elements such as
ethnicity or specific religious dogma. How can reality be realized
if society self-creates its form? Society must free itself from preconceived opinions, expectations, misconceptions, public opinion, and fear of discovery if it's ever going to comprehend reality's
true beingness. I say this because reality exists in its pure form in
spite of human thought—in spite of whatever humans think it is.

Human ideology cannot create or reshape reality according to its self-styled design and mold. Reality does not bend, stretch, or alter its shape to conform to human desires. Therefore, it's up to society to let go of these preconceived notions and just experience reality. My works have brought some of these experiences within reality to the public. It's that public's choice to accept or reject. My opinion or response to that choice is not relevant because it's nonexistent. I've already seen the raw beingness of reality and experienced a few of its many splendorous facets, unalterable by human opinion.

▸ *In* Earthway, *did the concept of the rainbow completing its arc below the ground to make a whole circle symbolize life's interconnectedness?*

Absolutely. Nature is circular, not linear. It was meant to represent the Great Web of Life on each shimmering connecting strand of which exist all living elements of life. The whole web is the life force of the Divine Essences' consciousness—the whole web is the reality of life, each and every strand and interconnecting thread creating a thoroughly integrated whole . . . a woven design of life emitting synergistic aspects of individualized yet responsive energy and consciousness.

The visible half of the rainbow is only that element of this living web that we perceive through our tactile senses, whereas the hidden half is that which humankind has yet to acknowledge because of lack of sensitivity. The philosophical ideology of indigenous peoples the world over that is identified by the phrase *all my relations* is associated with this Great Web of Life concept and my mentor's reference to the "full-circle rainbow." As above, so below. That which is seen is a reflection of the unseen. The obvious aspects of physics reflect the subtle.

Everything in reality consists of moving molecules and therefore has energy. This energy radiates out from its source and is imperceptible to the naked eye. The energy emits a specific type of influence in relation to the source's molecular composition. That radiated energy subtly affects its surroundings. In this manner, all of life becomes alive with energy and influencing forces of energy. Everything affects everything (and everyone) else. Every source of life is interconnected in this way and is subject to being influenced by same. All my relations. The Great Web of Life. The living rainbow circle. As above, so below.

► *I feel so alone in my beliefs because they're not aligned with any "traditional" religions, yet deep inside I know that I shouldn't be feeling this way because those beliefs are so strong. Am I wrong to be feeling this aloneness?*

Not exactly, because sometimes people have a tendency to misinterpret individuality as aloneness. If you can make a perceptual shift and equate your alone feeling to one of uniqueness of individuality, then perhaps that will help you. Frequently, the association of a negative term with a personal feeling can cause inner restlessness or dissatisfaction when all that's needed is to make the association to a more positive term or ideology. Just as one can call a concerned individual a cynic, one can also shift that negative connotation of cynic to a positive one of simple concern.

Let's look at this "aloneness" you feel.

Being a person who has discovered the freedom to express one's own individuality—in this case, regarding spiritual beliefs—can oftentimes give the sensation of being alone. You may feel separated from those holding to traditional belief systems—and being outside the circle the general populace draws around itself. Yet the very expression of that individuality is what makes us each unique. The fact that one has the potential and capability to think for oneself and feels no societal pressure to suppress that individualized expression directly relates to one's intellectual acknowledgment and personal appreciation of that beautiful right.

Individual thought is what generates social advances in beliefs and behaviors. History has proved this time and time again. Where would we be today if we still believed the popular concept of a flat earth? Or where would we be if Copernicus had been afraid to express his individual thought that the earth was not the center of the universe, that it was the sun that was positioned in the center of the solar system and the earth merely revolved in an orbit around that sun? Newton's revelation of his gravity theory was a real bell-ringer to the scientific community of his time. Though individual thought may at times seem exclusionary and seclusionary to the individual, it is a mark of one's uniqueness and is every person's right to enjoy and cherish.

Another aspect of specific individual thoughts, ideas, or perception that runs counter to public opinion is that it can carry various attitudes of self-perception. These are directly related to the quality or level of priority one personally places on the ego. If an individual views him- or herself through a mirror by which others see him or her, then individual thought will naturally be stifled because the person wants to avoid being viewed as different or as having odd or weird ideas. This individual places great importance on the acceptance of peers because her or his ego is getting in the way of the right to individualized thought. In this case, the person will perceive these thoughts and ideas as being a source of personal humiliation or criticism and will feel the need to smother them in deference to the opinions of others. This behavior is one that voluntarily suppresses individuality because the ego is allowed to take precedence in life.

You don't appear to me to be guilty of the above love of ego, yet your distinctive beliefs are making you feel somewhat like you're living on a deserted philosophical island. Yet that island is not a lone piece of earth sticking up out of a philosophical or spiritual sea, because each of us, intellectually, is an island. Each of us has a fertile mind that is meant to be nurtured with creative thought rather than stripped of nutrients through the practice of reseeding with the same variety of seeds (popular beliefs) year after year.

New thought can be a compelling force toward insightful inspiration and epiphanies. The practice of individual thinking in contemplation deepens one's understanding and expands one's comprehension of reality's vast possibilities. There are as many islands as there are people; the problem arises when folks just don't realize it.

Everyone needs to recognize the responsibility to think for him- or herself. Everyone has the right to cherish the beautiful gift of intellect and treasure the potential for self-discovery, for thinking for oneself is an element of wisdom. Few perceive individual thought as being an aspect of wisdom, yet if you spend time thinking about the idea, you'll eventually come to realize that your philosophy is one of your most precious natural facets of intellect that make you unique. Individualized thought and philosophy *becomes* you. It literally *becomes* one of the determining elements of your inherent beingness. Alone? Perhaps that could be one perception, but it is a viewpoint as superficial as a benign surface wave above the depths of the strong and natural ocean current. The acknowledgment and appreciation of one's right to individual thought far surpasses any momentary sense of aloneness it may whisper of.

I understand aloneness because I know what it feels like to experience it. Yet those experiences have only served to *enhance* one's sense of connection through the realization that no one is ever truly alone. Even within complete solitude you are never alone, for the consciousness of every living thing surrounds you. Along with your own shimmering beingness, you're surrounded by the vibrating energy of all of life. You are never alone. Cherish the wisdom you have whenever you think for yourself. That doesn't make you alone; it contributes toward helping you become wiser.

▸ *I find that Nature is a wonderful spiritual teacher. Was that part of the message* Earthway *was meant to convey?*

Nature is indeed a wonderful spiritual teacher. And *Earthway* certainly underscored that concept. Not only did it verify that Nature provides for our physiological needs through nourishing sustenance and beneficial healthful aids but it also brought out the aspect of Nature as a spiritual learning source—because it *is* natural. By this I mean that it's not judgmental, opinionated, full of egocentric attitudes, or selective in any way. It exists in its own purity of beingness and aids unconditionally. It is not full of affectations, wears no masks, and is not prejudicial in sharing its gifts. Nature is pure. Nature rejoices in its beingness and never feels the need to make excuses for that created beingness. Neither should we.

▸ *I don't understand why many New Age authors claim that we all have multidimensional bodies. Why an astral, ethereal, soul, and spirit body?*

Conceptually, it appears that there's a problem with terminology. It's not that we have multidimensional bodies but rather that our true consciousness is dimensionally all-inclusive and can quite naturally experience a simultaneous sensitivity and responsiveness to multiple levels of reality. Lucid dreaming is an example of this receptivity and sensitivity to these multiple levels in that the consciousness is fully aware of both being in a dream state and being semiawake enough to direct the dreamscape action. This in no way involves any other type of body other than your physical one in the third-dimensional plane of reality. This does, however, directly involve the consciousness's potential for simultaneous multidimensional experience.

Regarding the phenomenon of remote viewing, the consciousness of the individual is what makes a journey to a predetermined destination through the active directive of the conscious mind. Remote viewing does not involve anything other than controlling the surroundings in which the consciousness does its perceiving.

The out-of-body experiences are those in which the individual's awake-state consciousness carries an experiential awareness while accompanying the journey of the true consciousness. In other words, the individual is *aware* of being separated from the physical body. The consciousness fully understands what's happening, as in experiencing the personal observance of one's own surgical procedure in a hospital environment.

When third-dimension individuals experience the visual and recognize the identity of another person having an out-of-body event, the visitor may appear to have a translucent human form or she or he may present with the *appearance* of a normal solid body. This is because the true consciousness (as opposed to the awake-state consciousness) has the capability of manipulating the density of its vibrational energy field. This in no way equates to a separate body, but rather to the concept of the consciousness's ability to regulate its own energy.

Popular belief on this issue is simplistic. It addresses only the density of the body's energy fields by calling them separate bodies and giving the varying densities labels rather than going deeper—behind the surface—to address the basic generating factor that controls those varying densities.

So in essence, we have the potential to exhibit many gradations of spiritual bodies, from transparent all the way to a seemingly solid, three-dimensional form, yet each is a choice that the consciousness makes depending on the circumstance.

► *Why do you include patience as a quality of wisdom?*

I include it because it *is* one of the main qualities of wisdom.

Not only is patience a virtue but it is evidence of wisdom when it's practiced. Patience—true patience, not a forced or false presentation of it—reduces stress in one's life. It goes along with acceptance, another of wisdom's major qualities. To have patience is to have acceptance and an understanding of how time and destiny work as tandem concepts of reality. Patience negates the interference of one's ego, of one's selfish demands. Patience represents a deeper comprehension of spiritual philosophy (its expressed behavior) in that it displays a more mature perception of the reality of life rather than one that is self-centered and focused on the *I* of self. Patience attends the ability to control one's knee-jerk reactions and impetuosity. It conveys an understanding that many events in life must have a specified time for unfoldment to fulfillment. Just as a blossom will not unfurl from a planted seed before the sprout has grown to maturity, events in life must also be given their allotted time for all related aspects to perform their required interconnecting activities necessary for fruition. Wisdom's quality of patience embraces this concept. Everything manifests according to its *own* time, not *your* time. The practice of patience represents an understanding of this fact.

Having true patience gifts us with side benefits. It brings a new serenity to our beingness along with a new ability to appreciate the little blessings life gifts to us each day. When we're not stressing out over trying to make things happen, we notice that we're not as uptight and irritable as we were before. We become more aware of life and less focused on the narrowly confined issues related to self. We become more mellow and easygoing. We find that those negative knee-jerk reactions and animated theatrics have fallen by the wayside when our behavior reflects greater levels of acceptance. This is not to say or imply that we become as robots or think that we can do nothing to change certain things. Having patience and acceptance means that you have the wisdom to *recognize* that which you can't personally alter in life and you accept that situation with understanding and grace. Having patience and acceptance means that the things you *can* change, you do with reason, with a perceptive eye to timing and effective methodology, not with impetuosity.

People cringe when hearing the word *patience* because they

equate it with waiting or some type of suppression. Folks often think patience restricts their freedom to act at will or hampers their forward progress. Although these can be indirect effects in some circumstances, they're perceived in such constrictive negative lights only if the individual is focused on the self or has manipulative tendencies. The reality is that, in *every* situation, there is a time to act and a time to sit back and observe. We exhibit wisdom when we understand this and recognize the appropriate distinction.

► *Is having foresight the same as having a premonition?*

Foresight is more in the range of having intuitive acuity and/or an ability to access situations with a practiced eye for recognizing attending elements and probable possibilities. This skill is more directly related to one's intellectual ability to analyze and project outcomes, whereas a premonition is generated from a different aspect of our nature—a subtle perceptual sensitivity to reality as it relates to time.

► *Where did earthly society go wrong in respect to spiritual philosophy?*

Earthly society went wrong by placing emphasis on the ego and therefore experienced the recognition of separatism that accompanies that viewpoint. This is why I've so often stated that earth has become the ego planet. Humanity—all elements of it— was supposed to evolve into a unified "tan" race of human beings, but this can be reality only if all peoples aren't racially prejudicial. Once ego enters to color one's perspective, then the idea of separatism gains a strong enough foothold to allow myriad groups of people to perceive themselves as being better than others for a variety of reasons. The hate groups are born from these ideologies.

► *I get so disgusted with the nightly newscasts that I'm ashamed to be a part of the human race. Spiritually, this earth is a disgrace.*

This earth is one beautiful celestial body. It contains not one disgraceful aspect. What you mean to say is that the *humanity* living *upon* this earth is a disgrace. And, in many ways, I would not disagree with that perspective.

► *Is believing in Nature deities a paganistic belief?*

From my perspective, I'd say not at all. The term *pagan*, like the word *heretic*, is relative, is it not? In the days of King Henry VIII, when he broke from the Catholic Church and started what later became the Protestant Church of England, he declared the papists (Catholics) to be heretics. On the other hand, the church did likewise by claiming that all the Protestants were heretics.

Any separatist religious sect can claim that anyone outside its belief system is a pagan or a heretic, an infidel or a Gentile. The terms for "outsider" are numerous. Australian Aborigines could claim that those not believing as they do are ignorant of the living spiritual reality. This is what separatism creates. It creates a sense that all outsiders not sharing a specific belief are either wrong, being misled by the Devil, pagans, heretics, lost souls, or . . . Because of this, everyone, no matter what he or she believes, could be seen as being a pagan or heretic by someone else. We'd certainly be much better off and experience a greater depth of societal peace if each person's right to individualize spiritual beliefs were respected instead of criticized and persecuted.

► *I know you've said that we should honor all religious beliefs, but what of an atheist's?*

I didn't include a *but* in my statement. I said *all*. Is atheism a religious belief or a lack of one? Isn't that indicative of a nonbelief? That too is to be respected because each person has a right to believe as he or she is inherently inclined.

▸ *Was humankind supposed to have just one religion?*

No. It was supposed to have one unifying *spirituality*. No religion. No religions. Just a singular spiritual behavior pattern in which no separatism played a part.

▸ *My friend and I are always arguing over our respective religious beliefs. She's so stubborn that she can never see my side. What should I do?*

I suggest you also stop being stubborn. By arguing over this subject matter, you're not showing each other respect. Individualized religious beliefs are supposed to instill inner peacefulness, not verbal aggressiveness. You behave in a disrespectful manner and dishonor your own beliefs when you use them as a source for argument. There's nothing wrong with declaring one's beliefs or talking about them in a sharing manner, but to actually pit them against another's in a routine quarrelsome manner is lessening their sacredness, which, I assume, is a quality you believe they have. Though my books are full of my own spiritual philosophy as I've come to experience and witness realities through many forms and means, I'd never ever involve myself in a personal argument with anyone over our different beliefs. What's the point of it? This type of argument is only for the purpose of attempting to convince another of the "rightness" of your own belief. Why, I would ask, is that necessary? If you are completely content and at peace with your belief system, there's no need to have anyone else join you in that belief. Yes, you may be excited about it and want to share it, but so? Go share it—don't argue about it and try to push it down the throats of others. You can discuss it in an intelligent manner if you wish, but don't let it get away from you by ending up arguing over it. Then you're only dishonoring it by not treating it in a sacred manner. I suggest that you avoid the issue of you and your friend's separate religious beliefs altogether. You agree to disagree. You agree to respect each other's beliefs and leave it at that.

► *Do angels have wings? Is that just creative imagery?*

Creative imagery. But . . . on whose part? Humans' or the angels'? Remember, pure energy can alter its shape. Also remember that there is a difference between angels and angelic beings.

► *What does Satan really look like?*

Anything he wants. A nonphysical entity can create shape from thought. Just like the question regarding angel wings, thought is energy and energy can be reshaped. Satan can present himself as a human being, a shadow, a preacher, a street sweeper, whatever. Remember, he was a spirit created by God. With that in mind, I think the image of Satan as having red skin, horns, and an arrow-tipped tail is a bit ludicrous. That's the phantasmagorical imagery of a human mind. I would hope that we've advanced far beyond that kind of medieval thought.

► *The many hidden gnostic gospels that were discovered at the Najᶜ Hammādi site in December 1945 included the one that religious scholars suspect was written by the lower Sophia (Shekinah). For nearly two decades, you've been bringing us spiritual philosophy that has gradually unfolded to reveal one of feminine spirituality. Does the fact that you were born in December 1945 have a direct relationship to the discovery of the Sophia writings in that same month and year?*

This relationship is an example of simple synchronicity. I've noticed a societal tendency to attach esoteric and mysterious meanings to explain synchronic events, yet usually there is nothing more mysterious or meaningful associated with them than the basic fact that they're just plain and simple examples of how events can, at some point or another, be connected to others. Don't see things that aren't there. Don't read things into the spaces between lines. Don't make unfounded assumptions. Don't perceive implications that have never been claimed or implied, because this is precisely how someone's statements get twisted and turned into a convoluted braid of misunderstood concepts. Synchronicity happens. It's as simple as that. No hidden meanings, no secret messages. We exhibit intellectual wisdom when we restrain ourselves from making reactionary responses such as assumptions and quick conclusions that have no rational basis.

▸ *What is your image of God like?*

For me this is a rather odd question because I've no specific image of the Divine Essence, especially no image carrying shape or form. What comes to mind whenever I do think of the Divine is more in the way of a feeling than a shape or particular image— the feeling of powerful love, omnipotence, and compassion that relates more to a powerful energy rather than to the visual of some preconceived image.

▸ *Is there really a Hope Diamond curse?*

This incredible blue, 44.52-carat diamond, though believed by some to have caused the demise of Marie Antoinette and King Louis XVI of France, among others, does not carry a curse with it. That's the same superstitious type of perception that people attached to Tutankhamun's tomb and treasure. Or the evil eye and black cats.

▸ *Are you ever superstitious—just a little?*

No, not even a little, not even when no one's looking. In fact, I find it amusing to purposely walk beneath a ladder . . . on Friday the thirteenth. Not that I go out and look for a ladder to walk under, but if the situation presents itself, then I accommodate it.

This whole superstition concept involves a belief in luck— good luck, bad luck. If one doesn't believe in luck, then all those superstitious sayings and ideas hold no meaning. A gambler's lucky streak is nothing more than playing the right machines at the right time when their internal computer chip has cycled around to another hitting streak. It's got nothing to do with luck or a lucky charm one carries. And it's got nothing to do with positive thinking. Positive thinking and all the prayers in the world won't affect a casino computer chip. Sticking money in a machine when it's ready to give the royal flush is not an example of one's personal luck; it's an example of synchronicity because *someone*, whether it's you or someone else, will hit it as soon as the first few plays are made. All because it was the *machine* that was ready, not because of any *luck* the player thinks she or he had. Now this doesn't negate the fact that some folks can have natural intuitive *feelings* for which machine is about to cycle into a hitting spell. Some folks do well by using their intuition, but that still isn't luck. It's important to avoid using incorrect terminology.

▸ *Could New Age beliefs be categorized as a religion or a cult?*

Religion and *cult* are the same thing. I discovered this when I checked both definitions in my *Webster's New Universal Unabridged Dictionary*. I did this because I was getting sick of the television media calling every nontraditional religious belief a cult. Lo and behold, the dictionary didn't make any perceivable distinction between the two.

New Age beliefs are neither a religion nor a cult. They're a soft and subtle blend of spirituality and natural physics. If you read any popular science books by noted astrophysicists or biophysicists, you'll realize that the scientific community has recently discovered the existence of an interconnecting force between all of life. The Great Web of Life. All my relations. These scientists are realizing that the gap they once perceived as existing between physics and spiritual reality is narrowing. It's narrowing because they've come to acknowledge a type of consciousness perceptible within the nature of things. No, New Age ideas are not a religion or a cult. They've been around since ancient times and modern-day scientists are just now witnessing amazing revelations that expose threads connecting the concepts once thought to be miles apart. New Age ideas are mostly comprised of simple physics and the natural elements of our world reality. If you'd be interested in perusing some of these interesting and entertaining science books, here are a few of my favorites:

- *The Spiritual Universe—How Quantum Physics Proves the Existence of the Soul,* by Fred Alan Wolf, Ph.D., published by Simon & Schuster
- *The Holographic Universe,* by Michael Talbot, published by HarperCollins
- *Lifting the Veil—The Feminine Face of Science,* by Linda Jean Shepherd, Ph.D., published by Shambhala
- *Dancing Naked in the Mind Field,* by Kary Mullis (biochemist), published by Pantheon Books
- *Probability 1,* by Amir D. Aczel, Ph.D., published by Harcourt Brace & Company
- *The Tao of Physics,* by Fruitjof Capra, published by Shambhala

Though the scientific community has taken baby steps toward reaching its long-awaited epiphany, this is an exciting time because some of the New Age concepts once perceived as kooky and cultish by the general public are being concretely verified by science. The concepts of reality's physics were there all along and were recognized by the so-called New Age believers. These concepts were immutable; hence, they were stable enough to wait until the scientific community made its slow-paced way to their door.

Calling the physics of reality's basic nature (New Age concepts) a religion or cult is incredulous. It's laughable. It's none other than the pure nature of reality . . . *physics.* New Age concepts are the blending of spirituality and physics, so let's shed that medieval type of thinking about it once and for all. Let's get rid of the satanic connection to it that many folks love to make, because Nature and the workings of reality were created by the Divine. To call that creation a work of the Devil is an abomination. We're more intelligent than that—at least we should be by now.

► *What can I do about the spiritually bad thoughts I have?*

For the sake of being concise and preserving this correspondent's privacy, I'm going to clarify this question for the general readership.

Bad thoughts don't imply "dirty" or sexual thoughts but rather those thoughts we sometimes have that bring guilty feelings with them—the thoughts that can seem selfish, mean-spirited, or uncharacteristically unspiritual coming from the individual. Here we're referring to the unspiritual bad thoughts, not those of the "dirty" kind.

First, I need to remind everyone that no one is perfect. I suppose even the pope has a spiritually dirty thought or two during his busy week. Look at the famous evangelists who incite prejudicial attitudes and persecuting behavior toward those who are different. That's a prime example of unspiritual bad thoughts and behavior coming from an unlikely source.

We all have feelings. Too many people use the excuse of "I'm only human" as a way of shoving their responsibility off on the scapegoat of human nature, but in fact, we are human. Acknowledging our imperfect humanness in a rational and reasonable manner is not the same as constantly using that nature as an excuse for bad behavioral expressiveness. It's a fact that we're human and it's a fact that that psychological nature is extremely complex. It's a fact that the human nature has inherent emotional responses. It's a fact that that nature is not the *prime* scapegoat for *all* bad behavior.

The fact that you, like most of us, have a sense of guilt due to unspiritual thoughts is indicative of a desire to behave in a spiritual manner. That desire is what's most important to consider. None of us are unequivocable examples of perfect spiritual behavior. Though we may like to be, it's an unreasonable goal. It's unreasonable *because* of our human nature and its attendant emotions generated from our unique, complex psychological makeup.

Whenever I find myself having an unspiritual "bad thought," I make myself sit down and analyze the reason(s) behind it. Most times I realize that the thought was generated from a knee-jerk reaction and involved a perspective associated with the self rather than seeing the situation from a more generalized viewpoint. When this is clarified, the situation resolves itself through the understanding that the event in no way was intended to be a personal one and my bad thought was unfounded; hence, the guilt dissipates with the understanding.

The prime personal example of this involves my home situation in which my companion, Sally, and I need to give hourly care and monitoring to her elderly mother, Mary Belle, who is in stage 4 of Alzheimer's. Sally goes to town in the morning to pick up the mail at the post office (no home delivery) and sometimes won't return until dinnertime. Consequently, I'm left to monitor Mary Belle all day long while also trying to work on manuscripts. (I often have more than one that I'm working on simultaneously.) So once in a while I'll find myself getting more and more irritated as the hours pass. As I have to stop work and do this or attend to that, I think, *Where is Sally? Out having a good time while I'm stuck here taking care of Mary Belle? Does she think I'm her mother's babysitter?* Then the guilt swoops down like a black shadow for having those unspiritual "bad thoughts." So then I give them rational attention, and this is what I learn from my knee-jerk reaction.

This is Sally's own mother. There are limitless psychological factors involved in seeing your mother behave in such an uncharacteristic manner. It's hard. It's so hard seeing one's mother behave like a small child, doing socially and hygienically unacceptable things and voicing cruel, hateful and hurtful things. It's damn difficult hearing your mother accuse you of outrageous things and witnessing her paranoid and suspicious thought process. It's hard dealing with having to calm a suddenly combative parent who, before the illness, wouldn't have lifted a finger to a fly. It's hard to have to bathe your mother because she doesn't want to anymore and make sure she doesn't sleep in her clothes. It's frustrating to keep telling her the same things over and over again a hundred times each day because she forgets as soon as you say it. It's irritating to watch her put her dog outside four times in fifteen minutes because she forgets and glares at you as if you're lying when you remind her that the dog's just been out. It's tiring to hear her speak ill of you when talking to others on the phone as if you can't do anything right for her. It's hard to hear her tell relatives that she's not eating when, in reality, you spend a great deal of time cooking nutritious meals and she then hands the full plate back to you, saying, "The doctor told me not to eat." She gives people the impression that she's not fed well rather than telling people *why* she sometimes doesn't eat—it's because she refuses to because of the imagined doctor directive. Or she'll tell people that Sally won't take her to church but doesn't explain to them that she told us she didn't *want* to go anymore because "bearded mountain men were drinking wine out of the same chalice she was supposed to sip from." We've had to build a plywood Dutch door at the top of the stairway to keep Mary Belle from sneaking downstairs during the night and wandering outside in the woods. It's hard for a daughter to be suddenly awakened at 3 A.M. to the sound of her mother kicking at the door because she wants out and then getting combative and threatening to get the rifle and "take care of everybody" unless the door is kept unlocked. Yes. Oh yes, it's got to be incredibly hard for a daughter to see her mother behave so uncharacteristically. And I should always—always—realize this. I should always keep in mind how incredibly painful this is for Sally to deal with day after day, night after night. Some nights we get no sleep at all because "love never sleeps." So if my being here all day allows her some time away from the dementia and affords her a few hours of social contact in town, who the hell am I to deny her that? Those who have not had to be responsible for the hourly care of a patient with advanced Alzheimer's have no idea what the caregiver goes through and is exposed to. The surprises, the denial and forgetfulness, the cruel accusations and paranoid suspicions, the threats and violent behavior are ongoing behavioral characteristics related to the disease. The caregiver's complete understanding of these is paramount to proper management and care. The general public's comprehension of the whole issue is near nil unless they've experienced it firsthand. This is why Sally and I are planning on coauthoring a book on it to help the general public better understand and to maybe give some comfort to the existing caregivers themselves.

So when this selfish "bad thought" begins to enter my mind the next time Sally is away for the day, the guilt never has a chance to appear anymore because I've already analyzed the reasons for the thought and it doesn't get a chance to develop into a full-blown feeling anymore. Part of my thinking went like this: If Mary Belle weren't here, what would I be doing while Sally was in town? I'd be sitting at the computer working on a manuscript and taking breaks by doing laundry, letting the dogs out, and vacuuming or doing the dishes. Would I be out in town with Sally? No, not usually, because I prefer to stay home in the cabin rather than going out doing errands. So what was my deal? The deal was I was being selfish by feeling put upon and used as a handy babysitter. Well, how silly that was, because I'd be here anyway! How silly that was because I want Sally to feel confident that her mother is left with someone she can depend on. How ridiculous my reaction was because Sally has a great need to get out and away from the dementia to maintain her own balance of well-being. This last is one of the main pieces of strong advice given to the caregivers in every book we've read on Alzheimer's. The caregiver *must* make time for her- or himself and *not* slip into a situation of isolation. I can help Sally get those much-needed breaks. To have a put-upon perspective is a terrible unspiritual bad thought and I never have it anymore. It's elements such as this that we feel we can help other Alzheimer's caregivers come to terms with through our planned book.

So, to you, who want to know how to handle your unspiritual bad thoughts, my first suggestion is to sit down and analyze the feelings that brought them on. *Honestly* analyze them, and, nine times out of ten, you'll discover that they were unfounded or you will at least come to a better understanding of your thought process and the psychological elements of that process will have more defined clarity. If the thought(s) bring an attending sense of guilt, don't just mentally slap yourself on the hand and shove the thought away; you need to also analyze the why of them. When this analysis is done, the same thoughts rarely return.

As an addendum to the example I gave, Sally realized that she was staying away because she was in denial. She felt she was using the mechanism of escapism so she wouldn't have to deal with the exhausting grind of attending to her mother's condition. Not only did she not want to deal with it, but she subconsciously figured that if she stayed away, she could avoid getting emotionally hurt by that behavior. Though her analysis was good, it was only half right. An Alzheimer's caregiver *must* have some personal time away. It's a fact. It's a fact that isn't even associated with any psychological mechanism of guilt, denial, or hurtful emotional avoidance, it's just a very solid and basic fact of effective care giving. And, since Sally and I can never (or rarely) both leave the house at the same time, we've recently employed a friend to spell us for a couple of days a week. Though we've tried taking Mary Belle down to Colorado Springs with us when we needed to do shopping trips, she's tired out by the time we walk into the first store and demands to return home. So we've learned a lot, regarding not only the natural thoughts that come with caring for someone with this disease but also little helpful caregiving tricks that have become wonderful life- and mind-savers. Living with an individual with Alzheimer's is hard enough; I can't imagine how difficult it must be to have that person be your own mother. My heart is full of empathy for what Sally and others like her are going through.

Again, nobody's perfect. Don't let yourself become guilt ridden over what you identify as being unspiritual bad thoughts. Analyze the thoughts and the situation or relationship that generated them. Know yourself. Know your mind. Give yourself the courtesy of wanting to understand both. Treat yourself to the added inner strength and gained wisdom that naturally comes from that understanding.

▸ *How do I know God's plan for me?*

God's plan for you is for your spirit to become aligned to the Divine. How you accomplish that is *your* plan.

▸ *I look around and see people's repetitive lifestyle—work, eat, sleep, maybe go out to dinner once in a while—and I frequently think it all seems so shallow or useless. We're just going through the motions, passing time until we croak. What for?*

It's for the reason of choosing the *quality* of that passing time. How we fill in the spaces between the daily work-eat-sleep cycle is really what life's about. The working, eating, and sleeping only serve to financially sustain and physically fortify us for what we do during the spaces between these activities. Those spaces are the opportunities to practice unconditional goodness and, through spiritual works and behavior, raise our consciousness to higher levels of spirituality. I know the daily grind can seem useless and mundane, but you wouldn't be here unless your spirit had a good reason for choosing to return and, most times, that singular reason is because it foresaw its physical presence as making some type of difference. That difference may not be what you'd currently equate that concept with—nothing monumental—but rather the small differences one makes in the lives of others that accumulate into what is seen as an *entire* that generated many differences. Most times people don't even realize or become aware of the differences they make in the lives of those they touch. Sometimes just a kind word of encouragement voiced to another can end up making a huge difference in the other's life. We don't necessarily have to do something monumental or huge or even something publicly recognized to make a difference; often it's as subtle and simple as a smile or setting a behavioral example. There are many ways to touch the lives of others and you're probably already doing some of them without even realizing it.

If this planet was meant to have one religion, which one would it be?

None. It was meant to have a spirituality. Humans were meant to have a *spiritual behavior* rather than a specific type of religion or worship.

Have the individual religions ended up being bad or harmful to people?

Only in the sense that they've ended up being separatist, a means of dividing people and causing prejudicial attitudes and behavior involving persecution of those believing differently. I don't think that was what the Divine Minds had in mind and I certainly don't think it pleases Them to see it happening in the name of God.

No religion can be called wrong. It's the behavioral attitudes resulting from many of the humanmade tenets that make them misaligned with divine intent. It's the barnacles of dogma that weigh down the purity of simple spirituality.

sh Christianity—people did. What type of
nk he would've established had he lived

...ve to live longer to accomplish this. He didn't care
...aratism of any kind; therefore, he tried to get the message
across that it's one's spiritual behavior that counts. He emphasized this over and over again when he said, "I am the Way," meaning that people needed to follow the example of his *spiritual
behavior and words,* not some constricting religious dogma.

AFTERWORD

We're all looking to live meaningful lives and ways to improve our relationship with the Divine. You wouldn't have bought this book if you weren't searching for greater spiritual understanding of reality and ways to enhance that philosophical understanding. The responses I've given to my correspondents' questions are not the end-all word; they were provided as stepping-stones to further development through readers' ensuing contemplative inspiration. Our thought processes can be stimulated by a particular phrase or a simple word. The illumination of a philosophical epiphany can be ignited by a single spark of a specific sentence. This, then, is what this book has been about. You've written many questions regarding the subject matters covered within the pages of *Earthway*. This companion volume is offered as a way to not only respond to those inquiries but to also present associated ideas that convey the reality of multiconceptual interrelatedness. From the shimmering celestial bodies to the natural plants growing upon this verdant green earth, from the crystal mountain streams to the human hikers walking beside their lush banks, all of life is tightly interwoven in a beautiful pattern of living reality. All of life shares a Divine consciousness. The Great Web of Life verifies the sustaining breath of the Divine Essences as it gently touches our lives in myriad ways and, from everywhere, whispers its words of wisdom. The way of the earth, of reality's nature—the Earthway—is a living facet of Divine creation. It is a thriving, fertile gift of life . . . full of invaluable lessons and powerful wisdom.

INDEX

Acceptance, 22, 94, 154, 175, 292, 326, 327, 337
  in aging, 197
  of bad behavior, 177
  ego versus, 197–98
  of ignorance, 201
  of intolerant behavior, 202
  lack of, 260
  parental, 176
  patience and, 354–55
  power in, 345
  of who one is, 14
Acid/alkaline balance, 123–24
Acne, 131–32
Adult eating baby food (dream), 255
Affirmation
  in meditation, 293, 302
After-death experience, 322
Aging, fear of, 196–97
AIDS, 114–15, 147
Alien abduction dreams, 237–39
Aloneness, 350–52
Alternative healing methods, 121–22
Altitude, 48, 53, 63
Aluminum, 135, 136
Alzheimer's, 191, 342, 364–67

AMA (American Medical Association), 107–08, 114–15, 133, 134
Anasazi planetary belief system, 7–8
Angels, 359
Animal superimposed on human (dream), 211
Animal totems, 24
Animals
  astrological influences on, 15–16
  erratic reaction before earthquake, 48
  mean vibratory rates, 81, 98–99
  sixth sense, 253
Antisocial behavior, 159–60
Anxiety, 192–93
Aquarium (dream), 215–16
Archaeologist, 216
Arrogance, 31, 156
  see also Religious arrogance; Spiritual arrogance
Artist profession, 83
Artworks
  composite vibrational rate in, 100–101
As above, so below, 85, 106, 268
Asbestos, 135, 136
Asexuality, 85, 242
Assumptions, 237, 249–50
  regarding dreams, 208, 221, 222

Astrologer(s), 44
Astrological chart(s), 21, 79, 80, 89
  computer-generated versus manual, 36
  end times event on, 44–45
  for Jesus, 42
  major life events in, 41
  and marriage, 10–11, 31–33
  and occupation(s), 27–29
  of partner, 45–46
  as possibilities, 33–35
  showing fatal disease, 45
  of twins born on opposing sides of
    cusp, 46
Astrological influences, 24
  on animals, 15–16
  effect of mother's on baby, 39–40
  on inanimate objects, 19–20
  in life plan, 20–23
  in multiple births, 16–17
  of parents, 9–10
  from past lives, 17–18
  in pregnancy, 14–15
  on volcanoes, 12–13
  in war(s), 18–19
Astrological signs
  characteristic for psychism in, 40–41
  of partners, 77–78
  see also Birth signs
Astrology, 5–46
  Anasazi, 7
  as work of Satan, 35–36
Astronomers/astronomy, 5, 6, 38
Atheism, 357
Atmosphere, 48, 56, 61
Attitude(s), 59, 105, 106
  being born with, 165–66
  contaminating, 151–205
  how one uses, 183
  of optimism and joyfulness, 268
  perceptions altered by, 256
  and weight loss, 109–10
Attraction/repulsion
  mean vibratory rate in, 85–86
Aura, 79, 82
  and mean vibratory rate, 94–95
  vibrational frequency and, 98–99
Awake-state condition
  see Awake-state consciousness
Awake-state consciousness, 208, 278,
    282, 283, 284, 285, 287, 304, 354
  returning to, following meditation,
    301

Bacteria, 132–33, 145
Bad thoughts, 363–68
Balsa wood (dream), 254
Barbie dolls, 160–62
Barometric pressure, 72–73
  low, 56, 71, 72
Barren landscape (dream), 259–60
Beauticians
  exposure to chemicals, 148
Beauty
  real, 161–62
  society's perception of, 160
Beauty secrets, 116–17
Behavior
  is choice, 314–15
  is communication, 251
  defines beingness, 192
  religious beliefs and, 316–18
  see also Spiritual behavior
Beingness, 104
  balanced inner chi state of, 159
  and beauty, 117
  behavior defines, 192
  birth signs in, 13
  cherishing, 95, 201
  of child(ren), 176
  child as blend of, 93
  composite, 45, 85
  consciousness core of, 275
  consciousness equated with, 96
  in flux and turmoil, 262
  ignoring, 89
  individualized thought and philoso-
    phy in, 352
  love in, 243
  nurturing, 214
  of reality, 348–49
  outward expression of, 155
  and spirituality, 316
Belief systems, 286
Beliefs
  social advances in, 350–51
Bible, 38, 318, 329–30, 331
Biofeedback, 116
Biological elements
  in vibrational rate, 103
Biological warfare, 66
Biotin, 135
Birdcage (dream), 231–32
Birth signs, 6, 13–14, 15, 78
  color(s), associated with, 24–25
  of employees, 8–9

in hiring, 8–9, 23
of Jesus, 9
and occupations, 28
past lives, 17
and uniqueness, 25, 29–30
Bisexuality, 242
Bitterns (dream), 268
Blessings, 8, 172, 355
Divine, 266
food as, 140
smaller, 267
unrecognized, 263
Blood tests, 111
Bodies, 72
multidimensional, 353–54
Body language, 250–51
Body temperature
humidity and, 71–72
Books, 137, 138
dream interpretation, 223
learning from, 110
meditation, 275–76, 292
Boys, 162
Bubble bath products, 118–19

Cancer, 111–12
Candle lighting (dream), 227–29
Catalpa tree
dream symbology, 269
Catholicism, 329, 331–32, 343, 357
Cayce, Edgar, 107, 136–37, 249
Celestial affinity, 5–46
Celestial bodies
magnetic influences of, 5, 6, 10, 13
relationship with earth's physiologi-
cal activity, 12–13
Celestial event(s)
marking end times, 44–45
Cereal, colored, 148
Changes, The, 252
Channeler, 296
Channeler (dream), 219–20
Character, 13, 234
Character self-examination, 214–15
Chemicals, 123, 148
Chi (energy), 94, 112, 159, 279–80,
304–05
Chicken Little perspective, 67, 68
Chicory, 218
Chihuahua, 259
Children
fears of, 186

gift acknowledgment, 173–77
idols and heroes, 187–88
and meditation, 285–86
spiritual behavior in, 345–46
unique composite consciousness of,
93
Chiropractic treatment, 112, 121
Chocolate, 128
Choices, 13, 41, 137–38
and acceptance, 22
in behavior, 314–15
as evidence of individuality, 155
and mean vibrational rate, 88
responsibility for, 21, 23, 27
of young adults, 177
Christianity, 370
Chrysoberyl gem (dream), 224
Church
dream symbology, 263
women in/and, 312–14
Church of England, 357
Cleaning precautions
rodent droppings, 126–27
Climatological effects on human physiology, 63–64
Coffee (dream), 218
Color, 79–80
altered in dreams, 233
with birth signs, 24–25
in dreams, 212, 217–18, 261
and mean vibratory rate, 84
in Virtual Meditation, 281
Comets, 30–31, 33
Commitment, 254
Common courtesy, 173, 174–75, 177
Community-mindedness, 254
Completed spirits, returned, 19
Composite identity
vibratory rate in, 88
Composite spirit consciousness, 30, 32,
92, 96
Composite vibrationary rate, 90, 96, 97,
103, 159, 201
in artworks, 100–101
and mechanical equipment, 99–101
and relaxation, 291
and spiritual inclinations, 261–62
Computer memory (dream), 264
Concentration, 290
Concern, 193
Confession, 335–36
Conscious intent, 212

Consciousness, 63, 235
  concept of, 96
  dimensionally all-inclusive, 353–54
  Divine, 371
  dreams controlled by, 212
  expansion of, 273
  freeing, 348
  high states of, 94
  of infant(s), 165, 214
  in meditation, 274–75, 277, 278,
    279, 280–81, 282–83, 285–86,
    291, 293, 297, 298, 300, 301–02,
    305
  during sleep, 206, 217, 255
  survives death of body, 322–23
  totality of, 13, 16
Consciousness raising, 201, 312
Contemplation, 276, 291, 347, 352
Cooperation, 254
Copernicus, Nicolaus, 38–39, 351
Countries
  mean vibratory rate, 84–85
Creatrix, 313, 315
Criticism, 181–82
Crone, 246–47
Crystal stream, meditation as, 279–80
Crystals, energizing, 102–03
Cultures
  astrological beliefs, 41–42
  meditation in, 276–77
Cusp, being born on, 42, 46

Dancing Naked in the Mind Field (Mullis), 115
Dandelions (dream), 232
Dark forces, 300, 324
  see also Dark spirit entities
Dark spirit entities
  in hatred and intolerance, 314–15
Daybreak (Summer Rain), 203
Dead friends/relatives (dream), 237
de Becker, Gavin, 184, 185
Decisions, 13
  and acceptance, 22
  educated, 137
  responsibility for, 21, 23, 27–28, 32,
    68–69
Denial, 144, 231, 235, 239, 242, 245,
  264
Depression, 56, 72, 233
  electrically charged environments
    and, 102
  and health, 109

Deserving things, 172
  see also "I deserve" excuse
Devil, 324, 363
  in/and meditation, 279, 302
Diet(s), 132, 135
  and cancer, 111–12
  weight-loss, 106–10
Dietary aspects, 105–48
Digestive problems, 109, 130–31, 139
Disasters, 185–86
Discrimination, 8–9, 157, 158
Disease, 147
  psychosomatic, 120–21
  showing on astrological chart, 45
Diversity, 9, 14, 15, 166
Divine (the), 18, 35, 117–18, 337
  alignment to, 368
  communion with, 342, 345
  and concept of hell, 340
  Goddess aspect of, 213
  life is gift from, 186
  relationship with, 328, 335, 336,
    343, 371
  Sabbath and, 344
Divine Consciousness, 18
Divine Essences, 325–27, 328, 329,
  336, 337, 339, 349, 360, 372
Divine Feminine Aspect, 312, 316–17,
  328
DNA, 9–10, 14, 40, 112, 116, 243
Do no harm philosophy, 292, 331, 333,
  337
Dog(s) (dream), 224–25
Dogs smarter than humans (dream),
  253–54
Dream deprivation, 215
Dream interpretation, 206–69
Dream recall, 215
Dream symbology, 222–23, 236, 249–
  50
Dreams, 18
  adult eating baby food, 255
  alien abduction, 237–39
  balsa wood, 254
  barren landscape, 259–60
  bitterns, 268
  candle lighting in, 227–29
  of channeler, 219–20
  chrysoberyl gem, 224
  coffee in, 218
  color altered in, 233
  colors in, 212, 217–18, 261

computer memory, 264
controlled by consciousness, 212
dandelions, 232
dead friends/relatives in, 237
dogs smarter than humans, 253–54
estate sale, 265
flowers dying, 262–63
fortune teller, 265–66
foster care home for children, 266–67
gender transposed in, 241
ginkgo tree in, 225–26
Isis in, 233
jet stone, 257
Ku Klux Klan, 264
Lhasa Apso, 224–25
little people, 259
loading a moving van, 239
Manx cat, 236–37
meadow/thistles in, 229–30
meerkat, 254
milkwood in, 235–36
mirrors don't reflect image, 255–56
mist/fog, 256
moon in full lunar eclipse, 252
morganite in, 230–31
mushrooms in, 218
obsidian, 256–57
occupations in, 216
OOBE distinct from, 219
orchids in, 213
peridot gemstone, 267
pickup truck with three wheels, 260–61
picture covered with mold, 264–65
proboscis monkey in, 226–27
prophetic, 206–07, 222
psychic in, 234–35
redbud tree, 214–15
reflection of subconscious, 236
relationships in, 257–58
rock shop, 210
sand lily, 267
sea sponge in, 208–10
sensitivity to neighbor, 240–41
snow in summer, 252
snowbird, 210
specific time in, 257
spoonbill bird, 224
staurolite, 251–52
strangers manifesting behind face of friend in, 234
sugar glider in, 226
sugar maple, 253
Taco Bell dog, 258
thesaurus in, 250–51
time frames in, 223–24
Titanic, 217
trees bare of leaves, 252–53
unremembered, 62
upside-down objects in, 225
Viagra, 258–59
viper in, 229
walking down church steps wearing medieval costume, 263
watermelon tourmaline stone, 267–68
whippoorwill in birdcage, 231–32
Dress, "sloppy," 166–67
Drugs
and vibratory rate, 103–04

Earth, 13, 333–34, 357
magnetic field, 47–49, 54
Earth Mother, 313
Earthquakes, 48, 67, 85, 315
Earthway (Summer Rain), 6, 47, 48, 49, 77, 116, 117, 118, 121, 122, 123, 129, 135, 136, 279, 349, 353, 371
Eating too fast, 139–40
Eclipse (Summer Rain), 183, 204, 205, 247, 248, 340
Ego, 164, 192, 194–95, 314, 348
versus acceptance, 197–98
dominating personality, 211
emphasis on, 356
in jealousy, 151
negating intuitive thoughts, 240
patience and, 355
in prayer, 326
priority placed on, 351
sense of superiority, 332
in spiritual beliefs, 343
in trying to please others, 198, 200
Ego stroking, 158, 181, 214, 215
Egyptology, 91
El Niño, 49, 51
Elders, respect for, 188–92
Electrically charged work environments and vibratory rate, 102
Elevation(s)
high/low, 53, 56–57

Embryo, astrological influence on, 10,
    40
Emotional sensitivity
    in meditation, 298
Emotional sustenance, 235–36
Emotionality, negative
    and cancer, 112
Emotions, 62, 100, 132
    contaminating, 151–205
    releasing, 345
    in vibrational rate, 103
Employees
    astrology in hiring, 8–9
Encouragement, 210
End times, 44–45
Energy, 20, 98, 349–50
    see also Chi (energy)
Energy level
    and mechanical equipment, 99–100
Enlightenment
    meditation and, 283–84, 299
Envy, 152–53, 154–55
Epiphanies, 8, 39, 235, 299
    in dreams, 207
    new thought in, 352
Escapism, 67, 308
Escherichia coli (E. coli), 132
Estate sale (dream), 265
Ethnicity, 48, 158, 348
    and mean vibratory rate, 96–97
Exercise, 109, 112, 113
Expectation, 303, 307
Eye makeup removal product, 123

Fairy (dream), 259
Faith, 193
Faith healing, 117–18
Family meditation, 292
Family solidarity, 337
Fear, 183–86, 268
    in meditation, 294
Fear of discovery, 264
Fear of dying, 262–63
Fear of the unknown, 294
Feminine deity concept, 247–48
Feminine spirituality, 220, 246–48,
    328, 359–60
Feminism, 245–46, 248, 320–22
Fireside (Summer Rain), 160, 247, 323
Flatlanders, 58
Flowers dying (dream), 262–63
Fluoride, 65, 135

Folic acid, 135
Foods, 105, 120
    abundance of, 140
    acid/alkaline balance in, 123–24
    chemicals and growth hormones, in,
        123
    and digestive problems, 130–31
    freeze-dried, 141
    healthful benefits of, 134
    locally grown/shipped in, 124
    made by hand, 128–29
    medical reversals regarding, 107–08
    selection of, 137
    and terrorism, 144–45
    and vibratory rate, 103–04
    wild, 145
Foreknowledge, subconscious, 145
Foresight, 266, 356
Forgiveness, 335–36, 342
Fortune teller (dream), 265–66
Foster care home for children (dream),
    266–67
Free will, 38, 118, 191, 314, 325
Friends
    in dream, 268
Frustration, 197–98
Future (the)
    knowing, 265–66
    paranoia about, 183–86
    unknowability of, 192, 193

Gemini, 9, 46
Gender, 158, 181
    in language, 320–21
    in religion, 329
    transposed in dreams, 241
Gender equality, 246, 320
Genetic coding, 9–10, 103
Genetics, 96–97
Geographical choice
    mean vibratory rate and, 84
    partner and, 86–87
Geography
    emotional and physical reaction to,
        54–55, 63–64
Geologic content beneath home, 70–71
Geological events
    and relocation, 66–69
Geology, 13
G.I. Joes, 162
Gift acknowledgment, 173–77
Gift of Fear, The (Becker), 184

Ginkgo biloba, 224–26
Ginkgo tree (dream), 225–26
Girls
  and Barbie dolls, 160–63
  effects of bubble bath products on,
    118–19
  sexually abused, 165
Gnostic Gospels, 42–43, 248, 313,
  359–60
Goals, 186–87, 188, 269
God, 18, 321
  belief in, 97
  and health, 118
  and human grief/sorrow, 315
  image of, 360
  in individual lives, 325–26
  mind of, 329
  in Nature, 337–38
  plan(s) for individuals, 368
Goddesses, 181, 312–13, 321, 332
  term, 346–49
Goodness, 228
  see also Unconditional goodness
Gossip, 158
Grandmother Crone, 313
Grandmother Earth, 117, 134, 246
Grandmother Spider, 246, 313
Great Web of Life, 12, 13, 51–52, 98,
  195, 349–50, 361, 371–72
Group meditation, 290, 292
Growth hormones, 123
Guilt, 363, 364, 366, 367, 368
Gum problems, 129

Hair brushing, 134–35
Hantavirus pulmonary syndrome, 125–
  26
Happiness, 167–73
Harbingers of future
  comets as, 30–31
Hate crimes, 163, 194–96, 201
Hate groups, 312, 356
Hatred, 156, 157, 158, 163, 182, 194,
  195, 201, 202, 243, 281, 284,
  311–12, 331
  dark spirit entities in, 314–15
  forces negating, 326
  religion and, 339
  religious leaders incite, 318–19
Healing, 267
  magnets for, 49, 54
  mental visualization in, 115–16

Healing aspects, 105–48
Health, 105, 111
  effect of earth's magnetic field on,
    48–49
  humidity in, 55
  life perspective in, 268
  volcanoes and, 54
Hearing voices
  during meditation, 296
Heart attacks, red wine in preventing,
  118
Heaven, 322–23, 340
Hell, 340
Henry VIII, 343, 357
Herbal teas, 138–39
Herbs, 110–11, 117
Heroes/heroines, 187–88
Herpes virus, 128
Heterosexuality, 85
Hidden qualities, 232
HIV, 114–15
Holy Spirit, 333, 346
  as feminine deity, 247
Home(s), vibrational atmosphere, 101
Homeopathy, 106
Homosexual partners, 155–58
Homosexuality, 85, 203, 242
  and AIDS, 147
  as sin, 329–31
Honey, 123
Hope Diamond curse, 360
Human beings/humankind, 356, 357
  relatedness, 52–53, 71, 117
  rights of, 157
Human grief/sorrow
  God in/and, 315
Human nature
  as scapegoat, 363
Human races
  ethnic mean vibratory rate, 96–97,
    98
Humidifiers, 147
Humidity, 54–56, 57, 63, 71–72
Hypochondriacs, 121

"I deserve" excuse, 109–10, 113–14,
  151
Idols/idolatry, 187–88, 334–35
Ignorance, 201–02, 235
Illness, 71, 105–06
Inanimate objects
  astrological influences on, 19–20

Incense, 276, 291
Inclination, 81, 84, 85, 91–92, 165
  ignoring, 88–89
Indecision, 230–31
Individual thought
  importance of, 68–69, 137–38
Individuality, 22, 26, 79, 87, 198–201
  cherishing, 95
  of child, 94, 176
  choices evidence of, 155
  and criticism, 182
  degraded, 286
  of employees, 9
  expressing, 167
  is gift, 68
  and meditation, 295–96, 307
  persecuted, 202
  in spiritual beliefs, 350–52
Infallibility, 329
Infant(s)
  born with attitude, 165–66
  death of, 315
  dreaming, 214
  history of consciousness, 17
  magnetic influences of celestial bod-
    ies on, 10
  mother's astrological influences and,
    39–40
Inner tranquillity, 230
Inquisition, 235, 286, 329
Insight(s), 40, 41, 235
  in dreams, 207
  in meditation, 296, 298–99
Interconnectedness, 12, 15–16, 194,
    275, 338, 361
  rainbow symbolizing, 349–50
Interrelatedness of life
  see Interconnectedness
Intolerance, 158, 182, 201–02, 281,
    283, 284, 312
  dark spirit entities in, 314–15
  forces negating, 326
  of religious leaders, 318–19
Intuition, 40, 41, 235, 361
Intuitive inclinations, 81
Intuitive insight, 184, 240–41
Iron, 135, 136
Irritability, 56–57, 60
Isis (dream), 233

Jealousy, 151–55, 163, 202
Jesus, 19, 222, 319, 321, 329, 370

astrological birth sign, 9
astrological chart for, 42
in Bible, 329–30
birth of, 43
Jet stone (dream), 257
*Journal of the American Medical Associa-
  tion*, 115
Joyfulness, 268

Knowledge, 8, 117
  and wisdom, 65
Knox, John, 286, 343
Ku Klux Klan (dream), 264
Kundalini energy, 279–80, 304–05

L-arginine, 128
Labels/labeling, 159–60, 246, 249,
    322, 323
  spiritual beliefs, 343
Lead, 135
Lesbianism, 241–49, 347
Lhasa Apso (dream), 224–25
Libra, 30
Life
  emanates energy, 70
  gift of, 186, 193
  interconnectedness of, 12, 15–16
  perceived through dollar signs, 265
  purpose of features of, 68
  respect for, 163–64, 188, 194
  uselessness of, 259–60
  what is necessary in, 260–61
Life events, perspective of, 191–92
Life insurance beneficiary
  homosexual partner, 155–58
Life-forms
  affected by vibrational rate, 100
Life plan
  astrological influences in, 20–23
Life problem(s), 114
  solution to, in meditation, 298–99
Lifestyle
  repetitive, 368–69
  solitary, 159–60
Lifetimes, experiential, 13, 14, 17
Light orbs, 43–44
Little people (dream), 259
Live the moment, 8, 185
Liver, 127–28
Logic, 107, 110, 186, 259
Love, 11, 243
  as answer to hate crimes, 194–95

homosexual, 330–31
society and, 157
see also Unconditional love
Lucid dreaming, 212, 353
Luck, 360–61
Luna, goddess of wisdom, 36, 252

Madame Pele (goddess), 41
Magdalene Abbey, 122, 213, 339–40
Magnetism, 100
Magnets, 48–49, 54, 70–71
Manliness, 162
Manx cat (dream), 236–37
Marriage
astrological charts in, 10–11, 31–33
Mary Magdalene, 321, 330
*Mary Summer Rain's Guide to Dream
Symbology*, 213
Meadow/thistles (dream), 229–30
Mean vibratory rates, 77–104, 165
ancestral facet of, 97
animals, 81, 98–99
and artist profession, 83
in attraction/repulsion, 85–86
in attraction to stonework buildings,
92–93
and aura, 94–95
baseline, 103
chart of, 79–80, 81, 97, 101
and *chi* energy, 94
of children, 176
and choices, 88
and color, 84
of countries, 84–85
and differences in siblings, 93–94
genetics in, 96–97
and geographical choice, 84
of life partner, 77–78
never changes, 89–91
and occupation/profession, 78–79,
92
out of body and, 96
preexisting Egyptian influences in, 91
and relaxation, 291
religious beliefs and, 97
and sexual inclination, 85
and solitude versus social functions,
87–88
and spiritual beliefs, 97
and spiritual inclinations, 261–62
and violent/abusive behavior, 81–
82

Mechanical equipment
composite vibrationary rate and, 99–
100
Medical benefits
for homosexual partner, 155–58
Medical insurance conglomerates, 189
Medical reversals, 107–08, 115
Medicine
holistic, 115
traditional, 111, 117, 133–34
Medicines, 117
side effects, 146–47
weather and assimilation of, 72
Meditation, 187, 218, 273–74
age and intellectual capacity in, 285
children and, 285–86
in church, 300
concentration and, 290
as crystal stream, 279–80
in the dark, 276
dark forces entrance during, 300
Devil in/and, 302
emotional sensitivity in, 298
excuses for not doing, 307–08
expansion sensation in, 293
expectations of, 307
falling asleep in, 286–87
fear in, 294
as form of prayer, 308–09
frame of mind for, 300
frequency, 299, 306
as gift from God, 291
group, 290, 292
hearing voices in, 296
in helping the world, 292
in history, 289–90
on holy pictures, 291
incense in, 276, 291
individuality and, 295–96
letdown following, 301
level of advancement, 306
methodologies for, 275–77
while naked, 277
negative forces in, 285
as New Age idea, 286
orgasm in, 303
and personal life problems, 298–99
place for, 279, 297
position for, 299, 304–05
positive affirmation in, 293
on saying or visual, 276
sensations experienced in, 278

Meditation (*continued*)
  sensual perception intensified in, 301–02, 305–06
  and society's behavioral ills, 306–7
  and spiritual enlightenment, 283–84
  teacher not needed for, 284–85
  teaching in schools, 288–89
  thoughts interfering with, 287–88
  time of day for, 309–10
  venue for communication with dead, 282
  visuals during, 303–04
  see also Nonthought, meditation as
Meditation books, 275–76, 292
Meerkat (dream), 254
Melancholia/melancholy, 61–63, 72, 210, 233, 268
Memory, 226, 264
Menstrual cramping, weather and, 72
Menstrual cycle/menopause, 131
Mental (the)
  in health, 106
Mental illness, 56, 104
Mental visualization, 131
  in healing, 115–16
Metals, 70–71, 135–36
Meteor showers, 30, 31, 33, 36
Meterologic/geologic relatedness, 13, 47–73
Middle Ages, 30, 31, 263
Milk, 128, 129–30, 142
Milkweed (dream), 235–36
Mind, 120–21, 181, 235, 278
Minerals, 70–71, 136
Mirrors don't reflect image (dream), 255–56
Miscommunication, 236
Mist/fog (dream), 256
Moderation, 107, 108, 109, 110, 119, 128, 137
Moon, 36–37, 38, 39, 47
Moon in full lunar eclipse (dream), 252
Moon madness, 36–37, 48
Morganite (dream), 230–31
Mother Nature, 246, 313
Moving van, loading (dream), 239
Mullis, Kary, 115
Multiple births
  astrological influences in, 16–17
Mushrooms, 138, 218
Mythology, 41, 288–89

Najᶜ Hammādī 43, 313, 321, 348, 359
Naps, dreaming in, 254–55
Nature, 30, 33, 35–36, 73, 171
  aspects of, 117
  is circular, 349
  energy emanations, 98
  God in, 337–38
  polarity balance(s) in, 136
  priorities and, 187
  responses to, 58
  as spiritual teacher, 353
  weather and, 49–50, 51
Nature beings, 42
Nature deities, belief in, 357
Nature goddesses, 41–42
Neighbor, sensitivity to (dream), 240–41
New Age, 336, 346, 353–54
New Age beliefs, 40, 208, 209, 210, 273
  meditation as, 286
  as religion/cult, 361–63
New England Journal of Medicine, 108, 115
Night traveling, 207–08
Nonthought, meditation as, 274–75, 276, 277, 278, 282–83, 287, 290, 291, 292, 303, 304
Nursing homes, 188–92

Obsidian (dream), 256–57
Occupation(s)/career(s)
  astrological chart in, 27–29
  in dreams, 216, 219
  mean vibratory rate and, 78–79, 92
Opinions of others, 68, 295–96, 302, 351
Opportunities, 191–92, 226
Opportunistic personality, 224
Optimism, 110, 202–03, 218, 267
Orchids (dream), 213
Orgasm in meditation, 303
Oriental monks, 94
Out of body
  and mean vibratory rate, 96
Out-of-body experience (OOBE), 207, 217, 218–19, 354
Overabsorption, 208–9, 210
Overweight, 112–14

Paganism, 337–38, 346–50, 357
Paranoia about future, 183–86
Parents, 166, 181
  astrological influences of, 9–10
  and children's decisions, 27–28
Partner(s)
  astrological chart(s), 45–46
  and geographic choices, 86–87
  homosexual, 155–58
  mean vibratory rates of, 77–78
  and meditation, 297–98
Past-life characteristics, 45
Past-life experiences/influences, 17–18,
    30, 73, 82, 88, 201, 226
  carry-over influences, 32, 70, 91, 92
  of infant, 165
  in mean vibrational rate, 96, 103
  and occupations, 29, 78
Past-life identities, 34
  of children, 93
Patience
  as quality of wisdom, 354–56
Patriarchal domination, 339
  in religion, 312, 328
  in spiritual philosophy, 321
Patriarchal society, 247, 248, 346, 348
Penance, 342
Perception(s), 257–58
  cloudy (in dream), 256
  colored, 233
  density of, 251–52
  fear-based, 268
  skewed, 225
Peridot gemstone (dream), 267
Persecution, 243, 326, 337, 338, 369
Personal responsibility, 79, 188, 191,
    204
  avoiding, 144
  for behavior, 314–15, 327
  to care for others, 266–67
  for decisions and choices, 21, 22, 23,
    68–69
  dream symbology regarding, 220
  in healing, 118
  and prayers, 325–26
Personality, 13, 45, 234
Personality fragility, 214–15
Perspective, 105
  on fear, 183
  on happiness, 170
Pessimism, 109, 218, 257
Pet food, 148

Pharmaceutical companies, 146–
  47
Philosophy, individual, 352
  see also Spiritual philosophy
Physics, 35, 37, 38, 361–62
Physiological issues in dreams, 255
Physiological system
  effect of low barometric pressure on,
    56, 72
Pickup truck with three wheels (dream),
  260–61
Picture covered with mold (dream),
  264–65
Placebo, 120–21
Planetary influences, 30, 35, 37–
  39
  and spirit entities, 12, 19
Planets, realignment of, 23
Pollution, 64, 65, 137
Pope, infallibility of, 329
Positive thinking, 361
Power
  desire for, 187
  society's perception of, 344–45
  wisdom and, 323–24
Prayer, 335, 342
  asking/thank-you, 325–27
  meditation as form of, 308–09
Pregnancy, astrological influences in,
  14–15
Prejudice, 8–9, 156–57, 158, 163,
    201, 264, 281, 283, 284, 312,
    337, 369
  forces negating, 326
  religion in/and, 339
  of religious leaders, 318–19
Premonition, 240, 257, 356
Priests, 303
Priorities, 152, 153, 186–87, 269
  care for elderly in, 189, 190
Probabilities, 257
Proboscis monkey (dream), 226–27
Product tampering, 145
Prophetic dreams, 206–07, 222
Protection, 256–57
Protestants, 332, 357
Psyche
  in thunderstorm effects, 69–70
Psychic(s), 89
  in dream, 234–35
Psychic qualities, 324
Psychism, 40–41

Psychokinesis, 40, 41
Psychological aberrations
    with disturbance of earth's magnetic
        field, 47–48
Psychological aspects, 268
    in dreams, 255, 267
    in health, 105
    in psychosomatic illness, 121
    in vibrational rate, 103, 104
Psychological defense mechanisms, 211
Psychosexual abuse, 178–81
Psychosomatic illness, 120–21

Quantum consciousness, 273–310
Quantum Meditation, 273–74, 275,
        276–77, 278, 279–80, 281, 282,
        283, 284, 285, 290, 293, 297,
        347
    sequential, 211
Question and answer books, 203–05

Racism, 156, 163, 182–83, 201, 326,
        332
Rain, 60–61
Rainbow, 349–50
Raspberries
    in milk, 129–30
    and tumor growth, 133–34
Rationalization, 314, 347
Reading, 6–7, 209–10, 275
    books for spiritual (list), 325
Reality, 5, 12
    beingness of, 348–49
    comprehension of, 7–8, 352
    in human grief/sorrow, 315
    lack of understanding of, 325
    Nature is, 337
    nature of, 362
    perception of, 259, 260
    perceptual sensitivity to, 356
    in prophetic dream, 222
    and Virtual Meditation, 280–81,
        282, 283
Reason, 107, 186, 259
Red wine, 118, 128
Redbud tree (dream), 214–15
Reeve, Christopher, 172
Reincarnation, 12, 14, 84, 320
Relationships
    astrological signs in, 26–27
    in dreams, 257–58
    emotional distress in, 231–32

need to freshen up, 264–65
Relaxation
    in meditation, 277, 283, 284, 287,
        289, 291, 292, 294, 297, 299,
        300
Religion(s), 158, 338, 350
    dogmatic rules of, 341, 369, 370
    fighting over, 324–25
    harmful, 369
    Jesus and, 370
    meditation and, 274–75, 279
    New Age beliefs as, 361–63
    patriarchal, 248
    spirituality distinct from, 316–18,
        319, 324–25, 328, 331, 358, 369
    women in/and, 320, 327–28, 329
Religious arrogance, 336, 337, 338
Religious beliefs
    argument over, 358
    and behavior, 316–18
    and mean vibratory rate, 97
    model for, 331–32
    truth of, 339
    and vibratory rate, 104
Religious leaders, 318–19
Religious organizations, 344
Religious right, 182, 242, 332–33
Religious separatism, 332, 336–37,
        357, 369, 370
Relocation, 54–55, 66–69
Remote viewing, 353–54
Research, 6–7, 123–24, 137, 209
Resourcefulness, 226
Restaurant atmosphere, 140–41
Rights, 156, 157–58
    of women, 180
Rock shop (dream), 210
Rodent droppings, 124–27

Sabbath, 344
Saints, 341
Salem witch-hunts, 333
Salmon, dream symbology, 261
Salmonella, 132
Sand lily (dream), 267
Sappho, 221
Satan
    appearance of, 359
    astrology as work of, 35–36
    see also Devil
Scapegoat(s), 23, 69, 147, 220, 315,
        327

human nature as, 363
Science, 7
  and spirituality, 35
Science books (list), 362
Sea sponge (dream), 208–10
Second Coming, 221, 322
Self, 12
  denying nature of, 89
  false, 198, 200
  focus on, 190, 355, 356
  reluctance to express fully, 253
Self-absorption, 189, 190, 214
Self-aggrandizement, 195, 214, 317
Self-analysis, 225
Self-assuredness, 227
Self-control, 323–24
Self-esteem, 214–15, 255–56, 268
Self-gratification, eating for, 114
Self-hatred, 154
Self-image, 255–56
Self-perception, 258–59, 351
Self-pity, 260
Self-righteousness, 164
Self-soothing, eating for, 114
Sense of self, 153, 256
Separatism, 356, 357, 369, 370
Sequential dreaming, 211–12
Serenity, 159, 268
  from attainment of wisdom, 253
  through meditation, 273
  patience in, 355
  of solitude, 317
Sex, obsession with, 164–65
Sexism, 201, 281, 326, 332
Sexual abuse, 165
Sexual inclination, 242–43
  mean vibratory rate and, 85
Sexuality, 204
  of women, 196
Shekinah, 220, 221, 247, 313, 316,
  321, 328, 329, 333, 346, 359
Shellfish, 136–38
Siblings, 93–94
Silence, 323–24, 327, 345
Simplicity, 107, 170, 172
Sin, homosexuality as, 329–31
Singing Web, The (Summer Rain), 98
Sleep, 254–55
Sleep time
  and prophetic dreams, 206–07
Snow in summer (dream), 252
Snowbird (dream), 210

Social behavior, 311–12
Social functions
  mean vibratory rate in shunning,
    87–88
Social graces, 173–77
Societal apathy, 173
Societal vibration, 85
Society
  alien ideologies in, 238, 239
  apathetic toward elderly, 190
  attitude toward aging, 196–97
  conceptual falsehoods in, 233
  consciousness raising, 201–02, 312
  distant, removed from world, 140
  error in spiritual philosophy, 356
  failure to evolve intellectually, 195
  fearful of individual thought, 39
  fragmented, 156
  losing respect for life, 163–64
  meditation and behavioral ills of,
    306–07
  obsession with sex, 164–65
  pace of, 139
  perception of power in, 344–45
  and reality, 348
  is soft, 244–45
  spiritual behavior of, 332
  spiritual development of, 333–34
  taking blessings for granted, 263
Soft drinks, 119
Solar flares, 33
Solitary lifestyle, 159–60
Solitude, 87–88, 317
Song of Sophia, 313–14
Sophia (Goddess), 220–22, 248, 313–
  14, 316, 321, 328, 329, 346, 359
Sorrow, 298, 315
Sound, 57–59
  soothing, 60
Speaking without sound (dream), 236
Spirit consciousness, 66, 311
  past-life influences in, 88, 91
Spirit entities, 12, 300
  reincarnation, 14, 320
Spiritual arrogance, 215–16, 217, 326
Spiritual awareness, 263
Spiritual behavior, 90–91, 283, 284,
  314, 333, 338, 339, 370
  in children, 345–46
  expressed in prayer, 309, 326, 327
  making a difference, 368–69
  model for, 331–32

Spiritual behavior (*continued*)
power in, 345
representational, 334
of society, 332
and vibratory rate, 104
Spiritual beliefs, 268, 338
conflict in, 210
individuality in, 350–52, 357
labels for, 343
matriarchal, 332–33
and mean vibratory rate, 97
Spiritual development
society's level of, 333–34
stages of, 303
Spiritual downfall, 217
Spiritual inclinations, 261–62
Spiritual philosophy, 311–70
feminine, 320–22
patience in, 355
reality of, 347, 348
society's error regarding, 356
truth of, 339
Spiritual reading
books (list), 325
Spiritual redundancy, 208–09
Spiritual talents/abilities, 227–29, 240
Spiritual wisdom/enlightenment, 230
Spirituality, 230, 332, 368
distinct from religion, 316–18, 319,
324–25, 328, 331, 358, 369
feminine, 220, 246–48, 328, 359–
60
psychic qualities and, 324
science and, 35
and vibrationary rate changes, 90–
91
of women, 312–13
Spoonbill bird (dream), 224
Star seen by Wise Men, 42–44
Starborn races, 24
State of mind
and health, 130, 268
Statues, 334–35
Staurolite (dream), 251–52
Stonework buildings
mean vibratory rate in attraction to,
91–92
Storms, 71, 73
Stranger manifesting behind face of
friend (dream), 234
Stress, 132, 285
and cancer, 112

and digestive problems, 130–31
worry and, 193
Stretch marks and scars, treatment of,
122
Stuff (material possessions), 154, 172,
194, 345
Style(s), 166–67
Subconscious
in dreaming, 236, 237–38
in meditation, 304
and melancholy, 61–62
Sugar glider (dream), 226
Sugar maple (dream), 253
Sunburn, 53
Superstition, 360–61
Supportive force, 224–25, 235–36
Survival supplies, 141–44, 186
Symbolic representations in dreams,
207–08, 239
Synchronicity, 359–60, 361

Taco Bell dog (dream), 258
Talents/skills, 117, 165, 210, 253
and occupation, 92
Taurus, 46
Telepathy, 40
Temperature
earth's magnetic field and, 54
humidity and, 55, 71–72
Terrorism, 66
through food, 144–45
Thank-yous, 173–77
Therapeutic touch, 121
Thermoregulatory system, 71–72
Thesaurus (dream), 250–51
Thought
analytical, 186
individual, 68–69, 137–38, 350–
51, 352
Thought forms, 95
Thought process, 371
analyzing, 168
Thoughts
bad, 363–68
in meditation, 303–4
Thunder, The: Perfect Mind, 248, 313
Thunderstorms, 61, 69–70, 72–73
Time, specific
in dreams, 257
Time clocks, internal, 51
Time frames in dreams, 223–24
Titanic (dream), 217

Tobacco substitutes, 129
Tolerance, 194, 195, 292, 337, 345
Tornados, 61, 67
Totality of spirit consciousness, 45–46, 91
Traditional medicine, 111, 117, 133–34
Trees
  mean vibratory rate, 97–98
Trees bare of leaves (dream), 252–53
Trinity, 347
  divine aspects of, 18
  Divine Feminine Aspects of, 316–17
  Divine Mother aspect of, 248
  feminine aspects of, 220–22, 313, 321, 329, 348
  Mother aspect of, 346
  symbol for, 332, 333
Trying to please others, 95, 198–201
Tumor growth, raspberries and, 133–34
Tutankhamun's tomb, 360
Twins, 16, 46
Tylenol scare, 145

Unconditional goodness, 8, 187, 188, 194, 210, 228, 284, 292, 314, 317, 326, 327, 331, 337, 339
  acts of, 175, 177
  counterforce to hatred, 311–12
  opportunities to practice, 368
  power in, 345
Unconditional love, 187, 266, 292, 317, 326, 327, 331, 339
  counterforce to hatred, 371–72
  in dogs, 253
  in message of Jesus, 330
  power in, 345
Uniqueness, 9, 79, 155, 157
  and birth signs, 25, 29–30
  of siblings in multiple births, 16–17
Unpretentiousness, 236–37
Upside-down objects (dream), 225

Vegetable oil, 123
Vegetarianism, 105–06
Vehicles, dream symbology for, 261
Viagra (dream), 258–59
Vibrational frequency
  and foods, 128–29
  sensitivity to, 70–71
  see also Vibratory rate

Vibrational rate influences, ignoring, 88–89
  see also Vibratory rate
Vibrationary rate
  changes in, 89–91
  of crystals, 102–03
  see also Vibratory rate
Vibratory rate
  in composite identity, 88
  distinctive, 101
  drugs and foods in, 103–04
  emotional/biological, 103
  mental illness and, 104
  religious beliefs in, 104
  see also Composite vibrationary rate; Mean vibratory rate
Vindictiveness, 229
Violence, 158, 163, 243
  chemicals and growth hormones in food and, 123
  full moon, 36–37, 48
  hatred and, 156
  mean vibratory rate and, 81–82
Viper (dream), 229
Virgo, 13, 25–26
Virtual experience of Quantum Meditation, 218
Virtual Meditation, 273–310
Visions, 41
Visitation, The (Summer Rain), 247, 313
Visuals
  in dreams, 206, 221, 222–23
  in meditation, 303–04
Vitamin A, 129
Vitamins, 134, 135, 136
  in survival supplies, 141
Volcanos, 12–13, 54, 85

Walking down church steps wearing medieval costume (dream), 263
War(s)
  astrological influences in, 18–19
Water purification, 64–66, 141
Watermelon tourmaline stone (dream), 267–68
Weather, 67
  and assimilation of medicine, 72
  and irritability, 60
  mean vibratory rate and interest in, 92
  and menstrual cramping, 72
  physical and psychological effects of, 49–53

Weaver Woman, 246
Web page (proposed)
   dream interpretation, 233
Weddings, 19
Weight-loss diet, 106–10
Whippoorwill (dream), 231–32
Will to live, 117–18
Wind, 57–60
Winning lottery numbers, 240
Wisdom, 299, 311–70
   of aged women, 196–97
   in dream of moon in full lunar eclipse,
     252
   in knowing the future, 265–66
   knowledge and, 65
   moon represents, 36
   patience as quality of, 354–55
   and power, 323–24, 345
   quality of silence, 323–24, 327
   serenity from attainment of, 253
Wise Men, 42–44
Witch-hunts, 235, 333

Wizard of Oz (film), 239
Women
   in/and church, 312–14
   crimes against, 184–85
   fear of aging, 196–97
   fears of, 186
   Jesus and, 330
   and medicines, 146, 147
   in/and religion, 320, 327–28, 329
   rights of, 180
   society's perception of, 160, 162
   spirituality, 37
   subjugation of, 337, 339
Wooden cutting boards, 132–33
Words
   choosing and verbalizing, 250–51
   power of, 203, 204, 250, 323
Worrying, 192–94

Yellow Stick, 122
Yin-yang energy, 241

ABOUT THE AUTHOR

Spiritual philosopher and naturalist MARY SUMMER RAIN has written more than twenty books, selling more than a million copies worldwide, including the highly successful *Earthway*, and was featured on the NBC television special *Ancient Prophecies*. She lives in a rustic cabin high in the Colorado Rocky Mountains.